W9-BZT-634

Taste of Home 100

Family Meals

Bring the Family
Back to the Dinner Table

RDA ENTHUSIAST BRANDS, LLC • MILWAUKEE, WI

Taste *of* Home

©2016 RDA Enthusiast Brands, LLC 1610 N. 2nd St., Suite 102, Milwaukee WI 53212
All rights reserved. Taste of Home is a registered trademark of RDA Enthusiast Brands, LLC.

For other Taste of Home books and products, visit us at tasteofhome.com.

International Standard Book Number: 978-1-61765-582-1
Library of Congress Control Number: 2016948966

Cover Photographer: Jim Wieland
Set Stylist: Dee Dee Jacq
Food Stylist: Shannon Roum
Pictured on front cover: Slow-Cooked Chicken Tacos, page 55

Additional Photography:

Monkey Business Images/Shutterstock, pages 10, 92 and 93 (families); BlueOrange Studio/Shutterstock, page 278 (family with baby); wavebreakmedia/Shutterstock, pages 12 and 194 (families); Sandy DeGasser, pages 4 (wife and husband), 168 (family at table) and 193 (family photo); RAYphotographer/Shutterstock, pages 12, 52, 92, 130, 168, 194, 222, 248 and 278 (picture frames).

Printed in China.
1 3 5 7 9 10 8 6 4 2

CONTENTS

4 The Magic of the Family Meal

7 How to Use this Book

10 Conversation Starters

12 Beefy Favorites

52 Chicken and Turkey

92 Pork, Ham and More

130 Seafood and Meatless

168 No-Fuss Salads

194 Simple Sides

222 Easy Soups and Breads

248 Sweet Surprises

278 Odds and Ends

306 My Family Meals Journal

308 Indexes

Spaghetti Salad,
Page 80

Discover the Magic of *Family Meals!*

You'll be amazed at what happens when you sit down and share dinner.

It only takes a few nights a week to cook up a little magic in your home. Believe it or not, sitting down as a family and enjoying meals regularly can help kids develop great eating habits, raise their self-esteem and feel closer to their families. How does something as simple as a family meal turn into something "magic?" It's easy!

"The family meal is, in fact, the perfect place for families to connect," says therapist Anne K. Fishel, PhD, associate clinical professor of psychology at the Harvard Medical School. "We say food is what brings everybody to the table, but it's the other things that make it meaningful and enjoyable." Those other things include laughter, sharing memories and making new ones, learning about one another's day, instilling values and more.

If that seems like a lot to ask of a slice of meatloaf and a side of green beans, it's not—and that's proven by numerous studies. For instance, studies show that teens who are regulars at the dinner table say their parents know a lot about what's going on in their lives. In fact, many of those teens expressed a desire to have meals with their families more often.

"The family meal is, in fact, the perfect place for families to connect."

See the Franco family fiesta (above) on page 91; Nikki Barton's dinner (left) on page 193; and Gina Myers' mealtime staples (below) on page 51.

A MATTER OF TIME

These days, it's hard for parents and children to find a way to come together over anything. More children live in families with working parents, and some parents may work more than one job. In addition, with lessons, sports and various clubs, kids are scheduled tighter than airline flights these days.

Time was certainly a challenge for Debbie Halpern, her husband, Jeremy, and their 13-year-old twins, son Zach and daughter Izzy. "It's not that we never had dinner together. We did," says Debbie. "It was just stressful getting it on the table. We wanted to see the kids, but I didn't feel it played a role in our connection as a family. It just didn't have much meaning for us."

Through a colleague, Debbie heard about a movement that encouraged families to make sit-down meals a priority, even if it means cooking ahead and occasionally using convenience items to help get a meal on the table.

"Suddenly, dinner was a really wonderful time," Debbie explains. "It became an opportunity for us to find connection and fun. It became a place for us to share family values. For the kids, it reinforced the idea that no matter what else was going on, family is here for them and on their side."

It was a stress-free zone for Debbie, too, a benefit that was documented in a study from Brigham Young University. The results indicated that mothers benefited from regular family meals: Sitting down together as a family—even if the mother had to make dinner—offset the negative effects of long work hours and job stress. "It became an oasis from the stresses of the day," says Debbie.

GIVE YOURSELF A BREAK

While Debbie says she occasionally lights candles at dinner, a family meal doesn't need to be a big ceremony. The recipes can be as simple as you want them to be, and the menu doesn't have to be elaborate either.

Items such as deli meats, rotisserie chicken, bagged salad greens and boxed mixes can really speed up a menu. In fact,

continued on page 6

DINNER-TABLE RULES
Keep these ideas in mind when calling everyone to the table.

- **Banish all attention grabbers** such as cell phones, tablets and other devices. How can you listen to one another if a cell phone is demanding your attention? While you're at it, turn off the TV, too!

- **Wait to start eating** until everyone is at the table. This way, no one feels left out, and you can all enjoy every minute of the meal together.

- **Keep stressful discussions,** such as the empty gas tank or a messy bedroom, off the table. Studies show that raising unpleasant topics at the table negate all the benefits of sharing a meal.

- **Come prepared with conversation** starters to engage everyone. See the "Table Talk" items on pages 10 and 11 as well as those scattered throughout this book to get you started.

HEALTHY HABIT
Get the skinny on family mealtime.

The dinner table is a great place to learn about healthy eating habits. A Rutgers University review of 68 studies showed that regular family dinners are also an effective antidote to the effects of fast food.

Drive-thru dinners aren't the only calorie-bomb culprit. A study published in the Journal of the American Medical Association found that even at sit-down restaurant chains, the average meal contains 1,128 calories, 56 percent of the average daily intake recommended for healthy adults. Restaurant meals also average 89 percent of the total recommended daily intake of fat, 83 percent of the recommended intake of saturated fat and 151 percent of the amount of sodium that health experts recommend.

Weekday Beef Stew,
Page 40

> *"The point is to be together over some food. However you manage to do it is ultimately OK."*

Check out family-friendly pizza (above) from page 129; meet the Robles family (far left) on page 167; host a baking party (left) with the ideas on page 277; celebrate the seasons with the no-fuss sides (center) on page 221; and see how to make the kitchen the heart of your home (below) with the story on page 247.

more than 140 of the recipes in *100 Family Meals* are table ready in 30 minutes or less, making it easy to prepare dinners even on hectic nights.

Another timesaver? Let the kids help. From setting the table to mixing ingredients, your kitchen helpers not only get dinner on the table faster, but their involvement gets them more excited about sitting down as a family, teaches them techniques they'll rely on the rest of their lives and offers a chance to learn about healthy eating.

Speaking of which, little ones are more likely to eat their vegetables when they've been a part of the selection process. In other words, take them shopping, ask for their input or plant a garden. Studies found that children who grow vegetables are more inclined to eat them. "They want to try them because they've been part of the process," says Lynn Barendsen, Executive Director of The Family Dinner Project.

She suggests finding ways to get adolescents involved, too. "Let them pick some music to cook to, or let them pick music to play at dinner. The music also gives you something to talk about during the meal.

"Regardless, the important thing is to get the family together three or more days a week," she adds. "The point is to be together over some food. However you manage to do it is ultimately OK."

Family cook Debbie Halpern agrees. "For us, family dinners made an enormous change," she says. "It made me more intentional about making time for dinner, and I actually think it made me a better parent. Sharing family dinners turned out to be a really powerful thing."

Now it's your turn! Keep reading and you'll see how *100 Family Meals* can help bring your family back to the table. It's easy and the benefits are invaluable. Let's get started!

How to Use this Book

Making the commitment to sit-down dinners is easy with 100 Family Meals on your side!

Turn your dinner table into the family gathering spot it was meant to be. By enjoying an average of two sit-down meals a week for 12 months, you'll reach your 100-meal goal. It's easy with a small bit of planning and *100 Family Meals*. Simply turn this book into your ultimate kitchen helper!

Not only are these recipes shared by other family cooks, but every one was tested and approved by the *Taste of Home* Test Kitchen, so they're guaranteed to turn out perfect every time you prepare them. In addition, each dish call for items you likely have on hand or can easily pick up at the grocery store. You'll also discover step-by-step guidelines and Prep and Cook timelines to make it a snap to plan your time in the kitchen. A complete set of Nutrition Facts accompanies every recipe as well.

GET STARTED

There are so many great things about to happen at your dinner table—laughter, memories, heartwarming moments and, of course, incredible food! Let *100 Family Meals* help!

Begin by paging through the book and acquainting yourself with recipes, tips, meal ideas and conversation starters.

- It's easy to find the perfect entree because this book features the beef, poultry and other main-course chapters up front.

- Don't miss the chapter "Easy Soups and Breads" (p. 222). Not only do these recipes round out meals quickly, but many of the soups include hearty pastas or enough veggies for no-fuss meatless entrees.

- Similarly, check out the many side dishes and salads. The "Odds and Ends" chapter (p. 278) is also loaded with sandwiches, parfaits, beverages and all sorts of family favorites that make it a snap to complete meals.

- Throughout this book, you'll find motivating stories and smart tips from other home cooks who made the commitment to enjoy family meals regularly. Consider these stories when you're having a hard time fitting in family meals and need a little motivation.

Crumb-Coated Ranch Chicken, Page 76

Mom's Spanish Rice, Page 205

Garden Cucumber Salad, Page 181

GET PLANNING

For many, half of the home-cooking battle is deciding what to make and when. Remember that you'll need to serve an average of two family menus per week to make your 100-meal goal. Whether you plan for an entire week or just a few days, let *100 Family Meals* help!

- Each of the 100 entrees found here includes a "Goes Great With" tip box. These serving suggestions perfectly complement the meal. Some of the ideas are items you can pick up from the grocery store. Others are fast no-fuss recipes found within the book.

- This cookbook also offers 32 complete menus, each with its own cutout grocery list. See the Meal Planners at the end of the chapters for dinners your family is sure to enjoy.

- **Four At-a-Glance Icons** make it a snap to find recipes that fit your needs. Keep an eye out for these dishes as you plan your menus:

  FAST FIX In a hurry? Turn to these quick ideas for dinner in a flash. They come together in just 30 minutes or less.

  (5) INGREDIENTS You won't believe what you can make with just a handful of items. Not including water, salt, pepper, oils or optional ingredients, these fast dishes require only five ingredients.

  SLOW COOKER Let these comforting staples simmer to perfection while you are at work. What could be easier?

  EAT SMART Trying to serve healthier foods? Cutting back on fat or sodium? Anyone at the table following a diabetic diet? Consider dishes marked with this icon.

GET COOKING

You know what you're making...now get cooking! Grab your favorite skillet, plug in the slow cooker or preheat the oven, because it's time to turn your 100 family-meal resolution into a reality.

- Make dinner a family affair by getting everyone in on the fun. See the "Kids in the Kitchen" notes scattered throughout the book to learn how your little chefs can help prepare specific dishes.

- Watch for the step-by-step how-to tips and photos that can help you prepare foods more efficiently.

- You'll also find hints to streamline recipe prep, substitutions and reviews from others who made the dishes for their own families.

GET HAPPY

Now you're ready for the fun to begin! Call the gang to the dinner table and enjoy this special time together.

- Turn off all cell phones, tablets and other devices. Review the guidelines on page 5 for a great dinner experience.

- Get the conversation started with the "Table Talk" ideas on pages 10 and 11 or any those scattered throughout.

- Make notes for yourself regarding any changes or substitutions you made to the recipes. You'll find "Notes" boxes throughout *100 Family Meals*.

- Record your success! See the journal "My Family Meals" on page 306, and make a note of what you served. With every dinner, you're one meal closer to reaching your goal!

- When dinner is over, log onto your favorite social media account and share your success with other family cooks looking to create heartwarming moments at their own tables. Upload photos, funny things overheard at the table and more, using **#100FamilyMeals**.

MAKE IT
SERVE IT
SHARE IT

Take your journey to serving 100 family meals to social media!

Let other family cooks in on the fun when you post your dinnertime successes on social media! Upload photos of your gang enjoying dinners, little ones stirring up desserts and any of the special moments only found at your table.

Tell others about your favorite recipes from *100 Family Meals,* and explain how you dressed up a dish, made a substitution or used leftovers the next day. Don't forget to share any tips for getting dinner on the table when the clock was ticking or how you made an entree ahead of time.

GET SOCIAL

Join other home cooks who made the commitment to serve 100 family meals when you visit:

 Like Taste of Home on Facebook, and share your progress, photos and suppertime hits from the **100 Family Meals** cookbook.

 Share your tableside photos on Instagram by using the hashtag **#100FamilyMeals**. Don't forget to tag **@Tasteofhome** on all of your posts.

 Follow **@Tasteofhome** on Twitter and use the hashtag **#100FamilyMeals** whenever you post updates, shots of your favorite recipe or funny jokes told at the table.

 Discover ideas and recipes on Pinterest. Follow **Taste of Home** for additional entree recipes and cute snacks that make it easier to **hit your 100 family-meals goal**!

Looking for more dishes your gang is sure to love?
Visit www.TasteofHome.com. Serving 100 sit-down dinners has never been easier with *Taste of Home* at your fingertips!

Liven Up Meals with

Table Talk!

Look who's talking—YOUR FAMILY.

Make your time at the table as memorable as possible! Consider the following conversation starters, and liven up family meals at your home. You'll also find more "Table Talk" ideas scattered throughout the book. Give them a try and see just how fun dinnertime can be!

If you could only enjoy one dessert for the rest of your life, what would it be?

There's always room for dessert, but what if you could only have one? Share your sweet-tooth favorite with the family.

What is your favorite joke?

Get ready for some laughs! Take turns telling the best jokes you've ever heard and watch the room light up with smiles and laughter!

If you had to be stranded someplace for a month, where would that be?

Get out your passports, because you're about to take a trip for a month! Take turns discussing where the special destination might be.

What sports team do you think is the greatest?

From football to baseball and from basketball to hockey, there are plenty of all-time greats in the sporting arena. What team do you cheer for the most? Ask everyone if they have a favorite player from that team.

What is the nicest thing anyone has ever done for you?

Think about all the favors and gifts you've received. What kind things have people said to you or helped out with. Share them with one another.

Who is the greatest cartoon character?

Every generation has its own cast of colorful characters. Which one was your all-time favorite and why?

If you could create your own ice cream flavor, what would it taste like?

Take turns telling one another what ingredients you'd combine to create the ultimate frosty sensation. Would you combine a few flavors? Stir in some favorite treats? Top it off with sweet syrups? Take a vote on whose creation sounds the tastiest.

What is the one thing you wish you never would have thrown out or given away?

We all regret giving away that one special item. What's yours? Maybe it's something you lost and just can't forget.

What movie do you have to stop and watch as you flip through the channels?

Everyone has that one movie they need to stop and check out while flipping through the channels. What's yours? Maybe it's a TV show or talk show. What is it about that program that always makes you stop and take a look?

Which Olympic competitions do you like best?

Diving or gymnastics? Bobsled or figure skating? Explain which Olympic sport gets you cheering for the gold.

What's your favorite song to rock out to?

When it's time to let loose and get crazy, what song comes to mind first? Go ahead and play everyone's top pick during dessert.

Which Thanksgiving side dish to you look forward to the most?

Those mouthwatering sides strike a chord with everyone at your table. Use this time to discuss which one they can't wait to dig into!

What's the best party you ever attended?

Was there a birthday you liked best? Maybe it was a surprise party or a holiday get-together. What made it so memorable?

What is the best concert you ever saw? Why was it so special?

Everyone remember the first concert they saw. What was yours? Was that the best concert you ever attended? If not, what was? Share those memories with everyone at the table.

If you could be any superhero, who would it be?

Grab your cape, and take turns discussing the best of the best in the superhero world. Discuss which superhero would win an all-out battle, or share who you think is the most memorable villain of all time.

READY, SET, GO!

Ready to get started? It's time to begin your commitment to serving, sharing and enjoying 100 family meals. All the tools you need to succeed are at your fingertips. Simply turn the page, find a recipe that fits your family's tastes and start making mealtime memories today!

"Cooking is a wonderful way to express love for family. It generates smiles and hugs in return."

—Nancy Brown, Dahinda, Illinois

BEEFY FAVORITES

DIG INTO no-fuss dinners that are sure to satisfy everyone at your table!

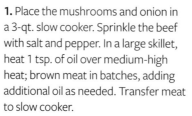

SLOW COOKER BEEF TIPS

These slow cooked beef tips remind me of a childhood favorite. I cook them with mushrooms and serve over brown rice, noodles or mashed potatoes.
—Amy Lents, Grand Forks, ND

....

Prep: 25 min. • **Cook:** 6¼ hours
Makes: 4 servings

- ½ lb. sliced baby portobello mushrooms
- 1 small onion, halved and sliced
- 1 beef top sirloin steak (1 lb.), cubed
- ½ tsp. salt
- ¼ tsp. pepper
- 2 tsp. olive oil
- ⅓ cup dry red wine or beef broth
- 2 cups beef broth
- 1 Tbsp. Worcestershire sauce
- 2 Tbsp. cornstarch
- ¼ cup cold water
  Hot cooked mashed potatoes

1. Place the mushrooms and onion in a 3-qt. slow cooker. Sprinkle the beef with salt and pepper. In a large skillet, heat 1 tsp. of oil over medium-high heat; brown meat in batches, adding additional oil as needed. Transfer meat to slow cooker.

2. Add wine to skillet, stirring to loosen browned bits from pan. Stir in broth and Worcestershire sauce; pour over meat. Cook, covered, on low for 6-8 hours or until meat is tender.

3. In a small bowl, mix cornstarch and cold water until smooth; gradually stir into slow cooker. Cook, covered, on high 15-30 minutes or until gravy is thickened. Serve with mashed potatoes.

Per serving: 1 cup (calculated without mashed potatoes) equals 212 cal., 7g fat (2g sat.fat), 46mg chol., 836mg sodium, 8g carb. (2g sugars, 1g fiber), 27g pro.
Diabetic Exchanges: ½ starch, 3 lean meat, ½ fat.

"Slip a love note under your sweetheart's plate. That's what great meals and memories are made of."

**—CHRISTINE PANZARELLA
BUENA PARK, CA**

GOES **GREAT** WITH

Panna cotta makes a refreshing end to a hearty meal. See the recipe on page 282.

Keep It Covered
Unless the recipe tells you to stir or add ingredients, don't lift the lid from the slow cooker. Every time you do, the temperature drops and you need to add cooking time. Resist the urge to take a peek!

GOES GREAT WITH

Pick up a bag of greens and stir up Pesto Buttermilk Dressing. You'll find the recipe on page 295.

(5) INGREDIENTS
PIZZA MACARONI BAKE

What do you get when you combine macaroni and cheese with pizza fixings? A hearty, family-pleasing casserole that's so easy and so tasty!
—Nancy Porterfield, Gap Mills, WV

Prep: 30 min. • **Bake:** 20 min.
Makes: 6-8 servings

- 1 pkg. (7¼ oz.) macaroni and cheese dinner mix
- 6 cups water
- 1 lb. ground beef
- 1 medium onion, chopped
- 1 small green pepper, chopped
- 1 cup (4 oz.) shredded cheddar cheese
- 1 jar (14 oz.) pizza sauce
- 1 pkg. (3½ oz.) sliced pepperoni
- 1 cup (4 oz.) shredded part-skim mozzarella cheese

1. Set the cheese packet from dinner mix aside. In a saucepan, bring water to a boil. Add the macaroni; cook for 8-10 minutes or until tender.
2. Meanwhile, in a large skillet, cook the beef, onion and green pepper over medium heat until the meat is no longer pink; drain. Drain macaroni; stir in the contents of cheese packet.
3. Transfer to a greased 13x9-in. baking dish. Sprinkle with cheddar cheese. Top with beef mixture, pizza sauce, pepperoni and mozzarella cheese.
4. Bake the dish, uncovered, at 350° for 20-25 minutes or until heated through.
Per serving: 1 serving equals: 365 cal., 20g fat (10g sat. fat), 68mg chol., 826mg sodium, 23g carb. (6g sugars, 2g fiber), 23g pro.

GOES GREAT WITH
Peel, boil and mash four sweet potatoes with butter and milk for an easy side.

EAT SMART | FAST FIX
COCOA-CRUSTED BEEF TENDERLOIN

It's amazing what a little coffee and cocoa can do to add richness and bold flavors to your steaks. This simple recipe is one to remember the next time you want to treat the family.
—Gina Myers, Spokane, WA

Takes: 30 min. • **Makes:** 4 servings

- 4 beef tenderloin steaks (1½ in. thick and 6 oz. each)
- ½ tsp. salt
- ½ tsp. coarsely ground pepper
- 3 Tbsp. baking cocoa
- 3 Tbsp. finely ground coffee

1. Preheat broiler. Sprinkle steaks with salt and pepper. In a shallow bowl, mix cocoa and coffee. Dip steaks in cocoa mixture to coat all sides; shake off excess.
2. Place steaks on a rack of a broiler pan. Broil 3-4 in. from heat for 9-11 minutes on each side or until the meat reaches the desired doneness (for medium-rare, a thermometer should read 145°; medium, 160°; well-done, 170°).
Per serving: 1 steak equals 252 cal., 10g fat (4g sat. fat), 75mg chol., 296mg sodium, 1g carb. (0 sugars, trace fiber), 37g pro.
Diabetic Exchanges: 5 lean meat.

KiDS in the KiTCHEN

Unleash your inner Picasso with a paper tablecloth! Invite everyone to draw a scene about their favorite family memory, and then take turns sharing the art...and the memories!

CHILI SLOPPY JOES

Teenagers are going to love this zesty take on an all-time classic. And the leftovers freeze great for last-minute meals later in the week.
—Brittany Allyn, Mesa, AZ

....

Prep: 15 min. • **Cook:** 20 min.
Makes: 6 servings

- 1 lb. lean ground beef (90% lean)
- 1 cup finely chopped sweet onion
- ½ cup finely chopped green pepper
- 1 jalapeno pepper, seeded and finely chopped, optional
- ½ cup chili sauce
- ½ cup water
- 1 to 2 chipotle peppers in adobo sauce, finely chopped
- 1 Tbsp. packed brown sugar
- 1 tsp. yellow mustard
- 6 hamburger buns or kaiser rolls, split
- 2 Tbsp. butter, softened

1. Preheat broiler. In a large skillet, cook beef, onion, green pepper and, if desired, jalapeno over medium heat 5-7 minutes or until beef is no longer pink, breaking up beef intro crumbles; drain.

2. Stir in the chili sauce, water, chipotle peppers, brown sugar and mustard; bring to a boil. Simmer, uncovered, 8-10 minutes or until slightly thickened, stirring occasionally.

3. Lightly spread cut sides of the buns with butter; arrange on a baking sheet, buttered side up. Broil 3-4 in. from heat until lightly toasted, about 30 seconds. Fill with beef mixture.

Freeze option: Freeze cooled meat mixture in freezer containers. To use, partially thaw in refrigerator overnight. Heat through in a saucepan, stirring occasionally and adding a little water if necessary.

Per serving: 1 sandwich equals 313 cal., 12g fat (5g sat. fat), 57mg chol., 615mg sodium, 32g carb. (11g sugars, 2g fiber), 19g pro. **Diabetic Exchanges:** 2 starch, 2 lean meat, 1 fat. meat, 1 fat.

GOES GREAT WITH
Bake up a bag of frozen french fries to round out the meal!

THREE-CHEESE MEATBALL MOSTACCIOLI

When my husband travels for work, I make a special dinner for my kids to keep their minds off missing Daddy. This tasty mostaccioli is meatball magic.
—Jennifer Gilbert, Brighton, MI

Prep: 15 min. • **Bake:** 35 min.
Makes: 10 servings

- 1 pkg. (16 oz.) mostaccioli
- 2 large eggs, lightly beaten
- 1 carton (15 oz.) part-skim ricotta cheese
- 1 lb. ground beef
- 1 medium onion, chopped
- 1 Tbsp. brown sugar
- 1 Tbsp. Italian seasoning
- 1 tsp. garlic powder
- ¼ tsp. pepper
- 2 jars (24 oz. each) pasta sauce with meat
- ½ cup grated Romano cheese
- 1 pkg. (12 oz.) frozen fully cooked Italian meatballs, thawed
- ¾ cup shaved Parmesan cheese
  Minced fresh parsley or fresh baby arugula, optional

1. Preheat the oven to 350°. Cook the mostaccioli according to the package directions for al dente; drain. In a small bowl, mix the eggs and ricotta cheese.

2. In a 6-qt. stockpot, cook beef and onion for 6-8 minutes or until beef is no longer pink, breaking up beef into crumbles; drain. Stir in brown sugar and seasonings. Add pasta sauce and mostaccioli; toss to combine.

3. Transfer half of the pasta mixture to a greased 13x9-in. baking dish. Layer with ricotta mixture and remaining pasta mixture; sprinkle with Romano cheese. Top with meatballs and Parmesan cheese.

4. Bake dish, uncovered, 35-40 minutes or until heated through. If desired, top with parsley or arugula.

Per serving: 1⅓ cups equals 541 cal., 23g fat (11g sat. fat), 105mg chol., 1335mg sodium, 55g carb. (13g sugars, 5g fiber), 34g pro.

GOES **GREAT** WITH

Ice cream is an ideal treat after any savory meal. Surprise your gang with homemade banana splits!

SLOW-COOKED ROUND STEAK

Quick and easy slow cooker recipes like this are a real plus for a busy family. You can serve these saucy steaks over boiled new potatoes or noodles.
—Dona McPherson, Spring, TX

Prep: 15 min. • **Cook:** 7 hours
Makes: 6-8 servings

- ¼ cup all-purpose flour
- ½ tsp. salt
- ⅛ tsp. pepper
- 2 lbs. boneless beef round steak, cut into serving-size pieces
- 6 tsp. canola oil, divided
- 1 medium onion, thinly sliced
- 1 can (10¾ oz.) condensed cream of mushroom soup, undiluted
- ½ tsp. dried oregano
- ¼ tsp. dried thyme

1. In a large resealable plastic bag, combine the flour, salt and pepper. Add beef, a few pieces at a time, and shake to coat. In a large skillet, brown meat on both sides in 4 tsp. oil. Place in a 5-qt. slow cooker.

2. In the same skillet, saute onion in remaining oil until lightly browned; place over beef. Combine the soup, oregano and thyme; pour over onion. Cover and cook on low for 7-8 hours or until meat is tender.

Per serving: 1 serving equals 224 cal., 9g fat (2g sat. fat), 65mg chol., 447mg sodium, 8g carb. (1g sugars, 1g fiber), 27g pro.

GOES GREAT WITH

Monkey Bread Biscuits come together in minutes with only a few ingredients. See page 225 for the no-fuss recipe.

"So good! The sauce was easy and yummy. I'm planning to use leftovers for sandwiches. This is one I will make again."

EAT SMART **SLOW COOKER**

BEEF BRISKET

One bite of this super-tender brisket and your family will be hooked! With its rich and satisfying gravy, it's perfect served with a side of mashed potatoes.
—Eunice Stoen, Decorah, IA

Prep: 15 min. • **Cook:** 8 hours
Makes: 6 servings

- 1   fresh beef brisket (2½ to 3 lbs.)
- 2   tsp. liquid smoke, optional
- 1   tsp. celery salt
- ½   tsp. pepper
- ¼   tsp. salt
- 1   large onion, sliced
- 1   can (12 oz.) beer or nonalcoholic beer
- 2   tsp. Worcestershire sauce
- 2   Tbsp. cornstarch
- ¼   cup cold water

1. Cut the brisket in half; rub with liquid smoke if desired, celery salt, pepper and salt. Place in a 3-qt. slow cooker. Top with onion. Combine beer and Worcestershire sauce; pour over meat. Cover and cook on low for 8-9 hours or until tender.
2. Remove the brisket and keep warm. Strain cooking juices; transfer to a small saucepan. Combine the cornstarch and water until smooth; stir into juices. Bring to a boil; cook and stir for 2 minutes or until thickened. Serve beef with the gravy.
Note: This is a fresh beef brisket, not corned beef.
Per serving: 1 serving equal 285 cal., 8g fat (3g sat. fat), 80mg chol., 430mg sodium, 7g carb. (3g sugars, trace fiber), 39g pro.
Diabetic Exchanges: ½ starch, 5 lean meat.

GOES GREAT WITH

Spruce up menus with Sweet Potato & Chickpea Salad on page 182. It's a healthy side dish that'll have your family running to the table.

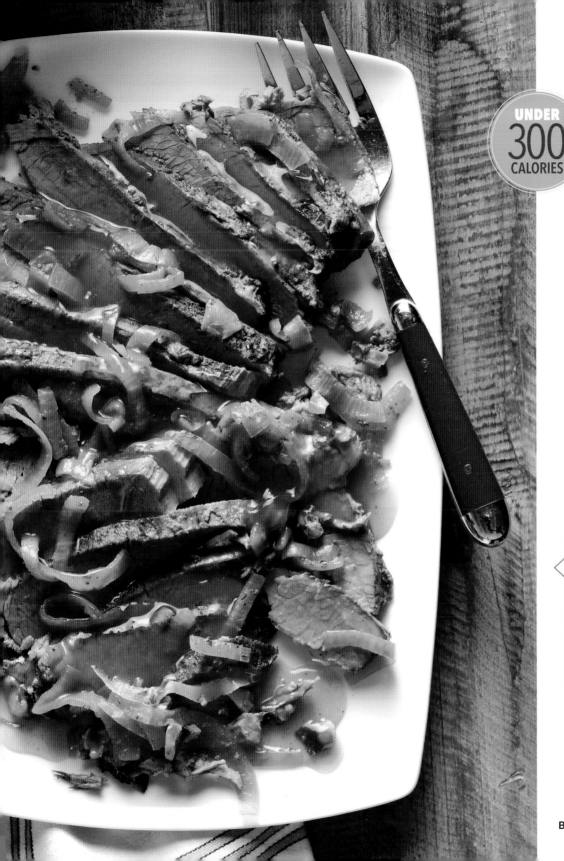

Tender Touch
To keep boneless roasts tender, be sure to slice the meat vertically across the grain into $\frac{1}{4}$ in. to $\frac{1}{2}$ in. slices. If the roast is tied, remove the string as you carve to help hold the roast together. roast together.

FAVORITE BAKED SPAGHETTI

Layering spaghetti and sauce keeps the pasta from drying out, so this cheesy dish is ideal for a potluck. It's also popular with my grandchildren.
—Louise Miller, Westminster, MD

Prep: 25 min. • **Bake:** 1 hour
Makes: 10 servings

- 1 pkg. (16 oz.) spaghetti
- 1 lb. ground beef
- 1 medium onion, chopped
- 1 jar (24 oz.) meatless spaghetti sauce
- ½ tsp. seasoned salt
- 2 large eggs
- ⅓ cup grated Parmesan cheese
- 5 Tbsp. butter, melted
- 2 cups (16 oz.) 4% cottage cheese
- 4 cups (16 oz.) part-skim shredded mozzarella cheese

1. Cook spaghetti according to package directions. Meanwhile, in a large skillet, cook beef and onion over medium heat until meat is no longer pink; drain. Stir in spaghetti sauce and seasoned salt; set aside.

2. In a large bowl, whisk eggs, Parmesan cheese and butter. Drain spaghetti; add to egg mixture and toss to coat.

3. Place half of the spaghetti mixture in a greased 3-qt. baking dish. Top with half of the cottage cheese, meat sauce and mozzarella cheese. Repeat layers.

4. Cover and bake at 350° for 40 minutes. Uncover; bake for 20-25 minutes longer or until cheese is melted.

Per serving: 1¼ cups equals 526 cal., 24g fat (13g sat. fat), 127mg chol., 881mg sodium, 45g carb. (9g sugars, 3g fiber), 31g pro.

GOES GREAT WITH

Herb Quick Bread bakes alongside this casserole just perfectly! Remove it from the oven when you uncover the spaghetti bake and let it cool as the entree finishes its baking time. See the recipe on page 236.

TOMATO STEAK SANDWICHES

When we were light on groceries one day, I came up with steak and tomatoes over bagels. They've been a favorite ever since, particularly when we need a quick dinner.
—Tessa Edwards, Provo, UT

Takes: 20 min. • **Makes:** 6 servings

- 2 tsp. canola oil
- 1 lb. beef top sirloin steak, cut into thin strips
- ⅛ tsp. salt
-    Dash pepper
- 3 plain bagels, split
- ⅓ cup cream cheese, softened
- 6 thick slices tomato
- 6 slices part-skim mozzarella cheese

1. Preheat broiler. In a large skillet, heat oil over medium heat. Add beef; cook and stir 3-5 minutes or until browned; drain. Stir in salt and pepper.

2. Spread cut sides of bagels with cream cheese. Transfer to an ungreased baking sheet; spoon beef over bagels. Top with tomato and mozzarella cheese. Broil 4-6 in. from heat for 3-5 minutes or until cheese is melted and lightly browned.

Per serving: 1 open-faced sandwich equals 381 cal., 15g fat (7g sat. fat), 63mg chol., 544mg sodium, 31g carb. (6g sugars, 1g fiber), 30g pro.

GOES **GREAT** WITH

Pasta salad from the deli, pickles and potato chips are an appealing way to round out these steak sandwiches.

BEEF POTATO MEAT LOAF

I've watched the film A Christmas Story *so many times since I was a kid. Now that I have a family of my own, I recreated the mom's meat loaf and mashed potatoes from that movie.*
—Christina Addison, Blanchester, OH

Prep: 15 min. • **Bake:** 50 min. + standing
Makes: 6 servings

2	large eggs, lightly beaten
½	cup ketchup
1	medium onion, finely chopped
1	small green or sweet red pepper, finely chopped
⅔	cup crushed saltines (about 12)
½	tsp. salt
1	tsp. pepper
1½	lbs. ground beef
4	cups hot mashed potatoes, divided
1	Tbsp. minced fresh parsley

1. Preheat oven to 375°. Place a rack in a 15x10x1-in. baking pan; place a 12x8-in. piece of foil in the center of the rack. In a large bowl, combine eggs, ketchup, onion, green pepper, crushed saltines, salt and pepper. Add beef; mix lightly but thoroughly. Place over foil rectangle and shape into a 9x6-in. loaf. Bake 50-60 minutes or until a thermometer reads 160°. Let stand 10 minutes before slicing.

2. Transfer meat loaf to a serving plate, discarding foil. Pipe or spread 1 cup mashed potatoes over meat loaf. Sprinkle with parsley. Serve with remaining mashed potatoes.

Per serving: 1 slice with ½ cup mashed potatoes equals 436 cal., 20g fat (7g sat. fat), 132mg chol., 1105mg sodium, 37g carb. (7g sugars, 3g fiber), 26g pro.

> *"Preparing nutritious meals is a part of everyday life, but I do it gladly because it's so satisfying."*
> —SUZIE SALLE, RENTON, WA

The Orange Spice Carrots from page 203 add the perfect touch to this dinner.

BURRITO BAKE

When I was in college, my roommate often made this shortcut Southwest casserole. Just one slice will fill you right up!

—Cindee Ness, Horace, ND

Prep: 25 min. • **Bake:** 30 min.
Makes: 6 servings

- 1   **lb. ground beef**
- 1   **can (16 oz.) refried beans**
- ¼   **cup chopped onion**
- 1   **envelope taco seasoning**
- 1   **tube (8 oz.) refrigerated crescent rolls**
- 1   **to 2 cups shredded cheddar cheese**
- 1   **to 2 cups shredded part-skim mozzarella cheese**
     Optional toppings: chopped green pepper, shredded lettuce, chopped tomatoes and sliced ripe olives

1. Preheat oven to 350°. In a large skillet, crumble and cook beef over medium heat until no longer pink; drain. Add the beans, onion and taco seasoning.
2. Unroll crescent roll dough. Press onto bottom and up the sides of a greased 13x9-in. baking dish; seal seams and perforations.
3. Spread beef mixture over the crust; sprinkle with cheeses. Bake, uncovered, until golden brown, about 30 minutes. If desired, sprinkle with toppings.
Per serving: 1 serving equals 509 cal., 29g fat (12g sat. fat), 78mg chol., 1403mg sodium, 32g carb. (4g sugars, 3g fiber), 29g pro.

GOES GREAT WITH

Be sure to have taco chips and salsa on the side of this meal-in-one favorite.

Table Talk

What was the best holiday gift you ever received?

Not only do kids like talking about their toys and games, but they'll love hearing about your all-time favorite childhood plaything. Next, ask everyone the favorite gifts they gave.

BALSAMIC BEEF HOAGIES

My boys like sandwiches, and balsamic beef is a welcome change from pulled barbecue chicken. We use the leftovers in quesadillas, on pizza or with rice.
—Blair Lonergan, Rochelle, VA

Prep: 25 min. • **Cook:** 5 hours
Makes: 8 servings

- 1 **cup beef broth**
- ½ **cup balsamic vinegar**
- 2 **Tbsp. brown sugar**
- 2 **Tbsp. Worcestershire sauce**
- 4 **garlic cloves, minced**
- 1 **boneless beef chuck roast (2 lbs.)**

SANDWICHES
- ½ **cup mayonnaise**
- 8 **hoagie buns, split and toasted**
- 4 **medium tomatoes, sliced**
- ½ **cup thinly sliced fresh basil**

1. In a small bowl, mix the first five ingredients. Place roast in a 4- or 5-qt. slow cooker. Pour broth mixture over top. Cook, covered, on low for 5-6 hours or until meat is tender.

2. Remove roast; shred beef with two forks. Skim fat from cooking juices. Return beef and cooking juices to slow cooker; heat through.

3. Spread mayonnaise on the buns. Using tongs, place shredded beef on buns; top with tomatoes and basil.

Freeze option: Freeze cooled meat mixture in freezer containers. To use, partially thaw in refrigerator overnight. Heat through in a saucepan, stirring occasionally and adding a little broth if necessary.

Per serving: 1 sandwich equals 549 cal., 26g fat (7g sat. fat), 79mg chol., 669mg sodium, 46g carb. (14g sugars, 2g fiber), 31g pro.

GOES GREAT WITH

Spruce up everyone's dinner plate with the tomato salad on page 207.

BACON CHEESEBURGER TATER TOT BAKE

My kids complete their chores quickly when they know this yummy casserole is on the menu!
—Deanna Zewen, Union Grove, WI

....

Prep: 15 min. • **Bake:** 35 min.
Makes: 12 servings

- 2 lbs. ground beef
- 1¼ cups chopped onion
       (about 1 large), divided
- 1 can (15 oz.) tomato sauce
- 8 oz. process cheese (Velveeta)
- 1 Tbsp. ground mustard
- 1 Tbsp. Worcestershire sauce
- 2 cups (8 oz.) shredded
       cheddar cheese
- 12 bacon strips, cooked
       and crumbled
- 1 pkg. (32 oz.) frozen Tater Tots
- 1 medium tomato, chopped
- ⅓ cup chopped dill pickles

1. Preheat the oven to 400°. In a large skillet, cook beef and 1 cup onion over medium heat for 6-8 minutes or until beef is no longer pink and onion is tender, breaking up beef into crumbles; drain. Stir in tomato sauce, process cheese, mustard and Worcestershire sauce. Cook and stir for 4-6 minutes or until cheese is melted.

2. Transfer the mixture to a greased 13x9-in. or 3½-qt. baking dish. Sprinkle with cheddar cheese and bacon. Top with Tater Tots. Bake, uncovered, for 35-40 minutes or until bubbly. Top with tomato, pickles and remaining onion.

Per serving: 1 serving equals 480 cal., 31g fat (12g sat. fat), 93mg chol., 1143mg sodium, 24g carb. (4g sugars, 3g fiber), 27g pro.

GOES GREAT WITH

Serve the gang chocolate shakes! They're a tasty treat alongside this cheeseburger casserole.

NOTES

_____
_____
_____
_____
_____
_____
_____
_____
_____

FAST FIX ▶

MEATBALL PIZZA

I always keep meatballs and pizza crusts in the freezer to make this specialty at the spur of the moment. Add a tossed salad and you have a delicious family dinner.
—Mary Humeniuk-Smith, Perry Hall, MD

Takes: 25 min. • **Makes:** 8 slices

- 1 prebaked 12-in. pizza crust
- 1 can (8 oz.) pizza sauce
- 1 tsp. garlic powder
- 1 tsp. Italian seasoning
- ¼ cup grated Parmesan cheese
- 1 small onion, halved and sliced
- 12 frozen fully cooked Italian meatballs (½ oz. each), thawed and halved
- 1 cup (4 oz.) shredded part-skim mozzarella cheese
- 1 cup (4 oz.) shredded cheddar cheese

1. Preheat oven to 350°. Place crust on an ungreased 12-in. pizza pan or baking sheet.
2. Spread sauce over crust; sprinkle with garlic powder, Italian seasoning and Parmesan cheese. Top with onion and meatballs; sprinkle with remaining cheeses. Bake for 12-17 minutes or until cheese is melted.
Per serving: 1 slice equals 321 cal., 16g fat (8g sat. fat), 36mg chol., 755mg sodium, 28g carb. (3g sugars, 2g fiber), 17g pro.

FAST FIX ▶

CHILI BEEF NOODLE SKILLET

A friend gave me this recipe. My husband likes this entree's hearty blend of beef, onion and tomatoes, but I like it because I can get it to the table so quickly.
—Deborah Elliott, Ridge Spring, SC

Takes: 30 min. • **Makes:** 8 servings

- 1 pkg. (8 oz.) egg noodles
- 2 lbs. ground beef
- 1 medium onion, chopped
- ¼ cup chopped celery
- 2 garlic cloves, minced
- 1 can (28 oz.) diced tomatoes, undrained
- 1 Tbsp. chili powder
- ¼ to ½ tsp. salt
- ⅛ tsp. pepper
- ½ to 1 cup shredded cheddar cheese

1. Cook noodles according to package directions. Meanwhile, in a large skillet, cook the beef, onion, celery and garlic over medium heat until meat is no longer pink and vegetables are tender; drain. Add the tomatoes, chili powder, salt and pepper. Cook and stir for 2 minutes or until heated through.
2. Drain noodles; stir into beef mixture and heat through. Remove from the heat. Sprinkle with cheese; cover and let stand for 5 minutes or until cheese is melted.
Per serving: 1 cup equals 344 cal., 14g fat (6g sat. fat), 90mg chol., 351mg sodium, 28g carb. (5g sugars, 3g fiber), 27g pro.

GOES GREAT WITH

Bread sticks make a welcome addition to this savory noodle skillet dish.

GOES GREAT WITH

Enjoy Chocolate-Covered Strawberry Cobbler from page 260 when you serve up this pizza.

Pile on the Flavor!

Pizzas are a great way to customize dinners to everyone's tastes. Feel free to add sliced mushrooms, chopped onion or diced green pepper to this easy meatball delight. You can even add a dash of red pepper flakes if you'd like to spice things up.

GOES GREAT WITH

Hit the bakery for a few cannoli on your way home. They'll make dinner time special tonight.

ONE PAN WONDERFUL

ONE SKILLET LASAGNA

Hands down, this is one of the best skillet lasagna recipes for a weekday meal. With classic flavors and cheesy layers, it's also definitely kid-friendly.
—*Taste of Home* Test Kitchen

....

Takes: 30 min. • **Makes:** 6 servings

- ¾ lb. ground beef
- 2 garlic cloves, minced
- 1 can (14½ oz.) diced tomatoes with basil, oregano and garlic, undrained
- 2 jars (14 oz. each) spaghetti sauce
- ⅔ cup condensed cream of onion soup, undiluted
- 2 large eggs, lightly beaten
- 1¼ cups 1% cottage cheese
- ¾ tsp. Italian seasoning
- 9 no-cook lasagna noodles
- ½ cup shredded Colby-Monterey Jack cheese
- ½ cup shredded part-skim mozzarella cheese

1. In a large skillet, cook beef and garlic over medium heat until the meat is no longer pink; drain. Stir in tomatoes and spaghetti sauce; heat through. Transfer to a large bowl.

2. In a small bowl, combine soup, eggs, cottage cheese and Italian seasoning.

3. Return 1 cup meat sauce to the skillet; spread evenly. Layer with 1 cup cottage cheese mixture, 1½ cups meat sauce and half of the noodles, breaking to fit. Repeat layers of cottage cheese mixture, meat sauce and noodles. Top with remaining meat sauce. Bring to a boil. Reduce heat; cover and simmer for 15-17 minutes or until noodles are tender.

4. Remove from the heat. Sprinkle with shredded cheeses; cover and let stand for 2 minutes or until cheeses are melted.

Per serving: 1 serving equals 478 cal., 20g fat (8g sat. fat), 128mg chol., 1552mg sodium, 43g carb. (15g sugars, 4g fiber), 31g pro.

"This recipe changed my life! It has all the taste and look of homemade lasagna but is done in a fraction of the time. I may never make the hard-labor lasagna again!"

—DEANNERUEDEMANN, TASTEOFHOME.COM

GOES **GREAT** WITH

Corn bread pairs well with this comforting beef roast. Yum!

SWEET & TANGY BEEF ROAST

Once while cleaning out the fridge, I found barbecue sauce, red pepper jelly and hoisin sauce—the perfect trio for creating a slightly tangy and sweet, utterly delicious roast.
—Rachel Van Orden, Annville, PA

Prep: 10 min. • **Cook:** 7 hours + standing
Makes: 8 servings

- 1 Tbsp. canola oil
- 1 boneless beef chuck roast (4 lbs.)
- 2 medium onions, sliced into ½-in. rings
- 1 cup plus 2 Tbsp. water, divided
- ¾ cup honey barbecue sauce
- ½ cup red pepper jelly
- 3 Tbsp. hoisin sauce
- 2 Tbsp. cornstarch

1. In a large skillet, heat oil over medium heat. Brown roast on all sides. Transfer to a 5-qt. slow cooker; add onions and 1 cup water.
2. In a small bowl, mix barbecue sauce, jelly and hoisin sauce; pour over meat. Cook, covered, on low for 7-9 hours or until meat is tender. Remove roast from slow cooker; tent with foil. Let stand 10 minutes before slicing.
3. Meanwhile, skim fat from cooking juices; transfer the juices to a small saucepan. Bring to a boil. Mix cornstarch and the remaining water until smooth. Stir into pan. Return to a boil; cook and stir for 1-2 minutes or until thickened. Serve with roast and onions.
Per serving: 4½ oz. cooked beef with ⅓ cup sauce and ¼ cup onion equals 457 cal., 22g fat (7g sat. fat), 120mg chol., 443mg sodium, 28g carb. (19g sugars, 1g fiber), 35g pro.

ONE-POT SAUCY BEEF ROTINI

We love pasta. On Spaghetti Day, as we call it, I make a one-pot saucy rotini that keeps everyone happy.
—Lorraine Caland, Shuniah, ON

Takes: 30 min. • **Makes:** 4 servings

- ¾ lb. lean ground beef (90% lean)
- 2 cups sliced fresh mushrooms
- 1 medium onion, chopped
- 3 garlic cloves, minced
- ¾ tsp. Italian seasoning
- 2 cups tomato basil pasta sauce
- ¼ tsp. salt
- 2½ cups water
- 3 cups uncooked whole wheat rotini (about 8 oz.)
- ¼ cup grated Parmesan cheese

1. In a 6-qt. stockpot, cook the first five ingredients over medium-high heat for 6-8 minutes or until beef is no longer pink, breaking up beef into crumbles; drain.
2. Add the pasta sauce, salt and water; bring to a boil. Stir in rotini; return to a boil. Reduce heat; simmer, covered, for 8-10 minutes or until pasta is al dente, stirring occasionally. Serve with cheese.
Per serving: 1½ cups equals 414 cal., 11g fat (4g sat. fat), 57mg chol., 806mg sodium, 49g carb. (12g sugars, 8g fiber), 28g pro.

GOES GREAT WITH

You can't beat a buttery loaf of garlic bread. Set a frozen loaf in the oven to bake alongside the rotini.

HASH BROWN-TOPPED STEAK

My husband and I enjoy cooking together. One night, craving grilled steak and cheese-stuffed baked potatoes, we were feeling a little impatient. So we invented this quicker meal-in-one.
—Judy Armstrong, Prairieville, LA

Takes: 30 min. • **Makes:** 4 servings

- 2 **Tbsp. butter**
- 1 **small onion, chopped**
- 3 **garlic cloves, minced**
- 2 **cups frozen shredded hash brown potatoes, thawed**
- ¾ **tsp. salt, divided**
- 1 **cup (4 oz.) shredded Jarlsberg cheese**
- 1 **beef top sirloin steak (1 in. thick and 1½ lbs.), cut into 4 portions**
- ½ **tsp. pepper**
- 2 **Tbsp. minced fresh chives**

1. In a large skillet, heat butter over medium-high heat. Add onion; cook and stir for 2-3 minutes or until tender. Add garlic; cook 2 minutes longer.

2. Stir in hash browns and ¼ tsp. salt; spread in an even layer. Reduce heat to medium; cook for 5 minutes. Turn the hash browns over; cook, covered, for 5-6 minutes longer or until heated through and bottom is lightly browned. Sprinkle with the cheese; cover and remove from heat. Keep warm.

3. Sprinkle beef with pepper and remaining salt. Grill, covered, over medium heat for 5-7 minutes on each side or until meat reaches desired doneness (for medium-rare, a thermometer should read 145°; medium, 160°; well-done, 170°).

4. Remove steaks from heat; top each with a fourth of the potato mixture. Sprinkle with chives.

Per serving: 1 serving equals 403 cal., 20g fat (10g sat. fat), 102mg chol., 703mg sodium, 10g carb. (1g sugars, 1g fiber), 45g pro.

NOTES

_____
_____
_____
_____
_____
_____
_____
_____
_____
_____

GOES GREAT WITH

Find Tomato-Onion Green Beans on page 210. They're great with the steak.

MAKE IT
SERVE IT
SHARE IT

Tweet with us!

Share your favorite at-the-table photos on Twitter! Don't forget the hashtag **#100FamilyMeals**.

WEEKDAY BEEF STEW

Beef stew capped with flaky puff pastry adds comfort and joy to the weeknight menu. Add a salad and your meal is complete.
—Daniel Anderson, Kenosha, WI

Takes: 30 min. • **Makes:** 4 servings

- 1 sheet frozen puff pastry, thawed
- 1 pkg. (15 oz.) refrigerated beef roast au jus
- 2 cans (14½ oz. each) diced tomatoes, undrained
- 1 pkg. (16 oz.) frozen vegetables for stew
- ¾ tsp. pepper
- 2 Tbsp. cornstarch
- 1¼ cups water

1. Preheat oven to 400°. Unfold puff pastry. Using a 4-in. round cookie cutter, cut out four circles. Place 2 in. apart on a greased baking sheet. Bake for 14-16 minutes or until golden brown.
2. Meanwhile, shred beef with two forks; transfer to a large saucepan. Add tomatoes, vegetables and pepper; bring to a boil. In a small bowl, mix cornstarch and water until smooth; stir into beef mixture. Return to a boil, stirring constantly; cook and stir for 1-2 minutes or until thickened.
3. Ladle stew into four bowls; top each with a pastry round.
Per serving: 1½ cups with 1 pastry round equals 604 cal., 25g fat (8g sat. fat), 73mg chol., 960mg sodium, 65g carb. (10g sugars, 9g fiber), 32g pro.

GOES **GREAT** WITH

Enjoy a slice of pie from the local bakery after this all-American meal.

Stir It In

Stir some shredded cheese, diced jalapeno pepper, Cajun seasoning or chopped chives in to the corn bread batter.

HEARTY BEEF CASSEROLE

Little ones who refuse to eat veggies won't complain one bit when you bring this cheesy casserole with a corn bread crust to the table. For picky eaters, try using less Cajun seasoning.
—Kelly Ciepluch, Kenosha, WI

Prep: 15 min. • **Bake:** 25 min.
Makes: 6 servings

- 1 pkg. (8½ oz.) corn bread/muffin mix
- 1 lb. ground beef
- 2 cans (14½ oz. each) diced tomatoes, drained
- 2 cups frozen mixed vegetables, thawed
- 1 can (6 oz.) tomato paste
- 1 to 2 tsp. Cajun seasoning
- 1 cup (4 oz.) shredded cheddar cheese
- 2 green onions, thinly sliced

1. Preheat oven to 350°. Prepare corn bread batter according to the package directions. Spread batter into a greased 11x7-in. baking dish.

2. In a large skillet, cook the beef over medium heat until no longer pink; drain. Add tomatoes, vegetables, tomato paste and seasoning. Bring to a boil. Reduce heat; simmer, uncovered, for 5 minutes. Pour over batter. Sprinkle with cheese.

3. Bake, uncovered, until golden brown, for 25-30 minutes. Sprinkle with onions.

Freeze option: Omit onion topping. Cool baked casserole; wrap and freeze. To use, partially thaw in refrigerator overnight. Remove 30 minutes before baking. Preheat oven to 350°; bake as directed, increasing time as necessary for a thermometer inserted in center to read 165°. Sprinkle cooked casserole with onions.

Per serving: 1 serving equals 449 cal., 19g fat (9g sat. fat), 111mg chol., 916mg sodium, 46g carb. (16g sugars, 6g fiber), 25g pro.

GOES GREAT WITH

Top off this meal with a quick idea for grapes. You'll find the recipe on page 298.

UNDER
400
CALORIES

BEEF & CHEESE SKILLET COBBLER

I tweaked my beefy skillet cobbler until it achieved the wow factor. I must have gotten it right, as it's now a family tradition. Top it with lettuce, avocado, cherry tomatoes and a dollop of sour cream.
—Gloria Bradley, Naperville, IL

....

Prep: 40 min. • **Bake:** 15 min. + standing
Makes: 8 servings

- 1 **lb. ground beef**
- 1 **can (15 oz.) black beans, rinsed and drained**
- 1 **can (14½ oz.) diced tomatoes with mild green chilies**
- 1 **can (10 oz.) enchilada sauce**
- 1 **tsp. ground cumin**
- 4 **Tbsp. chopped fresh cilantro or parsley, divided**
- 1½ **cups biscuit/baking mix**
- 1½ **cups (6 oz.) shredded Colby-Monterey Jack cheese, divided**
- 4 **bacon strips, cooked and crumbled**
- ⅔ **cup 2% milk**
- 1 **large egg, lightly beaten Sour cream, optional**

1. Preheat the oven to 400°. In a 10-in. ovenproof skillet, cook beef over medium heat for 5-7 minutes or until no longer pink, breaking into crumbles; drain. Stir in beans, tomatoes, enchilada sauce and cumin; bring to a boil. Reduce heat; simmer, uncovered, for 20 minutes to allow flavors to blend, stirring occasionally. Stir in 2 Tbsp. cilantro.

2. In a bowl, combine the baking mix, ½ cup cheese, bacon and remaining cilantro. Add milk and beaten egg; stir just until a soft dough is formed. Spoon over beef mixture.

3. Bake, uncovered, for 13-15 minutes or until golden brown. Sprinkle with remaining cheese; bake 2-3 minutes longer or until cheese is melted. Let stand for 10 minutes before serving. If desired, serve with sour cream.

Per serving: 1 serving (calculated without sour cream) equals 373 cal., 18g fat (9g sat. fat), 83mg chol., 949mg sodium, 30g carb. (4g sugars, 4g fiber), 23g pro.

GOES GREAT WITH

Cool down after a spicy meal with a bowl of Buttermilk Peach Ice Cream found on page 289.

(5) INGREDIENTS
EASY STUFFED SHELLS

I created a super-easy way to fill pasta shells—just use meatballs. If you put the kids on stuffing duty they'll be proud to help, and everyone will love the dish come dinnertime.
—Dolores Betchner, Cudahy, WI

Prep: 20 min. • **Bake:** 40 min.
Makes: 12 servings

- 36 uncooked jumbo pasta shells
- 1 jar (24 oz.) spaghetti sauce
- 36 frozen fully cooked Italian meatballs (½ oz. each), thawed
- 2 cups (8 oz.) shredded part-skim mozzarella cheese

1. Preheat oven to 350°. Cook pasta shells according to package directions; drain and rinse in cold water.
2. Spread ½ cup sauce into a greased 13x9-in. baking dish. Fill each shell with a meatball; place over sauce. Top with remaining sauce and the cheese.
3. Bake, covered, for 35 minutes. Uncover; bake 3-5 minutes longer or until bubbly and cheese is melted.
Per serving: 3 stuffed shells equals 334 cal., 17g fat (8g sat. fat), 45mg chol., 711mg sodium, 30g carb. (6g sugars, 3g fiber), 16g pro.

GOES GREAT WITH
Go green with the Lemon Pepper Roasted Broccoli on page 218.

on page 218.

SLOPPY JOE BISCUIT CUPS

I'm a busy teacher and mom, so meals with shortcuts are a huge help. These savory cups are a fun and easy way to change up sloppy joes.
—Julie Ahern, Waukegan, IL

Takes: 30 min. • **Makes:** 5 servings

- 1 **lb. lean ground beef (90% lean)**
- ¼ **cup each finely chopped celery, onion and green pepper**
- ½ **cup barbecue sauce**
- 1 **tube (12 oz.) medium refrigerated flaky biscuits (10 count)**
- ½ **cup shredded cheddar cheese**

1. Heat oven to 400°. In a large skillet, cook beef and vegetables over medium heat 5-7 minutes or until beef is no longer pink, breaking up beef into crumbles; drain. Stir in barbecue sauce; bring to a boil. Reduce heat; simmer, uncovered, for 2 minutes, stirring occasionally.

2. Separate dough into 10 biscuits; flatten to 5-in. circles. Press onto bottom and up sides of greased muffin cups. Fill with beef mixture.

3. Bake 9-11 minutes or until biscuits are golden brown. Sprinkle with the cheese; bake for 1-2 minutes longer or until the cheese is melted.

Per serving: 2 biscuit cups equals 463 cal., 22g fat (8g sat. fat), 68mg chol., 1050mg sodium, 41g carb. (16g sugars, 1g fiber), 25g pro.

GOES GREAT WITH

Classic mac and cheese is a perfect pairing for the beefy cups.

FAJITA IN A BOWL

Pull out the skewers and take a stab at grilling peppers, onions and corn for an awesome steak salad that's all summer and smoke.
—Peggy Woodward, Shullsburg, WI

....

Takes: 30 min. • **Makes:** 4 servings

- 1 Tbsp. brown sugar
- 1 Tbsp. chili powder
- ½ tsp. salt
- 1 beef flank steak (1 lb.)
- 12 miniature sweet peppers, halved and seeded
- 1 medium red onion, cut into thin wedges
- 2 cups cherry tomatoes
- 2 medium ears sweet corn, husks removed

SALAD

- 12 cups torn mixed salad greens
- 1 cup fresh cilantro leaves
- ½ cup reduced-fat lime vinaigrette
  Optional ingredients: Cotija cheese, lime wedges and tortillas

1. In a small bowl, mix brown sugar, chili powder and salt. Rub onto both sides of steak.

2. Place peppers and onion on a grilling grid; place on grill rack over medium heat. Grill, covered, for 9-11 minutes or until crisp-tender, stirring occasionally; add tomatoes during the last 2 minutes. Remove from grill.

3. Place steak and corn directly on grill rack; close lid. Grill steak 8-10 minutes on each side or until a thermometer reads 145° for medium-rare; grill corn 10-12 minutes or until lightly charred, turning occasionally.

4. Divide greens and cilantro among four bowls. Cut corn from cobs and thinly slice steak across the grain; place in bowls. Top with vegetables; drizzle with vinaigrette. If desired, serve with cheese, lime and tortillas.

Note: If you do not have a grilling grid, use a disposable foil pan with holes poked into the bottom with a meat fork.

Per serving: 1 serving (calculated without optional ingredients) equals 351 cal., 14g fat (5g sat. fat), 54mg chol., 862mg sodium, 33g carb., 7g fiber, 28g pro.

NOTES

_____
_____
_____
_____
_____
_____
_____

GOES **GREAT** WITH

Stir up Rosemary Lemonade from page 294 for a tasty addition to this meal.

SPEEDY SHEPHERD'S PIE

Turn mashed potatoes and a few pantry staples into cozy comfort food. This recipe is really flexible, so if you have extra veggies on hand, such as corn or peppers, stir them into the beef mixture for even more goodness.
—Sharon Tipton, Casselberry, FL

Takes: 20 min. • **Makes:** 4 servings

- 1½ lbs. ground beef
- 1 medium onion, chopped
- 2 garlic cloves, minced
- ½ cup water
- 1 envelope taco seasoning
- 2 cups (8 oz.) shredded cheddar cheese, divided
- 3 cups leftover or refrigerated mashed potatoes, warmed

1. Preheat broiler. In a large ovenproof skillet, cook beef, onion and garlic over medium heat until beef is no longer pink, breaking up beef into crumbles; drain. Stir in water and taco seasoning; heat through. Stir in 1 cup cheese. Remove from heat.
2. In a bowl, mix the mashed potatoes and the remaining cheese; spread over beef mixture. Broil 4-6 in. from heat for 5-6 minutes or until top is golden brown.
Per serving: 1 serving equals 782 cal., 45g fat (24g sat. fat), 206mg chol., 1756mg sodium, 40g carb. (5g sugars, 3g fiber), 52g pro.

GOES **GREAT** WITH

Round out the savory pie with cups of vegetable soup made easy from a can.

Table Talk

Describe a time you laughed so hard you cried.

Get ready to give your funny bone a good workout! Fill the kitchen with smiles as everyone at the table talks about the last time they were doubled over with laughter.

MEAL PLANNER

BEEFY ♥ FAVORITES

YOUR COMMITMENT TO SERVING 100 MEALS STARTS HERE!

MEAT LOAF MEAL

ENTREE:
Beef Potato Meat Loaf
page 26

SIDE:
Orange Spice Carrots
page 203

DESSERT:
Banana Pudding
page 266

TAG YOUR MEAL
MEMORIES WITH
#100 FAMILYMEALS

GROCERY LIST

KITCHEN STAPLES
- ○ Ketchup
- ○ Cornstarch
- ○ All-purpose flour
- ○ Sugar
- ○ Brown sugar
- ○ Ground cinnamon
- ○ Ground nutmeg
- ○ Vanilla extract
- ○ Salt
- ○ Pepper
- ○ Butter

PRODUCE
- ○ 4 large ripe bananas
- ○ 1 medium onion
- ○ 1 small green or sweet red pepper
- ○ 1 bunch parsley
- ○ 8 potatoes for mashing
- ○ 2 lbs. medium carrots or baby carrots

PANTRY
- ○ 1 box (16 oz.) saltine crackers
- ○ 1 box (11 oz.) vanilla wafers

MEAT
- ○ 1½ lbs. ground beef

DAIRY
- ○ 2% milk
- ○ ½ dozen large eggs

OTHER
- ○ 1 bottle (15.2 oz.) orange juice

FAMILY FAVORITE

ENTREE:
Beef & Cheese
Skillet Cobbler
page 43

SALAD:
Colorful Quinoa Salad
page 177

DESSERT:
Buttermilk Peach
Ice Cream
page 289

TAG YOUR MEAL
MEMORIES WITH
#100 FAMILYMEALS

GROCERY LIST

KITCHEN STAPLES
- ○ Olive oil
- ○ Honey
- ○ Sugar
- ○ Brown sugar
- ○ Ground cumin
- ○ Vanilla extract
- ○ Salt

PRODUCE
- ○ 2 lbs. ripe peaches
- ○ 1 lemon
- ○ 1 lime
- ○ 1 package (16 oz.) baby spinach
- ○ 1 package (8 oz.) grape tomatoes
- ○ 1 medium cucumber
- ○ 1 medium sweet orange pepper
- ○ 1 medium sweet yellow pepper
- ○ 1 bunch green onions
- ○ Small piece of gingerroot
- ○ 1 bunch cilantro or parsley

PANTRY
- ○ 1 can (15 oz.) black beans
- ○ 1 can (14½ oz.) diced tomatoes with mild green chilies
- ○ 1 can (10 oz.) enchilada sauce
- ○ 1 box (12 oz.) quinoa
- ○ 1 box (40 oz.) biscuit/ baking mix

MEAT
- ○ 1 lb. ground beef
- ○ 1 package (8 oz.) bacon strips

DAIRY
- ○ 1½ cups shredded Colby-Monterey Jack cheese, divided
- ○ 2% milk
- ○ 1 large egg
- ○ Sour cream
- ○ 1 bottle (32 oz.) buttermilk
- ○ ½ pint heavy whipping cream

MEAL PLANNER

BEEFY ♥ FAVORITES

YOUR COMMITMENT TO SERVING 100 MEALS STARTS HERE!

SUREFIRE PLEASER

ENTREE:
Cocoa-Crusted Beef Tenderloin
page 17

SIDES:
Kale Salad, *page 186*
Browned Butter Roasted Cauliflower, *page 209*

DESSERT:
Quick Apple Crisp
page 250

TAG YOUR MEAL
MEMORIES WITH
#100 FAMILYMEALS

GROCERY LIST

KITCHEN STAPLES
- Olive oil
- Baking cocoa
- All-purpose flour
- Brown sugar
- Ground cinnamon
- Ground nutmeg
- Salt
- Pepper

PRODUCE
- 9 medium tart apples
- 1 bunch kale
- 1 medium head cauliflower

- 1 bunch parsley
- 1 head of garlic

MEAT
- 4 beef tenderloin steaks (6 oz. each)

PANTRY
- 1 box (14.4 oz.) graham crackers
- 1 box (15 oz.) golden raisins
- 1 jar (3.5 oz.) capers

DAIRY
- Unsalted butter
- 1 pkg. (4 oz.) crumbled feta cheese

OTHER
- 1 bottle (2.5 oz.) lemon juice
- Salted pumpkin seeds or pepitas (2 oz.)
- Finely ground coffee
- Frozen whipped topping or ice cream

✂ -

CLASSIC TWIST

ENTREE:
Chili Sloppy Joes
page 19

SIDES:
Roasted Sweet Potato Wedges
page 214

DESSERT:
Coconut Macaroon Pie
page 253

TAG YOUR MEAL
MEMORIES WITH
#100 FAMILYMEALS

GROCERY LIST

KITCHEN STAPLES
- Olive oil
- Yellow mustard
- Brown sugar
- All-purpose flour
- Almond extract
- Butter
- Salt
- Pepper

PRODUCE
- 1 medium sweet onion
- 1 medium green pepper
- 1 jalapeno pepper

- 2 medium sweet potatoes (about 1 lb.)
- 1 bunch cilantro

PANTRY
- 1 bottle (12 oz.) chili sauce
- 1 can (7 oz.) chipotle peppers in adobo sauce
- Curry powder
- Smoked paprika
- 1 can (14 oz.) sweetened condensed milk
- Mango chutney

MEAT
- 1 lb. lean ground beef (90% lean)

DAIRY
- 2 large eggs

BAKERY
- 6 hamburger buns or kaiser rolls

OTHER
- 1 sheet refrigerated pie pastry
- 1 pkg. (14 oz.) flaked coconut

Kicking Up Mealtime

Cocoa-Crusted Beef Tenderloin (p. 17), Kale Salad (p. 186) and Browned Butter Roasted Cauliflower (p. 209)

YOU KNOW YOU HAVE A COOL DAD WHEN you get home from school and find out he's planned a father-daughter cook-off. That's what happened to Gina Myers of Spokane, Washington (above). As a high school freshman, she was a fan of *Chopped*, a TV show featuring chefs who each have to turn the contents of "mystery baskets" into great food on the fly.

"One day my dad had two mystery baskets waiting, ready for a competition," Gina says. The pair had such a blast, they staged several more cook-offs. Her mom and sister were the judges. Talk about taking family meals to new heights!

Gina was so inspired by the friendly food wars, she's now a student at The Culinary Institute of America in Hyde Park, New York. When she graduates, she hopes to use her skills for good: "I'd like to work with people in impoverished nations, helping to establish healthy and environmentally friendly food systems.

Who's the best cook in the family? "I always won," Gina says, "and Dad was always so cute about it."

Serve Gina's award-winning entree on a bed of mashed sweet potatoes (above), or create a little friendly competition of your own. Start off easy with an appetizer cook-off or a no-fuss desserts contest. Not only will you enjoy a fun family meal, but you'll build memories to last a lifetime.

"Any day is better when you're with the ones you love and good food."

—Becky Lohmiller
Monticello, Indiana

CHICKEN
and TURKEY

COOK UP memories with satisfying dinner staples like these.

"We make it a priority to sit down to dinner together at least six nights a week."

—BECKY LOHMILLER, MONTICELLO, IN

EAT SMART **SLOW COOKER**

SLOW COOKER CHICKEN TACOS

We enjoy this zesty chicken in several meals including tacos, sandwiches, omelets and enchiladas. My little guys love to help measure the seasonings.
—Karie Houghton, Lynnwood, WA

Prep: 10 min. • **Cook:** 3 hours
Makes: 8 servings

- 3 tsp. chili powder
- 1 tsp. each ground cumin, seasoned salt and pepper
- ½ tsp. each white pepper, ground chipotle pepper and paprika
- ¼ tsp. dried oregano
- ¼ tsp. crushed red pepper flakes
- 1½ lbs. boneless skinless chicken breasts
- 1 cup chicken broth
- 16 corn tortillas or flour tortillas
  Optional toppings: chopped tomatoes, sliced avocado, shredded cheddar cheese, thinly sliced green onions and torn romaine.

1. Mix seasonings; rub over chicken. Place in a 3-qt. slow cooker. Add broth. Cook, covered, on low 3-4 hours or until chicken is tender (a thermometer inserted in chicken should read at least 165°).
2. Remove chicken; cool slightly. Shred with two forks. Serve with tortillas and toppings as desired.

Per serving: 2 tacos (calculated without toppings) equals 204 cal., 4g fat (1g sat. fat), 48mg chol., 409mg sodium, 23g carb. (1g sugars, 4g fiber), 20g pro. **Diabetic Exchanges:** 3 lean meats, 1½ starch.

GOES **GREAT** WITH

Mom's Spanish Rice is a great addition to these tacos! You'll find the easy recipe on page 205.

Mom's Spanish Rice is a great addition to these tacos! You'll find the easy recipe on page 205.

BACON & SWISS CHICKEN SANDWICHES

I created this sandwich based on one my daughter tried at a restaurant. She prefers my version and likes to dip it in the extra honey mustard sauce.
—Marilyn Moberg, Papillion, NE

Takes: 25 min. • **Makes:** 4 servings

- ¼ cup reduced-fat mayonnaise
- 1 Tbsp. Dijon mustard
- 1 Tbsp. honey
- 4 boneless skinless chicken breast halves (4 oz. each)
- ½ tsp. Montreal steak seasoning
- 4 slices Swiss cheese
- 4 whole wheat hamburger buns, split
- 2 bacon strips, cooked and crumbled
  Lettuce leaves and tomato slices, optional

1. In a small bowl, mix the mayonnaise, mustard and honey. Pound chicken with a meat mallet to ½-in. thickness. Sprinkle chicken with steak seasoning. Grill chicken, covered, over medium heat or broil 4 in. from heat for 4-6 minutes on each side or until a thermometer reads 165°. Top with the cheese during the last 1 minute of cooking.

2. Grill buns over medium heat, cut side down, for 30-60 seconds or until toasted. Serve the chicken on buns with the bacon, mayonnaise mixture and, if desired, the lettuce and tomato.

Per serving: 1 sandwich equals 410 cal., 17g fat (6g sat. fat), 91mg chol., 667mg sodium, 29g carb. (9g sugars, 3g fiber), 34g pro.
Diabetic Exchanges: 2 starch, 4 lean meat, 2 fat.

EAT SMART

QUICK CHICKEN PARMESAN

Frozen chicken strips make this family favorite a snap when time is tight. The tangy sauce is simple and satisfying, and the longer it simmers, the better it tastes!
—Danielle Grochowski, Milwaukee, WI

Prep: 10 min. • **Cook:** 25 min.
Makes: 4 servings

- 12 **oz. frozen grilled chicken breast strips (about 3 cups)**
- 1 **can (14½ oz.) diced tomatoes, undrained**
- 1 **can (6 oz.) tomato paste**
- 2 **Tbsp. dry red wine or chicken broth**
- 1 **Tbsp. olive oil**
- 1½ **tsp. Italian seasoning**
- 1 **garlic clove, minced**
- ½ **tsp. sugar**
- ⅓ **cup shredded Parmesan cheese**
- ⅓ **cup shredded part-skim mozzarella cheese**
  Hot cooked pasta

1. Heat a large skillet over medium heat. Add the chicken strips; cook and stir for 5-8 minutes or until heated through. Remove from pan.
2. In the same skillet, combine tomatoes, tomato paste, wine, oil, Italian seasoning, garlic and sugar; bring to a boil, stirring occasionally. Reduce the heat; simmer, uncovered, 10-15 minutes to allow flavors to blend, stirring occasionally.
3. Stir in chicken. Sprinkle with cheeses; cook, covered, for 1-2 minutes longer or until cheese is melted. Serve with pasta.
Per serving: 1 cup (calculated without pasta) equals 248 cal., 9g fat (3g sat. fat), 86mg chol., 739mg sodium, 15g carb. (8g sugars, 3g fiber), 28g pro. **Diabetic Exchanges:** 3 lean meat, 2 vegetable, 2 fat.

GOES **GREAT** WITH

Zap a package of frozen green beans in the microwave to serve alongside this popular chicken entree.

TURKEY MUSHROOM TETRAZZINI

Get ready for your family to go wild over this Parmesan-topped tetrazzini. It's so rich, creamy and satisfying that no one will suspect it's low in fat.

—Irene Banegas, Las Cruces, NM

Prep: 25 min. • **Bake:** 25 min.
Makes: 6 servings

- ½ lb. uncooked spaghetti
- ¼ cup finely chopped onion
- 1 Tbsp. butter
- 1 garlic clove, minced
- 3 Tbsp. cornstarch
- 1 can (14½ oz.) reduced-sodium chicken broth
- 1 can (12 oz.) fat-free evaporated milk
- 2½ cups cubed cooked turkey breast
- 1 can (4 oz.) mushroom stems and pieces, drained
- ½ tsp. seasoned salt
  Dash pepper
- 2 Tbsp. grated Parmesan cheese
- ¼ tsp. paprika

1. Cook spaghetti according to package directions; drain.

2. In a large saucepan, saute the onion in butter until tender. Add the garlic; cook for 1 minute longer. Combine cornstarch and broth until smooth; stir into the onion mixture. Bring to a boil; cook and stir for 2 minutes or until thickened.

3. Reduce heat to low. Add milk; cook and stir for 2-3 minutes. Stir in the spaghetti, turkey, mushrooms, seasoned salt and the pepper.

4. Transfer to an 8-in. square baking dish coated with cooking spray. Cover and bake at 350° for 20 minutes. Uncover; sprinkle with cheese and paprika. Bake tetrazzini 5-10 minutes longer or until heated through.

Per serving: 1¼ cup equals 331 cal., 5g fat (2g sat. fat), 51mg chol., 544mg sodium, 41g carb. (10g sugars, 1g fiber), 28g pro. **Diabetic Exchanges:** 2 starch, 3 lean meat, 1 vegetable, ½ fat-free milk.

GOES GREAT WITH

Small bowls of fruit salad make a colorful addition to this meal-in-one casserole.

NOTES

_____
_____
_____
_____
_____
_____
_____

Talkin' Turkey
Turkey Mushroom Tetrazzini is a great way to use up leftover turkey (or even chicken). If you're going to cook poultry specifically for this dish, however, feel free to season it with ground sage, poultry seasoning or whatever herbs you like best.

FAST FIX ▶

SPEEDY CHICKEN MARSALA

I created my own version of a favorite restaurant dish. You can make it in a flash on a busy night.
—Trisha Kruse, Eagle, ID

Takes: 30 min. • **Makes:** 4 servings

- 8 oz. uncooked whole wheat or multigrain angel hair pasta
- 4 boneless skinless chicken breast halves (5 oz. each)
- ¼ cup all-purpose flour
- 1 tsp. lemon-pepper seasoning
- ½ tsp. salt
- 2 Tbsp. olive oil, divided
- 4 cups sliced fresh mushrooms
- 1 garlic clove, minced
- 1 cup dry Marsala wine

1. Cook the pasta according to package directions. Pound chicken with a meat mallet to ¼-in. thickness. In a large resealable plastic bag, mix the flour, lemon pepper and salt. Add chicken, one piece at a time; close bag and shake to coat.
2. In a large skillet, heat 1 Tbsp. oil over medium heat. Add the chicken; cook for 4-5 minutes on each side or until no longer pink. Remove from pan.
3. In the same skillet, heat remaining oil over medium-high heat. Add mushrooms; cook and stir until tender. Add garlic; cook 1 minute longer. Add wine; bring to a boil. Cook for for 5-6 minutes or until liquid is reduced by half, stirring to loosen the browned bits from pan. Return chicken to the pan, turning to coat with sauce; heat through.
4. Drain pasta; serve with chicken mixture.
Per serving: 1 serving equals 493 cal., 11g fat (2g sat. fat), 78mg chol., 279mg sodium, 50g carb. (4g sugars, 7g fiber), 40g pro.

Protein POWERHOUSE

GOES GREAT WITH

Lemon-Roasted Asparagus is a delightful addition to the chicken. See the recipe on page 203.

PECAN-CRUSTED CHICKEN NUGGETS

Every family goes through the chicken nugget phase. If you're stuck in a nugget rut, try this healthy homemade version.
—Haili Carroll, Valencia, CA

Takes: 30 min. • **Makes:** 6 servings

- 1½ cups cornflakes
- 1 Tbsp. dried parsley flakes
- 1 tsp. salt
- ½ tsp. garlic powder
- ½ tsp. pepper
- ½ cup panko (Japanese) bread crumbs
- ½ cup finely chopped pecans
- 3 Tbsp. 2% milk
- 1½ lbs. boneless skinless chicken breasts, cut into 1-in. pieces
  Cooking spray

1. Preheat oven to 400°. Place cornflakes, parsley, salt, garlic powder and pepper in a blender; cover and pulse until finely ground. Transfer to a shallow bowl; stir in bread crumbs and pecans. Place the milk in another shallow bowl. Dip chicken in milk, then roll in crumb mixture to coat.

2. Place on a greased baking sheet; spritz chicken with cooking spray. Bake for 12-16 minutes or until chicken is no longer pink, turning the nuggets once halfway through cooking.

Per serving: 3 oz. cooked chicken equals 206 cal., 9g fat (1g sat. fat), 63mg chol., 290mg sodium, 6g carb. (1g sugars, 1g fiber), 24g pro. **Diabetic Exchanges:** ½ starch, 3 lean meat, 1 fat.

GOES GREAT WITH

Buttered noodles make an easy addition to these nuggets.

SPEEDY SWAPS!

DON'T HAVE CHICKEN THIGHS?
Use boneless, skinless chicken breasts instead. Bake until the thickest part of the breast is no longer pink.

DON'T HAVE ALL THE HERBS?
Simply try a teaspoon of Italian Seasoning.

ROASTED CHICKEN THIGHS WITH PEPPERS & POTATOES

This homey dish is simpler than it looks. Add fresh herbs from your garden to make it even better.

—Pattie Prescott, Manchester, NH

Prep: 20 min. • **Bake:** 35 min.
Makes: 8 servings

- 2 lbs. red potatoes (about 6 medium)
- 2 large sweet red peppers
- 2 large green peppers
- 2 medium onions
- 2 Tbsp. olive oil, divided
- 4 tsp. minced fresh thyme or 1½ tsp. dried thyme, divided
- 3 tsp. minced fresh rosemary or 1 tsp. dried rosemary, crushed, divided
- ⅛ boneless skinless chicken thighs (about 2 lbs.)
- ½ tsp. salt
- ¼ tsp. pepper

1. Preheat oven to 450°. Cut the potatoes, peppers and onions into 1-in. pieces. Place vegetables in a roasting pan. Drizzle with 1 Tbsp. oil; sprinkle with 2 tsp. each thyme and rosemary and toss to coat. Place the chicken over vegetables. Brush chicken with remaining oil; sprinkle with remaining thyme and rosemary. Sprinkle vegetables and chicken with salt and pepper.

2. Roast for 35-40 minutes or until a thermometer inserted in chicken reads 170° and vegetables are tender.

Per serving: 1 chicken thigh with 1 cup vegetables equals 308 cal., 12g fat (3g sat. fat), 76mg chol., 221mg sodium, 25g carb. (5g sugars, 4g fiber), 24g pro. **Diabetic Exchanges:** 1 starch, 3 lean meat, 1 vegetable, ½ fat.

GOES GREAT WITH

Treat your taste buds to a sweet sorbet after dinner. Turn to page 274 for this make-ahead light dessert.

NOTES

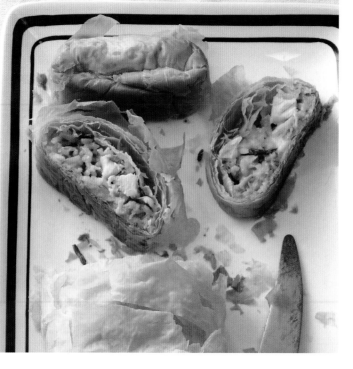

GOES GREAT WITH

Cranberry sauce isn't just for Thanksgiving! Try it alongside slices of the strudel.

CRISPY FRIED CHICKEN

My signature fried chicken can be served while it's hot or pulled out of the fridge to enjoy as leftovers the next day. It's an easy meal, and folks love it either way.
—Jeanne Schnitzler, Lima, MT

Prep: 10 min. • **Cook:** 10 min./batch
Makes: 8 servings

 4 cups all-purpose flour, divided
 2 Tbsp. garlic salt
 1 Tbsp. paprika
 3 tsp. pepper, divided
2½ tsp. poultry seasoning
 2 large eggs
1½ cups water
 1 tsp. salt
 2 broiler/fryer chickens
    (3½ to 4 lbs. each), cut up
    Oil for deep-fat frying

1. In a large resealable plastic bag, combine 2⅔ cups of the flour, garlic salt, paprika, 2½ tsp. pepper and poultry seasoning. In a shallow bowl, beat eggs and water; add salt and the remaining flour and pepper. Dip the chicken in the egg mixture, then place in the bag, a few pieces at a time. Seal the bag and shake to coat.
2. In a deep-fat fryer, heat oil to 375°. Fry the chicken, several pieces at a time, for 5-6 minutes on each side or until golden brown and juices run clear. Drain chicken on paper towels.
Per serving: 2 pieces equals 469 cal., 14g fat (4g sat. fat), 130mg chol., 1738mg sodium, 50g carb. (1g sugars, 2g fiber), 33g pro.

FAST FIX
CHICKEN & WILD RICE STRUDELS

Does your family's full schedule leave you feeling a little hectic and harried? With this easy recipe, you'll have savory strudel in the oven in 10 minutes flat. It's a lifesaver on busy weeknights.
—Johnna Johnson, Scottsdale, AZ

Takes: 30 min. • **Makes:** 6 servings

 1 pkg. (8.8 oz.) ready-to-serve long grain and wild rice
1½ cups coarsely chopped rotisserie chicken
 ½ cup shredded Swiss cheese
 ½ tsp. Italian seasoning
 ¼ tsp. salt
 ¼ tsp. pepper
12 sheets phyllo dough (14x9-in. size)
 6 Tbsp. butter, melted

1. Preheat oven to 400°. Place the first six ingredients in a bowl; toss to combine.
2. Place one sheet of phyllo dough on a work surface; brush lightly with melted butter. Layer with five additional sheets, brushing each layer with butter. (Keep the remaining phyllo covered with plastic wrap and a damp towel to prevent it from drying out.)
3. Spoon half of the rice mixture down the center of the phyllo dough to within 1 in. of ends. Fold up the short sides to enclose the filling. Roll up tightly, starting with a long side.
4. Transfer to a parchment paper-lined 15x10x1-in. baking pan, seam side down. Brush with additional butter. Repeat with the remaining ingredients to make second strudel. Bake strudels 20-25 minutes or until golden brown and heated through.
Per serving: 1 slice equal 323 cal., 18g fat (10g sat. fat), 70mg chol., 550mg sodium, 25g carb. (1g sugars, 1g fiber), 16g pro.

**Become a
Fry Guy**

If you don't have a
deep-fat fryer or
electric fry pan with
a thermostat, you can
use a kettle or Dutch
oven together with
a thermometer so
you can accurately
regulate the
temperature of the
oil. Never overload
the kettle, Dutch oven
or fryer. Fry foods in
batches instead. It's
safer and the food
will cook evenly.

GOES GREAT WITH

*Buttery corn bread makes
a finger-licking addition
to fried chicken.*

FAST FIX ▶

CHICKEN CAESAR PIZZA

When you think of toppings for a pizza, dressed salad greens probably aren't the first things that comes to mind. But try this fun take on the classic Caesar salad and you might agree—it's fantastic!
—Tracy Youngman, Post Falls, ID

Takes: 30 min. • **Makes:** 6 servings

- 1   tube (13.8 oz.) refrigerated pizza crust
- 1   Tbsp. olive oil
- 1   lb. boneless skinless chicken breasts, cut into ½-in. cubes
- 1½ tsp. minced garlic, divided
- 6   Tbsp. creamy Caesar salad dressing, divided
- 2   cups (8 oz.) shredded Monterey Jack cheese
- ½   cup grated Parmesan cheese
- 2   cups hearts of romaine salad mix
- 2   green onions, thinly sliced
- 2   plum tomatoes, chopped

1. Preheat oven to 400°. Unroll pizza crust and press to fit into a greased 15x10x1-in. baking pan, pinching edges to form a rim. Bake for 10 minutes or until the edges are lightly browned.

2. Meanwhile, in a large skillet, heat the oil over medium-high heat. Add chicken and ½ tsp. garlic; cook and stir until chicken is no longer pink. Remove from heat; stir in 2 Tbsp. salad dressing. Spread crust with 3 Tbsp. of salad dressing; sprinkle with the remaining garlic. Top with half of the cheeses and all of the chicken. Sprinkle with the remaining cheeses. Bake for 10-15 minutes or until the crust is golden brown and cheese is melted.

3. In a small bowl, toss the salad mix and green onions with the remaining dressing. Just before serving, top the pizza with salad and tomatoes.

Per serving: ⅙ of pizza equals 506 cal., 25g fat (10g sat. fat), 86mg chol., 927mg sodium, 34g carb. (4g sugars, 2g fiber), 34g pro.

"Really good! I used additional tomatoes, and I also used a Monterey pepper jack cheese, which gave it some bite. I added some sliced black olives for color. Excellent results. Leftovers were good, too."

—JLBJEANIE, TASTEOFHOME.COM

GOES GREAT WITH

A crisp cucumber salad makes a refreshing side dish for this change-of-pace pizza.

MAKE IT
SERVE IT
SHARE IT

Don't be shy!
Post your favorite recipes, time-saving hints and family photos on social media today.
#100FamilyMeals

FAMILY
FAVORITE

BARBECUE CHICKEN QUESADILLAS

These oven-baked quesadillas are fast to fix, fun to eat—and filling. My kids always asked for them when they were growing up. Stuff the tortillas with leftover or store-bought rotisserie chicken to keep prep easy.
—Pam Martin, Canandaigua, NY

Takes: 25 min. • **Makes:** 6 servings

- 3 **cups shredded cooked chicken**
- 1 **can (4 oz.) chopped green chilies**
- ½ **cup salsa**
- ⅓ **cup barbecue sauce**
- ¼ **cup taco sauce**
- 8 **flour tortillas (8 in.)**
- ¾ **cup shredded sharp cheddar cheese**
     Sour cream and additional salsa, optional

1. Preheat oven to 450°. In a large bowl, combine the first five ingredients; toss to combine. Divide four tortillas between two baking sheets; spread with chicken mixture. Sprinkle with cheese and top with remaining tortillas.

2. Bake for 6-8 minutes or until lightly browned and cheese is melted. Cut each quesadilla into six wedges. If desired, serve with sour cream and additional salsa.

Per serving: 4 wedges (calculated without sour cream and additional salsa) equals 446 cal., 15g fat (5g sat. fat), 77mg chol., 814mg sodium, 46g carb. (6g sugars, 3g fiber), 30g pro.

GOES GREAT WITH

Slices of fresh, colorful avocado make fun additions to these quesadillas.

"Very yummy and tasty! Even my teenagers loved it. I used a frozen Asian vegetable stir-fry blend with water chestnuts, and I loved the crunchiness of it."

—ISANCHEZ, TASTEOFHOME.COM

EAT SMART FAST FIX ▶

ASIAN TURKEY LETTUCE CUPS

Here's a cool, crisp idea for a light lunch or appetizers for a summer party. When I want to make it easier for my kids to eat, I mix it all up with shredded lettuce and serve it as a salad.
—Diana Rios, Lytle, TX

Takes: 30 min. • **Makes:** 4 servings

- 3 Tbsp. reduced-sodium soy sauce
- 2 tsp. sugar
- 2 tsp. sesame oil
- 1 tsp. Thai chili sauce, optional
- 1 lb. lean ground turkey
- 1 celery rib, chopped
- 1 Tbsp. minced fresh gingerroot
- 1 garlic clove, minced
- 1 can (8 oz.) water chestnuts, drained and chopped
- 1 medium carrot, shredded
- 2 cups cooked brown rice
- 8 Bibb or Boston lettuce leaves

1. In a small bowl, whisk soy sauce, sugar, sesame oil and, if desired, chili sauce until blended. In a large skillet, cook turkey and celery 6-9 minutes or until turkey is no longer pink, breaking up the turkey into crumbles; drain.

2. Add ginger and garlic to turkey; cook 2 minutes. Stir in soy sauce mixture, water chestnuts and carrot; cook for 2 minutes longer. Stir in rice; heat through. Serve in lettuce leaves.

Per serving: 2 filled lettuce cups equals 353 cal., 13g fat (3g sat. fat), 90mg chol., 589mg sodium, 35g carb. (5g sugars, 4g fiber), 24g pro. **Diabetic Exchanges:** 2 starch, 3 lean meat, 1 vegetable, ½ fat.

GOES **GREAT** WITH

Consider serving Edamame Corn Carrot Salad when Asian Turkey Lettuce Cups are on the menu. You'll find it on page 176.

CHICKEN PENNE CASEROLE

I make this family favorite casserole every week or two, and we never tire of it. I like that I can put it all together and then relax while it bakes.
—Carmen Vanosch, Vernon, BC

....

Prep: 35 min. • **Bake:** 45 min.
Makes: 4 servings

1½	cups uncooked penne pasta
1	Tbsp. canola oil
1	lb. boneless skinless chicken thighs, cut into 1-in. pieces
½	cup chopped onion
½	cup chopped green pepper
½	cup chopped sweet red pepper
1	tsp. dried basil
1	tsp. dried oregano
1	tsp. dried parsley flakes
½	tsp. salt
½	tsp. crushed red pepper flakes
3	garlic cloves, minced
1	can (14½ oz.) diced tomatoes, undrained
3	Tbsp. tomato paste
¾	cup chicken broth
2	cups (8 oz.) shredded part-skim mozzarella cheese
½	cup grated Romano cheese

1. Preheat oven to 350°. Cook pasta according to the package directions. Meanwhile, in a large saucepan, heat oil over medium heat. Add chicken, onion, peppers and seasonings; saute until the chicken is no longer pink. Add garlic; cook 1 minute longer.

2. In a blender, pulse the tomatoes and tomato paste, covered, until blended. Add to chicken mixture. Stir in the broth; bring to a boil over medium-high heat. Reduce the heat; cover and simmer until slightly thickened, 10-15 minutes.

3. Drain pasta; toss with chicken mixture. Spoon half of the mixture into a greased 2-qt. baking dish. Sprinkle with half of the cheeses. Repeat layers.

4. Cover and bake 30 minutes. Uncover; bake the casserole until heated through, 15-20 minutes longer.

Per serving: 1½ cups equals 579 cal., 28g fat (12g sat. fat), 128mg chol., 1357mg sodium, 36g carb. (9g sugars, 4g fiber), 47g pro.

GOES GREAT WITH

Nutella Hand Pies are a great finale to any meal, including this casserole! See the recipe on page 262.

GOES GREAT WITH

Give Eddie's Favorite Fiesta Corn a try if this chicken entree is on the menu. See the recipe on page 206 for the no-fuss details.

SWEET TEA BARBECUED CHICKEN

Some marinades use coffee or espresso, so I decided to try the same concept with sweet tea and apple juice. The tea lends a pleasing Southern twist to the barbecue sauce for this grilled chicken.
—Kelly Williams, Forked River, NJ

Prep: 15 min. • **Cook:** 1 hour
Makes: 8 servings

- 1 cup unsweetened apple juice
- 1 cup water
- 2 tsp. seafood seasoning
- 1 tsp. paprika
- 1 tsp. garlic powder
- 1 tsp. coarsely ground pepper
- 1 broiler/fryer chicken (4 to 5 lbs.), cut up
- 1 cup barbecue sauce
- ½ cup sweet tea

1. Preheat oven to 350°. Pour apple juice and water into a large shallow roasting pan. Mix the seafood seasoning, paprika, garlic powder and pepper; rub over the chicken. Place in roasting pan.
2. Bake, covered, until juices run clear and a thermometer reads 170° to 175°, about 50-60 minutes. Transfer the chicken to a foil-lined 15x10x1-in. baking pan. Whisk barbecue sauce and sweet tea; brush over the chicken.
3. Place chicken on greased grill rack; grill over medium heat 3-4 minutes per side, brushing occasionally with the remaining barbecue sauce.
Per serving: 1 piece equals 374 cal., 17g fat (5g sat. fat), 104mg chol., 608mg sodium, 19g carb. (16g sugars, 1g fiber), 33g pro.

GOES GREAT WITH
Grab a tube of buttermilk biscuit dough, and bake the biscuits up as this stew finishes simmering.

EAT SMART   SLOW COOKER
SPRING-THYME CHICKEN STEW

One particularly long winter, we were in need of something warm, comforting but also bright to get us in the mood for spring. This stew, so reminiscent of my mom's chicken soup, did the trick.
—Amy Chase, Vanderhoof, BC

Prep: 15 min. • **Cook:** 7 hours
Makes: 4 servings

- 1 lb. small red potatoes, halved
- 1 large onion, finely chopped
- ¾ cup shredded carrots
- 3 Tbsp. all-purpose flour
- 6 garlic cloves, minced
- 2 tsp. grated lemon peel
- 2 tsp. dried thyme
- ½ tsp. salt
- ¼ tsp. pepper
- 1½ lbs. boneless skinless chicken thighs, halved
- 2 cups reduced-sodium chicken broth
- 2 bay leaves
- 2 Tbsp. minced fresh parsley

1. Place potatoes, onion and carrots in a 3-qt. slow cooker. Sprinkle with flour, garlic, lemon peel, thyme, salt and pepper; toss to coat. Place chicken over top. Add broth and bay leaves.
2. Cook, covered, on low for 7-9 hours or until the chicken and vegetables are tender. Remove the bay leaves. Sprinkle individual servings with parsley.
Per serving: 1 serving equals 395 cal., 13g fat (3g sat. fat), 113mg chol., 707mg sodium, 32g carb. (5g sugars, 4g fiber), 37g pro. **Diabetic Exchanges:** 1½ starch, 5 lean meat, 2 vegetable.

MOM'S CHICKEN TETRAZZINI

I toss together baked chicken spaghetti when my family craves a warm, cozy meal. If I have leftover turkey on hand, I'll use that instead.
—Jennifer Petrino, Newnan, GA

Prep: 35 min. • **Bake:** 25 min. + standing
Makes: 6 servings

- 8 oz. uncooked spaghetti
- 2 tsp. plus 3 Tbsp. butter, divided
- 8 bacon strips, chopped
- 2 cups sliced fresh mushrooms
- 1 small onion, chopped
- 1 small green pepper, chopped
- ⅓ cup all-purpose flour
- ¼ tsp. salt
- ¼ tsp. pepper
- 3 cups chicken broth
- 3 cups coarsely shredded rotisserie chicken
- 2 cups frozen peas (about 8 oz.)
- 1 jar (4 oz.) diced pimientos, drained
- ½ cup grated Romano or Parmesan cheese

1. Preheat oven to 375°. Cook spaghetti according to the package directions for al dente. Drain; transfer to a greased 13x9-in. baking dish. Add 2 tsp. butter and toss to coat.

2. Meanwhile, in a large skillet, cook the bacon over medium heat until crisp, stirring occasionally. Remove the bacon with a slotted spoon; drain on paper towels. Discard the drippings, reserving 1 Tbsp. in pan. Add mushrooms, onion and green pepper to drippings; cook and stir over medium-high heat 5-7 minutes or until tender. Remove from pan.

3. In same pan, heat the remaining butter over medium heat. Stir in flour, salt and pepper until smooth; gradually whisk in broth. Bring to a boil, stirring occasionally; cook and stir 3-5 minutes or until slightly thickened. Add chicken, peas, pimientos and the mushroom mixture; heat through, stirring occasionally. Spoon the chicken mixture over spaghetti. Sprinkle with the bacon and cheese.

4. Bake, uncovered, 25-30 minutes or until golden brown. Let stand for 10 minutes before serving.

Per serving: 1½ cups equals 533 cal., 23g fat (10g sat. fat), 107mg chol., 1133mg sodium, 44g carb. (6g sugars, 4g fiber), 38g pro.

GOES **GREAT** WITH

Turn to page 177 for Apple-Pecan Salad with Honey Vinaigrette. It's a tasty addition to the tetrazzini.

FAMILY
FAVORITE
♥

Revisiting
A Classic

Carefully hold spaghetti in boiling water and ease it down into the water as it softens, pushing it around the edge of the pan. When fully immersed in the water, stir the spaghetti to separate strands.

CRUMB-COATED RANCH CHICKEN

Ranch dressing and seasonings add zesty flavor to a crunchy coating of cornflakes in this five-ingredient recipe.
—LaDonna Reed, Ponca City, OK

Prep: 10 min. • **Bake:** 30 min.
Makes: 4 servings

- ⅔ cup ranch salad dressing
- 2 cups coarsely crushed cornflakes
- 1 Tbsp. Italian seasoning
- 1 tsp. garlic powder
- 4 boneless skinless chicken breast halves (6 oz. each)

1. Preheat oven to 400°. Place the salad dressing in a shallow bowl. In a separate shallow bowl, mix the cornflakes, Italian seasoning and garlic powder. Dip chicken in the dressing, then in cornflake mixture, patting to help coating adhere.
2. Place on a greased baking sheet. Bake 30-35 minutes or until a thermometer reads 165°.
Per serving: 1 serving equals 495 cal., 20g fat (4g sat. fat), 99mg chol., 642mg sodium, 41g carb. (5g sugars, trace fiber), 37g pro.

GOES GREAT WITH

See page 197 for a colorful side dish just perfect for the chicken. Cheese Tortellini with Tomatoes and Corn is sure to be a new favorite.

THAI CHICKEN TACOS

Not only are these an awesome way to jazz up taco night, but with rotisserie chicken you can rely on a fast prep. If you have a little extra time, let the carrot and cucumber marinate in some rice vinegar.
—Melissa Halonen, Spokane, WA

Takes: 25 min. • **Makes:** 6 servings

- 12 **taco shells**
- 1 **rotisserie chicken, skin removed, shredded**
- 1 **bottle (11½ oz.) Thai peanut sauce, divided**
- 1 **medium cucumber, julienned**
- 1 **medium carrot, julienned**
- ⅓ **cup minced fresh cilantro**

1. Heat taco shells according to package directions. Meanwhile, in a large skillet, combine chicken and ½ cup peanut sauce; heat through.

2. In a small bowl, mix cucumber, carrot and cilantro. Serve chicken in taco shells with cucumber mixture and remaining peanut sauce.

Per serving: 2 tacos equals 434 cal., 21g fat (4g sat. fat), 62mg chol., 589mg sodium, 31g carb. (14g sugars, 1g fiber), 29g pro.

GOES GREAT WITH

While picking up the rotisserie chicken, grab some seafood pasta salad from the deli to serve with the tacos.

GOES GREAT WITH

Slices of the Honey Beer Bread on page 238 make a welcome addition to this pasta dinner.

FAST FIX ▶

GARDEN PASTA WITH CHICKEN

Here's a great 30-minute meal that everyone will love. If you don't feel like grilling, prepare the chicken sausages under the broiler or on the stovetop.
—Karie Houghton, Lynnwood, WA

Takes: 30 min. • **Makes:** 8 servings

3¼ cups uncooked mini penne pasta
1 pkg. (12 oz.) fully cooked roasted garlic chicken sausage links or flavor of your choice
4 medium tomatoes, chopped (about 3 cups)
1 round (8 oz.) Brie cheese, cubed
1 cup shredded Parmesan cheese
1 cup loosely packed basil leaves, thinly sliced
3 garlic cloves, minced
½ tsp. salt
½ tsp. pepper
¼ cup olive oil

1. Cook pasta according to the package directions. Meanwhile, grill the sausages, covered, turning occasionally, over medium heat or broil 4 in. from heat for 7-9 minutes or until a thermometer reads 165°. Remove sausage from the grill; cut into slices.

2. Drain pasta; transfer to a large bowl. Stir in sausage, tomatoes, cheeses, basil, garlic, salt and pepper. Drizzle with oil; toss to coat.

Per serving: 1½ cups equals 445 cal., 22g fat (9g sat. fat), 71mg chol., 739mg sodium, 40g carb. (3g sugars, 3g fiber), 24g pro.

"We always seem to have our very best conversations in the kitchen."

—YVONNE NAVE, LYONS, KS

FAST FIX ▶

SPAGHETTI SALAD

We love chilled chicken pasta salad brimming with fresh veggies. If you prefer a meatless version, omit the chicken and toss in more edamame.
—Cindy Heinbaugh, Aurora, CO

....

Takes: 30 min. • **Makes:** 8 servings

- 1 pkg. (16 oz.) whole wheat spaghetti
- 1 cup frozen shelled edamame
- 1 tsp. minced fresh gingerroot
- 1 cup reduced-fat sesame ginger salad dressing
- 3 cups cubed cooked chicken breast
- 1 English cucumber, chopped
- 1 medium sweet red pepper, chopped
- 1 small sweet yellow pepper, chopped
- 1 small red onion, finely chopped
- 3 green onions, sliced

1. Cook spaghetti according to package directions, adding edamame during the last 5 minutes of cooking. Rinse in cold water and drain well. Meanwhile, stir ginger into salad dressing.
2. In a large bowl, combine spaghetti, chicken, cucumber, peppers and red onion. Add the dressing; toss to coat. Sprinkle with green onions.
Per serving: 1¾ cups equals 353 cal., 5g fat (1g sat. fat), 40mg chol., 432mg sodium, 53g carb. (6g sugars, 8g fiber), 26g pro.

GOES GREAT WITH

Visit the Asian-foods aisle at the store and pick up a box of fortune cookies for a fun addition to this meal.

Table Talk

If you could create a ride at an amusement park, what would it be?

Fasten your seatbelt and hold on tight! You're in for a crazy ride when your family takes turns describing their dream roller coaster, water slide or other park attraction.

SPANISH RICE WITH CHICKEN & PEAS

My mom made some fantastic meals while I was growing up. This juicy chicken and rice was one of her specialties. She made it every Wednesday, and now I'm proud to serve it to my family.
—Josee Lanzi, New Port Richey, FL

Prep: 15 min. • **Cook:** 30 min.
Makes: 6 servings

- 1 lb. boneless skinless chicken breasts, cut into 1½-in. pieces
- 1 Tbsp. all-purpose flour
- ½ tsp. pepper
- ½ tsp. salt, divided

GOES GREAT WITH

Give canned refried beans a makeover by stirring in a little butter and ground cumin.

- 4 tsp. plus 1 Tbsp. olive oil, divided
- 1 small sweet red pepper, chopped
- 1 small onion, chopped
- 1 celery rib, chopped
- 1½ cups uncooked long grain rice
- 1 tsp. ground cumin
- 1 tsp. chili powder
- 2¼ cups chicken broth
- 1 can (14½ oz.) diced tomatoes, undrained
- 1 cup frozen peas, thawed

1. In a small bowl, toss chicken with flour, pepper and ¼ tsp. salt. In a Dutch oven, heat 4 tsp. of oil over medium-high heat. Brown the chicken, stirring occasionally; remove from pan.

2. In same pan, heat remaining oil over medium heat. Add pepper, onion and celery; cook and stir for 2-4 minutes or until onion is tender. Add the rice, cumin, chili powder and remaining salt; stir to coat rice. Stir in remaining ingredients; bring to a boil. Reduce the heat; simmer, covered, 10 minutes.

3. Place the browned chicken over rice (do not stir in). Cook, covered, 5 minutes longer or until rice is tender and chicken is cooked through.

Per serving: 1½ cups equals 367 cal., 8g fat (1g sat. fat), 44mg chol., 755mg sodium, 50g carb. (5g sugars, 4g fiber), 22g pro. **Diabetic Exchanges:** 3 starch, 2 lean meat, 1 vegetable, 1 fat.

UNDER
400
CALORIES

SLOW COOKER CHEESY WHITE LASAGNA

Here's the best version of my favorite food—lasagna! Even though this recipe requires a little more prep than most, it leaves you plenty of time to put together the remainder of the meal while it gently bakes to perfection in the slow cooker.
—Suzanne Smith, Bluffton, IN

Prep: 30 min. • **Cook:** 3 hours + standing
Makes: 8 servings

- 1 lb. ground chicken
- 2 tsp. canola oil
- 1¾ cups sliced fresh mushrooms
- 1 medium onion, chopped
- 2 medium carrots, chopped
- 2 garlic cloves, minced
- 2 tsp. Italian seasoning
- ¾ tsp. salt
- ½ tsp. pepper
- ½ cup white wine or chicken broth
- 1 cup half-and-half cream
- 4 oz. cream cheese, softened
- 1 cup (4 oz.) shredded white cheddar cheese
- 1 cup (4 oz.) shredded Gouda cheese
- 1 large egg, beaten
- 1½ cups (12 oz.) 2% cottage cheese
- ¼ cup minced fresh basil or 4 tsp. dried basil
- 9 no-cook lasagna noodles
- 4 cups (16 oz.) shredded part-skim mozzarella cheese
  Additional minced fresh basil, optional

1. Fold two 18-in.-square pieces of heavy-duty foil into thirds. Crisscross the strips and place on bottom and up sides of a 6-qt. slow cooker. Coat strips with cooking spray.

2. In a 6-qt. stockpot, cook chicken over medium heat until no longer pink, for 6-8 minutes, breaking into crumbles; drain. Set chicken aside.

3. In same pot, heat oil over medium-high heat. Add the mushrooms, onion and carrots; cook and stir just until tender, 6-8 minutes. Add garlic, Italian seasoning, salt and pepper; cook 1 minute longer. Stir in the wine. Bring to a boil; cook until liquid is reduced by half, 4-5 minutes. Stir in the cream, cream cheese, cheddar and Gouda cheeses. Return chicken to pot. In a large bowl, combine the egg, cottage cheese and basil.

4. Spread 1 cup meat mixture into slow cooker. Layer with 3 noodles (breaking noodles as necessary to fit), 1 cup meat mixture, ½ cup cottage cheese mixture and 1 cup mozzarella cheese. Repeat layers twice. Top with remaining meat mixture and cheese. Cook, covered, on low until noodles are tender, 3-4 hours. Remove slow cooker insert and let stand for 30 minutes. If desired, sprinkle with additional basil.

Per serving: 1 serving equals 603 cal., 35g fat (19g sat. fat), 165mg chol., 1086mg sodium, 28g carb. (7g sugars, 2g fiber), 40g pro.

GOES GREAT WITH

A big dinner calls for a big dessert! Turn to page 265 and give fancy Caramel Fluff & Toffee Trifle a try. It comes together in no time flat!

SPEEDY SWAPS!

It's easy to customize this recipe and make it your own.

DON'T HAVE GROUND CHICKEN?
Simply use a pound of lean ground beef instead.

NOT SURE ABOUT THE CHEESES?
If Gouda and white cheddar aren't exactly family favorites, try Parmesan or Colby—or just increase the mozzarella.

FAMILY FAVORITE

TURKEY BISCUIT STEW

Chunky stew makes a hearty supper, and it's especially comforting during the cold fall and winter months. I love that everything cooks in one handy skillet.
—Lori Schlecht, Wimbledon, ND

....

Prep: 15 min. • **Bake:** 20 min.
Makes: 8 servings

- ⅓ **cup chopped onion**
- ¼ **cup butter, cubed**
- ⅓ **cup all-purpose flour**
- ½ **tsp. salt**
- ⅛ **tsp. pepper**
- 1 **can (10½ oz.) condensed chicken broth, undiluted**
- ¾ **cup milk**
- 2 **cups cubed cooked turkey**
- 1 **cup cooked peas**
- 1 **cup cooked whole baby carrots**
- 1 **tube (10 oz.) refrigerated buttermilk biscuits**

1. In a 10-in. ovenproof or cast-iron skillet, saute onion in butter until tender. Stir in the flour, salt and pepper until blended. Gradually add broth and milk. Bring to a boil. Cook and stir for 2 minutes or until thickened and bubbly. Add turkey, peas and carrots; heat through. Separate the biscuits and arrange over the stew.
2. Bake at 375° for 20-25 minutes or until biscuits are golden brown.
Per serving: 1 serving equals 263 cal., 10g fat (5g sat. fat), 45mg chol., 792mg sodium, 27g carb.(4g sugars, 2g fiber), 17g pro.

GOES GREAT WITH

Surprise the gang with ice cream sandwiches for dessert! Not only are they sized right in single servings, but there's no cleanup.

ROASTED CHICKEN WITH POTATO WEDGES

I grow herbs and dry them for use in recipes all year long. Knowing that the rosemary and thyme are from my garden makes this classic dinner even better.
—Tanya Borkholder, Milford, IN

....

Prep: 10 min. • **Bake:** 30 min.
Makes: 4 servings

- 2 **large potatoes (about 1½ lbs.)**
- 2 **tsp. olive oil**
- 2 **tsp. Montreal steak seasoning**
- 4 **bone-in chicken thighs**
- 4 **chicken drumsticks**
- 1 **Tbsp. hot water**
- 2 **tsp. butter**
- 1 **tsp. dried rosemary, crushed**
- 1 **tsp. dried thyme**
- ¼ **tsp. kosher salt**
- ¼ **tsp. pepper**

1. Preheat oven to 450°. Cut each potato lengthwise into 12 wedges; toss with oil and steak seasoning. Arrange in a single layer in a greased 15x10x1-in. baking pan. Roast on a lower oven rack 30-35 minutes or until the wedges are tender and lightly browned, turning occasionally.
2. Place chicken in a large bowl. In a small bowl, mix remaining ingredients; add to the chicken and toss to coat. Transfer to a rack in a broiler pan, skin side up. Place on an oven rack above the potatoes; roast for 30-35 minutes or until a thermometer inserted in the chicken reads 170°-175°. Serve with potato wedges.
Per serving: 1 thigh and 1 drumstick (skin removed) with 6 potato wedges equals 447 cal., 17g fat (5g sat. fat), 133mg chol., 596mg sodium, 33g carb. (1g sugars, 4g fiber), 41g pro. **Diabetic Exchanges:** 5 lean meat, 2 starch, 2 fat.

GOES GREAT WITH

Corn on the cob adds color and flavor to this mealtime classic.

Table Talk

Which movie do you wish had a different ending? How so?

Let everyone settle into their own director's chair and describe how Hollywood got it wrong. What was the problem with the original ending? How should the movie have ended?

UNDER
300
CALORIES

GOES GREAT WITH

White rice is a great way to enjoy the tangy sauce this entree offers.

EAT SMART

CHICKEN-STUFFED CUBANELLE PEPPERS

This is my take on traditional stuffed peppers. Substitute chicken for beef and use Cubanelle peppers in place of green peppers to add a little more bite.
—Bev Burlingame, Canton, OH

Prep: 20 min. • **Bake:** 1 hour
Makes: 6 servings

- 6 **Cubanelle peppers or mild banana peppers**
- 2 **large eggs, lightly beaten**
- 3 **cups shredded cooked chicken breast**
- 1 **cup salsa**
- ¾ **cup soft bread crumbs**
- ½ **cup cooked long grain rice**
- 2 **cups meatless pasta sauce**

1. Preheat oven to 350°. Cut and discard tops from peppers; remove seeds. In a large bowl, mix eggs, chicken, salsa, bread crumbs and rice. Spoon into peppers.
2. Spread pasta sauce onto bottom of a 13x9-in. baking dish coated with cooking spray. Top with peppers. Bake, covered, 60-65 minutes or until peppers are tender and a thermometer inserted in stuffing reads at least 165°.

Note: To make soft bread crumbs, tear bread into pieces and place in a food processor or blender. Cover and pulse until crumbs form. One slice of bread yields ½ to ¾ cup crumbs.

Per serving: 1 stuffed pepper equals 230 cal., 4g fat (1g sat. fat), 125mg chol., 661mg sodium, 20g carb. (7g sugars, 5g fiber), 26g pro. **Diabetic Exchanges:** 1 starch, 3 lean meat, 2 vegetable.

NOTES

SLOW COOKER 🍲

BUFFALO CHICKEN PASTA

Buffalo chicken is a favorite in our house. Combine it with pasta and you have the ultimate comfort food. Not a fan of spicy food? The addition of sour cream, ranch salad dressing and mozzarella cheese provides a creamy contrast that nicely tempers the heat.

—Katherine White, Clemmons, NC

Prep: 10 min. • **Cook:** 4 hours.
Makes: 8 servings

- 2 lbs. boneless skinless chicken breasts, cut into 1-in. cubes
- 2 cans (10¾ oz. each) condensed cream of chicken soup, undiluted
- 1 cup Buffalo wing sauce
- 1 medium onion, finely chopped
- 1½ tsp. garlic powder
- ½ tsp. salt
- ½ tsp. pepper
- 1 pkg. (16 oz.) penne pasta
- 2 cups (8 oz.) shredded part-skim mozzarella cheese
- 2 cups (16 oz.) sour cream
- ½ cup ranch salad dressing
  Finely chopped celery, optional

1. In a 5-qt. slow cooker, combine the first seven ingredients. Cook, covered, on low 4-5 hours or until chicken is tender. Cook pasta according to package directions for al dente; drain.

2. Remove insert from slow cooker. Stir in the cheese until melted. Add pasta, sour cream and ranch dressing. If desired, top with celery.

Per serving: 1½ cups equals 806 cal., 42g fat (20g sat. fat), 165mg chol., 2013mg sodium, 58g carb. (9g sugars, 4g fiber), 43g pro.

GOES GREAT WITH

While the main course simmers on its own, prepare Coconut Macaroon Pie from page 253.

MEAL PLANNER

CHICKEN ❤ TURKEY

DINNERS ARE A SNAP WITH THESE EASY MENU IDEAS

FAST FEAST

ENTREE:
Asian Turkey Lettuce Cups
page 69

SIDE:
Edamame Corn
Carrot Salad
page 176

DESSERT:
Monkey Bars
page 263

TAG YOUR MEAL
MEMORIES WITH
#100 FAMILYMEALS

GROCERY LIST

KITCHEN STAPLES
- ○ Canola oil
- ○ Butter
- ○ Baking powder
- ○ Sugar
- ○ Brown sugar
- ○ Confectioners' sugar
- ○ Vanilla extract
- ○ Salt
- ○ Pepper

PRODUCE/SALAD BAR
- ○ 1 medium ripe banana
- ○ 1 head Bibb or Boston lettuce
- ○ 1 bunch celery
- ○ 1 medium carrot
- ○ 2 packages (10 oz. each) julienned carrots
- ○ 1 bunch green onions
- ○ 1 small piece gingerroot
- ○ 1 head of garlic
- ○ 1 bunch fresh cilantro

PANTRY
- ○ 1 can (8 oz.) water chestnuts
- ○ 1 box (14 oz.) brown rice
- ○ 1 jar (16 oz.) creamy peanut butter

MEAT
- ○ 1 lb. lean ground turkey

FREEZER SECTION
- ○ 2 bags (16 oz. each) frozen shelled edamame
- ○ 1 bag (12 oz.) frozen corn kernels

DAIRY
- ○ 1 large egg

OTHER
- ○ 1 bottle (8 oz.) lemon juice
- ○ 1 bottle (10 oz.) reduced-sodium soy sauce
- ○ 1 bottle (5 oz.) sesame oil
- ○ 1 bottle (16.5 oz.) Thai chili sauce
- ○ Rice vinegar
- ○ Whole wheat flour

CASUAL COMFORT

ENTREE:
Chicken Penne Casserole
page 71

SALAD:
Bacon-Tomato Salad
page 183

DESSERT:
Nutella Hand Pies
page 262

TAG YOUR MEAL
MEMORIES WITH
#100 FAMILYMEALS

GROCERY LIST

KITCHEN STAPLES
- ○ Canola oil
- ○ Confectioners' sugar
- ○ Dried basil
- ○ Dried oregano
- ○ Dried parsley flakes
- ○ Red pepper flakes
- ○ Salt

PRODUCE
- ○ 1 orange
- ○ 2 cups grape tomatoes
- ○ 1 package (12 oz.) iceberg lettuce blend
- ○ 1 medium green pepper
- ○ 1 medium sweet red pepper
- ○ 1 small onion
- ○ 3 garlic cloves

PANTRY
- ○ 1 box (16 oz.) penne pasta
- ○ 1 jar (7.7 oz.) Nutella
- ○ 1 can (14.5 oz.) chicken broth
- ○ 1 can (14.5 oz.) diced tomatoes, undrained
- ○ 1 can (6 oz.) tomato paste

MEATS
- ○ 1 lb. boneless skinless chicken thighs
- ○ 1 package (16 oz.) bacon

DAIRY
- ○ 2 cups shredded part-skim mozzarella cheese
- ○ ¾ cup shredded cheddar cheese
- ○ ½ cup grated Romano cheese
- ○ 1 large egg

OTHER
- ○ 1 jar (15 oz.) coleslaw salad dressing
- ○ 1 box (17.3 oz.) frozen puff pastry sheets

MEAL PLANNER

CHICKEN ♥ TURKEY

DINNERS ARE A SNAP WITH THESE EASY MENU IDEAS

TWIST ON TACOS

ENTREE:
Slow Cooker Chicken Tacos
page 55

SIDE:
Mom's Spanish Rice
page 205

DESSERT:
Mexican Crinkle Cookies
page 259

TAG YOUR MEAL
MEMORIES WITH
#100 FAMILYMEALS

GROCERY LIST

KITCHEN STAPLES
- ○ Light corn syrup
- ○ Brown sugar
- ○ All-purpose flour
- ○ Baking soda
- ○ Confectioners' sugar
- ○ Chili powder
- ○ Crushed red pepper flakes
- ○ Dried oregano
- ○ Garlic powder
- ○ Ground chipotle pepper
- ○ Ground cinnamon
- ○ Ground cumin
- ○ Paprika
- ○ Pepper

- ○ White pepper
- ○ Salt
- ○ Seasoned salt

PRODUCE/SALAD BAR
- ○ 1 bunch green onions
- ○ 1 package (10 oz.) leafy romaine
- ○ 4 tomatoes
- ○ 1 avocado
- ○ 1 large onion
- ○ 1 medium green pepper

PANTRY
- ○ 1 can (14.5oz.) chicken broth
- ○ 1 can (15 oz.) tomato sauce
- ○ 1 can (14.5 oz.) no-salt-added diced tomatoes

- ○ 1 box (14 oz.) brown rice

DAIRY
- ○ Butter
- ○ 1 large egg
- ○ 1 package (8 oz.) shredded cheddar cheese

MEATS
- ○ 1 lb. lean ground beef (90% lean)
- ○ 1½ lbs. boneless skinless chicken breasts

OTHER
- ○ 2 packages (11.6 oz.) corn or flour tortillas
- ○ 2 oz. unsweetened chocolate

✂ -

CLASSIC DINNER

ENTREE:
Roasted Chicken Thighs
with Peppers & Potatoes
page 63

SIDE:
Monkey Bread Biscuits
page 225

DESSERT:
Watermelon Chocolate
Chip Sorbet
page 274

TAG YOUR MEAL
MEMORIES WITH
#100 FAMILYMEALS

GROCERY LIST

KITCHEN STAPLES
- ○ Olive oil
- ○ Italian seasoning
- ○ Sugar
- ○ Salt
- ○ Pepper

PRODUCE
- ○ 1 lime
- ○ 1 small seedless watermelon
- ○ 2 lbs. red potatoes (about 6 medium)
- ○ 2 large sweet red peppers
- ○ 2 large green peppers

- ○ 2 medium onions
- ○ Fresh thyme
- ○ Fresh rosemary
- ○ 1 head of garlic

MEAT
- ○ 8 boneless skinless chicken thighs (about 2 lbs.)

DAIRY
- ○ Butter
- ○ 1 canister (8 oz.) grated Parmesan cheese

OTHER
- ○ 1 tube (16.3 oz.) large refrigerated flaky biscuits
- ○ 1 bag (12 oz.) miniature semisweet chocolate chips
- ○ 1 cup orange juice

Family Fiesta

Adan and Missy Franco (above) enjoy meals spent with Grandma Delfina (at left) and extended family.

IT'S SUNDAY AFTERNOON, and the comforting aroma of beans and rice wafts through Grandma Delfina Delgadillo's bustling home. Each week, her big family comes together around faith and a home-cooked Mexican meal.

Young grandkids bound through the living room; cousins set the table; and aunts tote spicy chicken, cookies and tortillas to the kitchen to prepare for the come-as-you-are feast. Every week, nearly 20 people pop by Grandma's house, including the newest family member, Missy Franco. Missy and her

husband, Adan, married a few years ago, but she knew how close-knit his family was from the start. "The first time I met Adan's family was at a summer party for their grandma. Imagine being introduced to more than 75 people in one sitting!" Missy says, laughing. "It was intimidating and wonderful all at once."

Adan's grandparents came to Milwaukee from Mexico, and as the family grew, the dinners became a touchstone. "My family gathers every Sunday afternoon for a meal," Adan says. "Birthdays blend with holidays

and turn into picnics and parties." Adan says that chicken tacos are menu staples. "Chicken is a no-brainer when it comes to mealtime—from weekday suppers to special weekend meals."

Adan, a professional chef, credits these meals for more than the delicious food. "Not only do I believe in sharing weeknight meals with immediate family, but my appreciation for cooking came from watching my mother and grandmother cook," he says. "Endless support—and rice—keep our family tradition alive every week!"

"The dinner table is the place where we reconnect. It's the hub of our busy lives."

–Cindy Reams
Philipsburg, Pennsylvania

PORK, HAM and MORE

SINK YOUR TEETH into these hearty dinners you'll turn to time and again.

PORK TENDERLOIN WITH MANGO RELISH

A colorful mango relish is a refreshing counterpoint to the heat in the rub I use to pep up pork dishes. These roasted tenderloins turn out juicy, and you can use the relish with other dishes, too!
—Gloria Bradley, Naperville, IL

....

Prep: 15 min. • **Bake:** 45 min.
Makes: 6 servings

- 1½ tsp. ground coriander
- 1 tsp. ground cumin
- ½ tsp. salt
- ½ tsp. sugar
- ½ tsp. ground chipotle pepper
- ½ tsp. smoked Spanish paprika
- 2 pork tenderloins (¾ lb. each)

MANGO RELISH
- 1 medium mango, peeled and chopped
- 2 plum tomatoes, seeded and chopped
- ⅓ cup chopped onion
- ⅓ cup chopped seeded peeled cucumber
- ¼ cup minced fresh cilantro
- 1 jalapeno pepper, seeded and chopped
- 3 Tbsp. lime juice

1. In a small bowl, combine the first six ingredients. Set aside ½ tsp. for relish; rub remaining spice mixture over tenderloins. Place in a lightly greased 13x9-in. baking pan. Bake, uncovered, at 350° for 45-50 minutes or until a meat thermometer reads 160°. Let stand for 5 minutes.

2. Meanwhile, in a small bowl, combine the mango, tomatoes, onion, cucumber, cilantro and jalapeno. Combine lime juice and reserved spice mixture; add to mango mixture and toss to coat. Slice pork; serve with relish.

Note: Wear disposable gloves when cutting hot peppers; the oils can burn skin. Avoid touching your face.

Per serving: 3 oz. cooked pork with ⅓ cup relish equals 171 cal., 4g fat (1g sat. fat), 63mg chol., 245mg sodium, 9g carb. (7g sugars, 2g fiber), 23g pro. **Diabetic Exchanges:** ½ starch, 3 lean meat.

GOES GREAT WITH

Served with fresh fruit, Mexican Chocolate Dip from page 281 will be a new staple at your house! Enjoy it after this pork dinner.

Tick Tock

As if this entree isn't easy enough to prepare, you can make the relish and set it in the fridge a day early. Similarly, season the pork with the rub, cover the tenderloins and store in the refrigerator until you're ready to cook the next day.

PIGS IN A PONCHO

For my pigs in a blanket, I rely on refried beans for a unique touch. Spice things up even more with pepper jack, jalapenos and guacamole if you'd like.
—Jennifer Stowell, Smithville, MO

Prep: 25 min. • **Cook:** 5 min./batch
Makes: 8 servings

    8   hot dogs
    1   can (16 oz.) refried beans
    8   flour tortillas (10 in.)
    1   can (4 oz.) chopped green chilies
    1   can (2¼ oz.) sliced ripe
        olives, drained
    2   cups (8 oz.) shredded
        Monterey Jack cheese
        Oil for frying
        Sour cream and salsa

1. Heat hot dogs according to package directions. Spread beans over the center of each tortilla; layer with green chilies, olives and cheese. Place hot dog down center of tortilla. Fold bottom and sides of tortilla over filling and roll up; secure with a toothpick.
2. In a deep skillet or electric skillet, heat 1 in. of oil to 375°. Fry wraps in batches, seam side down, for 2-3 minutes on each side or until golden brown. Drain on paper towels. Discard toothpicks before serving. Serve with sour cream and salsa.
Per serving: 1 poncho (calculated without sour cream and salsa) equals 726 cal., 50g fat (14g sat. fat), 50mg chol., 1494mg sodium, 48g carb. (4g sugars, 5g fiber), 21g pro.

GOES GREAT WITH

Enjoy these spicy ponchos with cool slices of melon on the side.

HAM BARBECUE

I've turned to this recipe countless times. The sandwiches are so easy to make, and they taste great. Leftovers are terrific for lunches later in the week.
—Jennifer Middlekauff, New Holland, PA

Prep: 10 min. • **Cook:** 4 hours
Makes: 12 servings

- 2 lbs. thinly sliced deli ham
- 1 cup water
- 1 cup ketchup
- ¼ cup packed brown sugar
- ¼ cup Worcestershire sauce
- 2 Tbsp. white vinegar
- 2 tsp. prepared mustard
- 12 hamburger buns, split and toasted

Place the ham in a greased 3-qt. slow cooker. In a large bowl, combine water, ketchup, brown sugar, Worcestershire sauce, vinegar and mustard; pour over ham and stir well. Cover and cook on low 4-5 hours or until heated through. Serve on buns.

Per serving: 1 sandwich equals 241 cal., 4g fat (1g sat. fat), 34mg chol., 1250mg sodium, 34g carb. (12g sugars, 1g fiber), 17g pro.

GOES GREAT WITH

Make it a soup-and-sandwich night by whipping up Bacon-Potato Corn Chowder from page 244.

GOES **GREAT** WITH

Pick up a bagged Caesar salad kit from the grocery store to complete this meal.

FAST FIX

PIZZA PANCAKES

Anything goes in these pancakes for pizza lovers. We like pepperoni and mozzarella in the batter, but garlic is a great addition, too!
—Maxine Smith, Owanka, SD

Takes: 30 min. • **Makes:** 14 pancakes

- 2 cups biscuit/baking mix
- 2 tsp. Italian seasoning
- 2 large eggs
- 1 cup 2% milk
- ½ cup shredded part-skim mozzarella cheese
- ½ cup chopped pepperoni
- 1 plum tomato, chopped and seeded
- ¼ cup chopped green pepper
- 1 can (8 oz.) pizza sauce, warmed

1. In a bowl, combine biscuit mix and Italian seasoning. In another bowl, whisk eggs and milk until blended. Add to dry ingredients, stirring just until moistened. Stir in the cheese, pepperoni, tomato and pepper.

2. Preheat griddle over medium heat; grease lightly. Pour batter by ¼ cupfuls onto griddle; cook until bubbles on top begin to pop and bottoms are golden brown. Turn; cook until second side is golden brown. Serve with pizza sauce.

Per serving: 2 pancakes with 2 tablespoons pizza sauce equals 272 cal., 13g fat (5g sat. fat), 70mg chol., 827mg sodium, 28g carb. (4g sugars, 2g fiber), 10g pro.

"My family loves this recipe! We make these fairly often, and sometimes we use different vegetables such as mushrooms and onions. I have even tripled the batch for a crowd."
—BFRANK, TASTEOFHOME.COM

SLOW-COOKED PORK STEW

Try this comforting stew that's easy to put together but tastes like you've been working hard in the kitchen all day. It's even better when served over polenta, egg noodles or mashed potatoes.
—Nancy Elliott, Houston, TX

Prep: 15 min. • **Cook:** 5 hours
Makes: 8 servings

- 2   pork tenderloins (1 lb. each), cut into 2-in. pieces
- 1   tsp. salt
- ½   tsp. pepper
- 2   large carrots, cut into ½-in. slices
- 2   celery ribs, coarsely chopped
- 1   medium onion, coarsely chopped
- 3   cups beef broth
- 2   Tbsp. tomato paste
- ⅓   cup pitted dried plums, chopped
- 4   garlic cloves, minced
- 2   bay leaves
- 1   fresh rosemary sprig
- 1   fresh thyme sprig
- ⅓   cup Greek olives, optional
       Chopped fresh parsley, optional
       Hot cooked mashed potatoes, optional

1. Sprinkle the pork with salt and pepper; transfer to a 4-qt. slow cooker. Add the carrots, celery and onion. In a small bowl, whisk broth and tomato paste; pour over vegetables. Add plums, garlic, bay leaves, rosemary, thyme and, if desired, olives. Cook, covered, on low 5-6 hours or until meat and vegetables are tender.

2. Discard the bay leaves, rosemary and thyme. If desired, sprinkle the stew with parsley and serve with potatoes.

Per serving: 1 cup (calculated without potatoes) equals 177 cal., 4g fat (1g sat. fat), 64mg chol., 698mg sodium, 9g carb. (4g sugars, 1g fiber), 24g pro.

GOES GREAT WITH

The olives and herbs in the stew make Olive & Onion Quick Bread an ideal side. You'll find the easy recipe on page 240.

> "A big hit for a quick dinner is what we call 'make-your-own night.' By putting all the ingredients on the table for subs or burgers, every family member can assemble their creation to their specific tastes."
> —JULIE JAHNKE GREEN LAKE, WI

GOES GREAT WITH

Sweet potato chips make a speedy addition to piled-high sandwiches.

FAST FIX ▶

HAM & VEGGIE CASSEROLE

I have paired ham with broccoli and cauliflower for years. To complete this casserole dinner, I serve it with warm dinner rolls.

—Sherri Melotik, Oak Creek, WI

Takes: 30 min. • **Makes:** 4 servings

- 1 pkg. (16 oz.) frozen broccoli florets
- 1 pkg. (16 oz.) frozen cauliflower
- 2 tsp. plus 2 Tbsp. butter, divided
- ¼ cup seasoned bread crumbs
- 2 Tbsp. all-purpose flour
- 1½ cups 2% milk
- ¾ cup shredded sharp cheddar cheese
- ½ cup grated Parmesan cheese
- 1½ cups cubed fully cooked ham (about 8 oz.)
- ¼ tsp. pepper

1. Preheat oven to 425°. Cook broccoli and cauliflower according to package directions; drain.
2. Meanwhile, in a small skillet, melt 2 tsp. butter. Add bread crumbs; cook and stir over medium heat for 2-3 minutes or until lightly toasted. Remove from heat.
3. In a large saucepan, melt the remaining butter over medium heat. Stir in flour until smooth; gradually whisk in milk. Bring to a boil, stirring constantly; cook and stir for 1-2 minutes or until thickened. Remove from heat; stir in cheeses until blended. Stir in ham, pepper and vegetables.
4. Transfer to a greased 8-in. square baking dish. Sprinkle with toasted crumbs. Bake, uncovered, 10-15 minutes or until heated through.
Per serving: 1½ cups equals 420 cal., 23g fat (13g sat. fat), 89mg chol., 1233mg sodium, 25g carb. (10g sugars, 6g fiber), 28g pro.

EAT SMART SLOW COOKER 🍲

SESAME PULLED PORK SANDWICHES

I wanted to build a better pork sandwich, and this Asian-style filling was a huge hit in my house. I love letting my slow cooker do all the work!

—Jennifer Berry, Lexington, OH

Prep: 15 min. • **Cook:** 4½ hours
Makes: 12 servings

- 3 pork tenderloins (1 lb. each)
- 1¾ cups reduced-fat sesame ginger salad dressing, divided
- ¼ cup packed brown sugar

SLAW
- 1 pkg. (14 oz.) coleslaw mix
- 4 green onions, chopped
- ¼ cup minced fresh cilantro
- 2 Tbsp. reduced-fat sesame ginger salad dressing
- 2 tsp. sesame oil
- 1 tsp. sugar
- 1 tsp. reduced-sodium soy sauce

TO SERVE
- 12 multigrain hamburger buns, split
  Wasabi mayonnaise, optional

1. Place tenderloins in a 5-qt. slow cooker coated with cooking spray; pour ¾ cup salad dressing over pork, turning to coat. Cook, covered, on low 4-5 hours or until meat is tender.
2. Remove pork; cool slightly. Shred meat into bite-size pieces; return to the slow cooker. Stir in brown sugar and remaining salad dressing. Cook, covered, for 30-45 minutes longer or until heated through.
3. Combine slaw ingredients. Serve pork on the buns with the slaw and, if desired, Wasabi mayonnaise.
Per serving: 1 sandwich (calculated without mayonnaise) equals 324 cal., 9g fat (2g sat. fat), 64mg chol., 756mg sodium, 33g carb. (14g sugars, 3g fiber), 27g pro. **Diabetic Exchanges:** 2 starch, 3 lean meat.

GOES GREAT WITH
Warm-from-the-oven croissants make for buttery bites alongside this hearty ham casserole.

Make a Change

Cooked ham makes this hot dish a fast fix and a great way to use up leftovers. If you don't have any ham in the fridge, however, feel free to sub in cooked chicken or turkey. You could even leave the meat out altogether and simply increase the veggies.

Table Talk

What's the best article of clothing you've ever owned?

Fashion trends come and go, but some items last forever in our closets. Explain why that certain sweater, Sunday dress or comfy sweatshirt is or was a go-to item for you.

GOES GREAT WITH

Tell humdrum dinners to take a hike when you shake up menus with Chipotle Lime Avocado Salad. See page 170 for the details.

BARBECUE PORK TACOS WITH APPLE SLAW

At my house we like to celebrate taco Tuesdays, so I keep things interesting by switching up the varieties. These pork tacos are super simple to make.
—Jenn Tidwell, Fair Oaks, CA

Prep: 15 min. • **Cook:** 2¼ hours
Makes: 8 servings

- 2 pork tenderloins (1 lb. each)
- 1 can (12 oz.) root beer

SLAW
- 6 cups shredded red cabbage (about 12 oz.)
- 2 medium Granny Smith apples, julienned
- ⅓ cup cider vinegar
- ¼ cup minced fresh cilantro
- ¼ cup lime juice
- 2 Tbsp. sugar
- ½ tsp. salt
- ½ tsp. pepper

ASSEMBLY
- 1 bottle (18 oz.) barbecue sauce
- 16 taco shells

1. Place pork in a 3-qt. slow cooker. Pour root beer over top. Cook, covered, on low 2 to 2½ hours or just until tender (a thermometer inserted in pork should read at least 145°).

2. Meanwhile, in a large bowl, toss slaw ingredients. Refrigerate slaw, covered, until serving.

3. Remove tenderloins to a cutting board; let stand, covered, for 5 minutes. Discard cooking juices.

4. Coarsely chop pork; return to slow cooker. Stir in barbecue sauce; heat through. Serve in taco shells; top with some of the slaw. Serve remaining slaw on the side.

Per serving: 2 tacos with 1 cup slaw equals 396 cal., 9g fat (2g sat. fat), 64mg chol., 954mg sodium, 53g carb. (31g sugars, 3g fiber), 25g pro.

"I like to nurture my family with their favorite nutritious foods. I truly believe that doing so helps keep us on the road to healthy living."

—ANNE SMITHSON
CARY, NORTH CAROLINA

BACON, MUSHROOM & ONION GRILLED CHEESE SANDWICHES

Little ones might like plain grilled cheese, but why not kick things up a notch for everyone else at the table? Add bacon and baby portobello mushrooms to grilled cheddar cheese for this specialty. It's good to the last crumb.
—Blair Lonergan, Rochelle, VA

Takes: 25 min. • **Makes:** 4 servings

- 3 Tbsp. butter, softened, divided
- 8 oz. sliced baby portobello mushrooms
- 1 small onion, halved and thinly sliced
- 8 thin slices cheddar cheese (about 3 oz.)
- 8 slices Texas toast
- 4 bacon strips, cooked and crumbled

1. In a large nonstick skillet coated with cooking spray, heat 1 Tbsp. butter over medium-high heat. Add mushrooms and onion; cook and stir 4-5 minutes or until tender. Remove from the pan. Wipe the skillet clean.

2. Place one slice cheese on each of four bread slices. Top with the mushroom mixture, bacon and remaining cheese and bread. Lightly spread the outsides of the sandwiches with remaining butter.

3. In the same skillet, toast sandwiches in batches over medium heat 45-60 seconds on each side or until golden brown and cheese is melted.

Per serving: 1 sandwich equals 406 cal., 21g fat (11g sat. fat), 54mg chol., 729mg sodium, 39g carb. (5g sugars, 2g fiber), 16g pro.

GOES GREAT WITH

Cream of potato soup is a hearty accompaniment to these sandwiches.

NOTES

FAST FIX ▸
APPLE-TOPPED HAM STEAK

When it's time to dine, I like to serve ham with a tangy sauce of sweet and tart apples, zingy mustard and a dash of sage.
—Eleanor Chore, Athena, OR

Takes: 30 min. • **Makes:** 8 servings

- 4 fully cooked boneless ham steaks (8 oz. each)
- 1 cup chopped onion
- 3 cups apple juice
- 2 tsp. Dijon mustard
- 2 medium green apples, thinly sliced
- 2 medium red apples, thinly sliced
- 2 Tbsp. cornstarch
- ¼ cup cold water
- 1 Tbsp. minced fresh sage or 1 tsp. rubbed sage
- ¼ tsp. pepper

1. In a large skillet coated with cooking spray, brown ham steaks in batches over medium heat; remove and keep warm.
2. In same skillet, saute onion until tender. Stir in apple juice and mustard; bring to a boil. Add apples. Reduce heat; cover and simmer for 4 minutes or until the apples are tender.
3. Combine cornstarch and water until smooth; stir into the apple juice mixture. Bring to a boil; cook and stir for 2 minutes. Stir in sage and pepper. Return steaks to skillet; heat through.
Per serving: 1 serving equals 219 cal., 4g fat (1g sat. fat), 58mg chol., 1213mg sodium, 25g carb. (18g sugars, 2g fiber), 21g pro.

GOES GREAT WITH

Keep a canister of stuffing mix on hand. The side dish comes together quickly in the microwave. Corn-bread stuffing mix pairs particularly well with ham.

EAT SMART **FAST FIX** ▸
BUSY-DAY PORK CHOPS

It was time to use or lose some pork chops I had in the fridge, so I dressed them in bread crumbs and Parmesan and baked them up. Necessity sure is the mother of invention!
—Dee Maltby, Wayne, OH

Takes: 25 min. • **Makes:** 4 servings

- ¼ cup fat-free milk
- ¼ cup seasoned bread crumbs
- ¼ cup grated Parmesan cheese
- ¼ tsp. salt
- ¼ tsp. garlic powder
- ⅛ tsp. pepper
- 4 boneless pork loin chops (4 oz. each) Cooking spray

1. Preheat oven to 375°. Place milk in a shallow bowl. In another shallow bowl, toss crumbs with cheese and seasonings.
2. Dip pork chops in milk, then coat with crumb mixture. Place on a baking sheet coated with cooking spray; lightly spritz chops with cooking spray.
3. Bake 8-10 minutes on each side or until a thermometer reads 145°. Let stand for 5 minutes before serving.
Per serving: 1 pork chop equals 178 cal., 7g fat (3g sat. fat), 57mg chol., 207mg sodium, 3g carb. (trace sugars, trace fiber), 23g pro.
Diabetic Exchanges: 3 lean meat.

GOES GREAT WITH

Flavor quick-cooking couscous with a little Italian seasoning for a tasty side dish that's perfect with the pork chops.

SWEET BARBECUED PORK CHOPS

I often prepare a double recipe of these tangy chops, then freeze half to keep on hand for fast family dinners. They're so easy and taste so fresh, no one ever guesses my quick entree was frozen!
—Susan Holderman, Fostoria, OH

Takes: 25 min. • **Makes:** 8 servings

- 2   Tbsp. canola oil
- 8   boneless pork loin chops
     (¾ in. thick and 8 oz. each)
- ½   cup packed brown sugar
- ½   cup chopped sweet onion
- ½   cup each ketchup, barbecue sauce,
     French salad dressing and honey

1. In a large skillet, heat oil over medium heat. In batches, brown pork chops 2-3 minutes on each side. Return all to pan.
2. In a small bowl, mix the remaining ingredients; pour over chops. Bring to a boil. Reduce the heat; simmer, covered, 4-5 minutes or until a thermometer reads 145°. Let stand 5 minutes before serving.
Freeze option: Place the pork chops in freezer containers; top with sauce. Cool and freeze. To use, partially thaw chops in refrigerator overnight. Heat through in a covered saucepan, gently stirring sauce and adding a little water if necessary.
Per serving: 1 pork chop equals 82 cal., 12g fat (3g sat. fat), 14mg chol., 533mg sodium, 41g carb. (37g sugars, 1g fiber), 6g pro.

GOES **GREAT** WITH

Serve baked potatoes alongside these chops. Forget the butter and sour cream, however, and top them with the tangy barbecue sauce instead.

Beef Up On Veggies

Sneak more vegetables into family meals. Add a handful of frozen corn kernels or peas into the cabbage layer or work in chopped zucchini.

PORK SHEPHERD'S PIE

Of all the shepherd's pie recipes I've tried through the years, this one is definitely the best. I enjoy cooking for my family, who all agree this meat pie is a keeper.
—Mary Arthurs, Etobicoke, ON

Prep: 30 min. • **Bake:** 45 min.
Makes: 6 servings

PORK LAYER
- 1 lb. ground pork
- 1 small onion, chopped
- 2 garlic cloves, minced
- 1 cup cooked rice
- ½ cup pork gravy or ¼ cup chicken broth
- ½ tsp. salt
- ½ tsp. dried thyme

CABBAGE LAYER
- 1 medium carrot, diced
- 1 small onion, chopped
- 2 Tbsp. butter or margarine
- 6 cups chopped cabbage
- 1 cup chicken broth
- ½ tsp. salt
- ¼ tsp. pepper

POTATO LAYER
- 2 cups mashed potatoes
- ¼ cup shredded cheddar cheese

In a skillet over medium heat, brown the pork until no longer pink. Add onion and garlic. Cook until vegetables are tender; drain. Stir in rice, gravy, salt and thyme. Spoon into a greased 11x7-in. baking dish. In the same skillet, saute the carrot and onion in butter over medium heat for 5 minutes. Stir in cabbage; cook for 1 minute. Add broth, salt and pepper; cover and cook for 10 minutes. Spoon over pork layer. Spoon or pipe mashed potatoes on top; sprinkle with cheese. Bake, uncovered, at 350° for 45 minutes or until browned.

Per serving: 1 cup equals 365 cal., 19g fat (8g sat. fat), 66mg chol., 1045mg sodium, 28g carb. (5g sugars, 4g fiber), 19g pro.

GOES GREAT WITH

Green beans add color, flavor and nutrition to this family staple.

FLORENTINE SPAGHETTI BAKE

My daughter, a Montana wheat rancher's wife, says she serves this often to satisfy her hardworking family.
—Lorraine Martin, Lincoln, CA

Prep: 30 min. • **Bake:** 1 hour + standing
Makes: 9 servings

- 8 oz. uncooked spaghetti
- 1 lb. bulk Italian sausage
- 1 cup chopped onion
- 1 garlic clove, minced
- 1 jar (26 oz.) spaghetti sauce
- 1 can (4 oz.) mushroom stems and pieces, drained
- 1 large egg, lightly beaten
- 2 cups (16 oz.) 4% cottage cheese
- 1 pkg. (10 oz.) frozen chopped spinach, thawed and squeezed dry
- ¼ cup grated Parmesan cheese
- ½ tsp. seasoned salt
- ¼ tsp. pepper
- 2 cups (8 oz.) shredded part-skim mozzarella cheese

1. Cook pasta according to the package directions. Meanwhile, in a large skillet, cook sausage and onion over medium heat until sausage is no longer pink. Add garlic; cook 1 minute longer. Drain. Stir in spaghetti sauce and mushrooms. Bring to a boil. Reduce heat; cover and cook for 15 minutes or until heated through.

2. Drain pasta. In a large bowl, combine egg, cottage cheese, spinach, Parmesan cheese, seasoned salt and pepper. Spread 1 cup of the sausage mixture in a greased 13x9-in. baking dish. Top with spaghetti and the remaining sausage mixture. Layer with the spinach mixture and shredded mozzarella cheese.

3. Cover and bake at 375° for 45 minutes. Uncover; bake 15 minutes longer or until lightly browned and heated through. Let stand for 15 minutes before cutting.

Per serving: 1 serving equals 491 cal., 28g fat (12g sat. fat), 96mg chol., 1243mg sodium, 33g carb. (10g sugars, 3g fiber), 26g pro.

GOES GREAT WITH

Bake up some breadsticks to serve with this piping hot spaghetti dish.

NOTES

FAMILY
FAVORITE
♥

READY IN 20 MINUTES

FAST FIX ▶

BEAN & BACON GRIDDLE BURRITOS

These griddle burritos with bacon and veggies make an awesome handheld meal. I use fresh pico de gallo when I can, but a jar of salsa works if that's what you've got on hand.
—Stacy Mullens, Gresham, OR

....

Takes: 20 min. • **Makes:** 4 servings

- 1 can (16 oz.) fat-free refried beans
- ½ cup salsa, divided
- 4 flour tortillas (8 in.)
- ½ cup crumbled cotija cheese or shredded Monterey Jack cheese
- 3 bacon strips, cooked and coarsely chopped
- 2 cups shredded lettuce

1. In a small bowl, mix beans and ¼ cup salsa until blended. Place the tortillas on a griddle; cook over medium heat 1 minute, then turn over. Place bean mixture, cheese and bacon onto centers of tortillas; cook 1-2 minutes longer or until tortillas begin to crisp.

2. Remove from the griddle; immediately top with lettuce and remaining salsa. To serve, fold the bottom and sides of tortilla over the filling.

Per serving: 1 burrito equals 375 cal., 10g fat (4g sat. fat), 21mg chol., 1133mg sodium, 52g carb. (1g sugars, 8g fiber), 18g pro.

GOES GREAT WITH

Sliced tomatoes and avocados tossed with a bit of Italian salad dressing makes a zesty change-of-pace salad. Add some fresh cilantro or a dash of lemon juice if you'd like!

⑤INGREDIENTS | SLOW COOKER 🍲
BBQ COUNTRY-STYLE RIBS

With 10 minutes of prep time, this dinner goes great with a salad and corn on the cob. My family practically lets out a cheer whenever I make it!
—Cheryl Mann, Winside, NE

Prep: 10 min. • **Cook:** 6 hours
Makes: 6 servings

- 3 lbs. boneless country-style pork ribs
- ½ tsp. salt
- ½ tsp. pepper
- 1 large onion, cut into ½-in. rings
- 1 bottle (18 oz.) hickory smoke-flavored barbecue sauce
- ⅓ cup maple syrup
- ¼ cup spicy brown mustard
   Thinly sliced green onions, optional

1. Sprinkle ribs with salt and pepper. Place onion in a 6-qt. slow cooker. Top with ribs. In a large bowl, combine barbecue sauce, maple syrup and mustard; pour over ribs. Cook, covered, on low 6-8 hours or until meat is tender.

2. Transfer the meat to a serving platter; keep warm. Pour cooking liquid into a large saucepan; bring to a boil. Reduce heat; simmer, uncovered, 10 minutes or until sauce is thickened. Serve with pork. If desired, sprinkle with onions.

Per serving: 6 oz. cooked pork with ⅓ cup sauce equals 598 cal., 21g fat (8g sat. fat), 131mg chol., 1443mg sodium, 56g carb. (46g sugars, 1g fiber), 41g pro.

GOES **GREAT** WITH

Deli coleslaw makes an easy addition to this meal. Stir in some raisins and a dash of caraway seeds for extra flair.

WAFFLE MONTE CRISTOS

Adults love the sweet-smoky flavor of these sandwiches, and kids like the waffles. Ready in no time, they're an ideal way to break up weeknight meals.
—Kelly Reynolds, Urbana, IL

Takes: 20 min. • **Makes:** 4 servings

½	**cup apricot preserves**
8	**frozen waffles**
4	**slices deli turkey**
4	**slices deli ham**
4	**slices Havarti cheese (about 3 oz.)**
4	**bacon strips, cooked**
2	**Tbsp. butter, softened**
	Maple syrup, optional

1. Preheat the griddle over medium heat. Spread preserves over four waffles. Layer with turkey, ham, cheese and bacon; top with the remaining waffles. Lightly spread outsides of waffles with butter.

2. Place on griddle; cook for 4-5 minutes on each side or until golden brown and heated through. Serve with maple syrup for dipping if desired.

Per serving: 1 sandwich (calculated without syrup) equals 511 cal., 23g fat (10g sat. fat), 70mg chol., 1163mg sodium, 57g carb. (22g sugars, 2g fiber), 21g pro.

GOES GREAT WITH

Breakfast for dinner anyone? Scramble a few eggs and serve them alongside these sandwiches.

SLOW COOKER 🍲

PB&J PORK SANDWICHES

I came up with this recipe for one of my daughters who loves peanut butter. The result has become a family favorite at our house, and everyone asks for it for dinner often. Give it a try!
—Jill Cox, Lincoln, NE

Prep: 15 min. • **Cook:** 6 hours
Makes: 6 servings

- 3 to 4 lbs. boneless pork shoulder butt roast
- 1 tsp. salt
- ½ tsp. pepper
- 1 can (14½ oz.) reduced-sodium chicken broth
- 1 cup creamy peanut butter
- ¾ cup apricot preserves
- ¼ cup packed brown sugar
- ¼ cup finely chopped onion
- ¼ cup cider vinegar
- 3 Tbsp. Dijon mustard
- 1 garlic clove, minced
- 2 Tbsp. butter, melted
- 6 ciabatta rolls, split
  Coleslaw, optional

1. Sprinkle roast with salt and pepper; transfer to a 5-qt. slow cooker. In a large bowl, whisk the broth, peanut butter, preserves, brown sugar, onion, vinegar, mustard and garlic; pour over the meat. Cook, covered, on low 6-8 hours or until the meat is tender.

2. Preheat broiler. Remove roast; cool slightly. Shred pork with two forks. Return pork to slow cooker; heat through. Brush butter over cut sides of rolls. Place rolls, buttered side up, on an ungreased baking sheet. Broil 3-4 in. from heat for 30-60 seconds or until golden brown. Using a slotted spoon, spoon pork mixture onto roll bottoms; top with coleslaw if desired. Replace tops.

Per serving: 1 sandwich (calculated without coleslaw) equals 862 cal., 49g fat (15g sat. fat), 145mg chol., 1207mg sodium, 59g carb. (32g sugars, 3g fiber), 51g pro.

GOES GREAT WITH

Serve Garden Tomato Salad (page 184) with the sandwiches. The cider vinegar in both recipes makes them a perfect pairing.

"Mom and Dad made sure we ate dinner as a family. That was important to them, and once I had a family, it became important to me as well."

—KAREN BAILEY, GOLDEN, CO

Served On The Side

If you're using coleslaw on your sandwiches, buy enough to serve some as a quick and easy side dish. French fries, pickle spears and fresh fruit also round out the meal nicely.

Swing by the grocery store or bakery and pick up a loaf of rye bread to round out this skillet dish.

⟨5⟩INGREDIENTS FAST FIX▸

SPAGHETTI SQUASH & SAUSAGE EASY MEAL

I first created my son's favorite dish using homegrown squash, kielbasa and salsa. This variation uses only four ingredients. What could be easier?
—Pam Mascarenas, Taylorsville, UT

Takes: 30 min. • **Makes:** 6 servings

- 1 **medium spaghetti squash**
- 1 **Tbsp. olive oil**
- 1 **pkg. (14 oz.) smoked sausage, halved lengthwise and sliced**
- 1 **cup pico de gallo**
- ¼ **tsp. salt**
- ⅛ **tsp. pepper**

1. Cut squash lengthwise in half; discard seeds. Place halves on a microwave-safe plate, cut side down. Microwave squash, uncovered, on high for 15-20 minutes or until tender.
2. Meanwhile, in a large skillet, heat the oil over medium heat. Add sausage; cook and stir 4-5 minutes or until lightly browned.
3. When squash is cool enough to handle, use a fork to separate into strands. Add squash, pico de gallo, salt and pepper to the sausage; heat through, tossing well to combine.
Note: This recipe was tested in a 1,100-watt microwave.
Per serving: 1 cup equals 326 cal., 22g fat (8g sat. fat), 44mg chol., 901mg sodium, 24g carb. (2g sugars, 5g fiber), 12g pro.

Table Talk

How do you cheer yourself up when you're having a bad day?

Everyone get the blues now and then. Give each other a pep talk and share ways to turn a frown upside down. Promise to help one another the next time the going gets tough.

PIZZA MACARONI & CHEESE

My grandma made this for us once during a visit and I never forgot just how good it was. Since my kids love anything with pepperoni and cheese, I bake it so they can enjoy it as much as I did.
—Juli Meyers, Hinesville, GA

Prep: 30 min. • **Bake:** 25 min.
Makes: 12 servings

- 2 pkg. (14 oz. each) deluxe macaroni and cheese dinner mix
- ½ cup sour cream
- 1 can (14½ oz.) petite diced tomatoes, drained
- 1 can (15 oz.) pizza sauce
- 1 small green pepper, chopped
- 1 small sweet red pepper, chopped
- 2 cups (8 oz.) shredded Italian cheese blend
- 2 oz. sliced pepperoni

1. Preheat oven to 350°. Cook macaroni according to the package directions for al dente. Drain; return to the pan. Stir in the contents of the cheese packets and sour cream. Transfer mixture to a greased 13x9-in. baking dish.

2. In a small bowl, combine tomatoes and pizza sauce; drop by spoonfuls over the macaroni. Top with peppers, cheese and pepperoni. Bake, uncovered, for 25-30 minutes or until bubbly.

Per serving: 1 cup equals 340 cal., 14g fat (7g sat. fat), 37mg chol., 927mg sodium, 37g carb. (5g sugars, 3g fiber), 14g pro.

GOES GREAT WITH

Set a packaged prebaked pizza crust in a hot oven until warmed through and crispy. Slice it into wedges.

GOES GREAT WITH

A hint of lime makes Colorful Quinoa Salad a tasty match for the pork chops. Turn to page 177 for the recipe.

EAT SMART **FAST FIX**

CITRUS-GLAZED PORK CHOPS

A wonderful, sweet-sour citrus glaze makes my recipe for tender chops tangy and tasty. The grilled chops are perfect for weeknight dinners and weekend barbecues alike.

—Jacqueline Correa, Landing, NJ

Takes: 25 min. • **Makes:** 4 servings

- ⅓ cup orange marmalade
- 1 jalapeno pepper, seeded and finely chopped
- 2 Tbsp. lime juice
- 1 tsp. grated fresh gingerroot
- 4 bone-in pork loin chops (8 oz. each)
- 4 tsp. minced fresh cilantro Lime wedges

1. For glaze, in a small saucepan, combine the marmalade, jalapeno, lime juice and ginger; cook and stir over medium heat 4-6 minutes or until marmalade is melted.
2. Moisten a paper towel with cooking oil; using long-handled tongs, rub on grill rack to coat lightly.
3. Grill chops, covered, over medium heat or broil 4 in. from heat for 6-8 minutes on each side or until a thermometer reads 145°, brushing with glaze during the last 5 minutes. Let stand 5 minutes. Sprinkle with cilantro; serve with lime wedges.
Note: Wear disposable gloves when cutting hot peppers; the oils can burn skin. Avoid touching your face.
Per serving: 1 pork chop equals 286 cal., 8g fat (3g sat. fat), 86mg chol., 85mg sodium, 18g carb. (0 sugars, 1g fiber), 34g pro.
Diabetic Exchanges: 1 starch, 4 lean meat.

NOTES

_____
_____
_____
_____
_____
_____
_____
_____
_____

SAUSAGE & SWISS CHARD LASAGNA

Rustic and comforting, this rich and cheesy lasagna is a great way to get kids to eat greens—it's such a tasty casserole they'll never even know the nutritious Swiss chard is there!
—Candace Morehouse, Show Low, AZ

Prep: 45 min. • **Bake:** 55 min. + standing
Makes: 6 servings

- 1 lb. bulk Italian sausage
- 1¾ cups sliced fresh mushrooms
- 2 garlic cloves, minced
- 1 bunch Swiss chard (about 10 oz.)
- 3 Tbsp. butter
- ¼ cup all-purpose flour
- 3 cups 2% milk
- 1 cup (4 oz.) shredded Gruyere or Swiss cheese, divided
- 1 Tbsp. minced fresh parsley or 1 tsp. dried parsley flakes
- 1 Tbsp. minced fresh oregano or 1 tsp. dried oregano
- 1 tsp. grated lemon peel
- ½ tsp. salt
- ⅛ tsp. pepper
- 6 no-cook lasagna noodles

1. Preheat oven to 350°. In a large skillet, cook sausage, mushrooms and garlic over medium heat for 8-10 minutes or until the sausage is no longer pink and mushrooms are tender, breaking up the sausage into crumbles. Remove from pan with a slotted spoon. Remove drippings.

2. Remove stems from the Swiss chard; coarsely chop leaves. In same skillet, heat butter over medium heat. Stir in flour until smooth; gradually whisk in milk. Bring to a boil, stirring constantly; cook and stir for 1-2 minutes or until thickened. Add ¾ cup cheese, parsley, oregano, lemon peel, salt and pepper; stir until cheese is melted. Stir in Swiss chard leaves.

3. Spread one-fourth of the cheese sauce into a greased 8-in.-square baking dish. Layer with each of the following: two noodles, one-third of the meat mixture and one-fourth of the cheese sauce. Repeat the layers twice. Sprinkle with remaining cheese.

4. Bake, covered, for 45 minutes. Uncover; bake 8-10 minutes longer or until cheese is melted. Let stand 10 minutes before serving.

Freeze option: Cool unbaked lasagna; cover and freeze. To use, partially thaw in refrigerator overnight. Remove from refrigerator 30 minutes before baking. Preheat oven to 350°. Cover lasagna with foil; bake as directed, increasing covered time to 55-60 minutes or until heated through and a thermometer inserted in center reads 165°. Uncover; bake for 10-12 minutes longer or until bubbly.

Per serving: 1 serving equals 470 cal., 31g fat (14g sat. fat), 87mg chol., 896mg sodium, 26g carb. (7g sugars, 1g fiber), 22g pro.

GOES GREAT WITH

In just half an hour, you can enjoy Ham & Green Onion Biscuits from page 232. The savory bites make a yummy addition to the cheesy lasagna.

GOES GREAT WITH

Mint ice cream, almond cookies or citrus sherbet make perfect desserts after this one-dish dinner.

READY IN
30
MINUTES

EAT SMART FAST FIX ▶

EGG ROLL NOODLE BOWL

At our house, we love egg rolls. They can be challenging to make, however, so I simplified everything with this tasty deconstructed version made on the stovetop in minutes!
—Courtney Stultz, Weir, KS

Takes: 30 min. •**Makes:** 4 servings

- 1   Tbsp. sesame oil
- ½   lb. ground pork
- 1   Tbsp. soy sauce
- 1   garlic clove, minced
- 1   tsp. ground ginger
- ½   tsp. salt
- ¼   tsp. ground turmeric
- ¼   tsp. pepper
- 6   cups shredded cabbage (about 1 small head)
- 2   large carrots, shredded (about 2 cups)
- 4   oz. thin rice noodles
- 3   green onions, thinly sliced
     Additional soy sauce, optional

1. In a large skillet, heat oil over medium-high heat. Add pork; cook for 4-6 minutes or until browned, breaking into crumbles. Stir in soy sauce, garlic and seasonings. Add the cabbage and carrots; cook for 4-6 minutes longer or until vegetables are tender, stirring occasionally.
2. Cook rice noodles according to package directions; drain and immediately add to pork mixture, tossing to combine. Sprinkle with green onions. If desired, serve with additional soy sauce.
Per serving: 1½ cups equals 302 cal., 12g fat (4g sat. fat), 38mg chol., 652mg sodium, 33g carb. (2g sugars, 4g fiber), 14g pro. **Diabetic Exchanges:** 1½ starch, 2 medium-fat meat, 2 vegetable, ½ fat.

MEAL PLANNER

PORK, HAM ♥ MORE

DIG INTO HEARTY FLAVOR WITH THESE MUST-TRY MEALS!

SAVORY SUPPER

ENTREE:
Sausage & Swiss Chard
Lasagna
page 124

SIDES:
Ham & Green
Onion Biscuits
page 232

DESSERT:
Creamy Hazelnut Pie
page 254

TAG YOUR MEAL
MEMORIES WITH
#100 FAMILYMEALS

GROCERY LIST

KITCHEN STAPLES
- ○ All-purpose flour
- ○ Baking powder
- ○ Sugar
- ○ Confectioners' sugar
- ○ Garlic salt
- ○ Salt
- ○ Pepper

PRODUCE
- ○ 1 lemon
- ○ 2 cartons (8 oz. each) sliced mushrooms
- ○ 1 bunch fresh parsley
- ○ 1 bunch fresh oregano
- ○ 1 head of garlic

- ○ 1 bunch Swiss chard
- ○ 1 bunch green onions

PANTRY
- ○ 1 box (9 oz.) no-cook lasagna noodles
- ○ 1 jar (13 oz.) Nutella
- ○ 1 chocolate crumb pie crust (9 in.)

MEATS
- ○ 1 lb. bulk Italian sausage
- ○ 1 package (8 oz.) fully cooked ham

DAIRY
- ○ Butter
- ○ 1 half gallon (64 oz.) 2% milk
- ○ 1 cup (4 oz.) shredded Gruyere or Swiss cheese
- ○ 1 package (8 oz.) cream cheese

OTHER
- ○ 1 carton (8 oz.) frozen whipped topping

SANDWICH TIME

ENTREE:
PB&J Pork Sandwiches
page 118

SALAD:
Garden Tomato Salad
page 184

DESSERT:
Berry Dream Cake
page 255

TAG YOUR MEAL
MEMORIES WITH
#100 FAMILYMEALS

GROCERY LIST

KITCHEN STAPLES
- ○ Olive oil
- ○ Brown sugar
- ○ Salt
- ○ Pepper

PRODUCE
- ○ 4 cups fresh strawberries
- ○ 1 small onion
- ○ 3 large tomatoes
- ○ 1 large sweet onion
- ○ 1 large cucumber
- ○ 1 bunch fresh basil
- ○ 1 bunch fresh chives
- ○ 1 head of garlic

PANTRY
- ○ 1 bottle (16 oz.) cider vinegar
- ○ 1 bottle (12 oz.) Dijon mustard
- ○ 1 can (14½ oz.) reduced-sodium chicken broth
- ○ 1 jar (16 oz.) creamy peanut butter
- ○ 1 jar (12 oz.) apricot preserves
- ○ 1 package (3 oz.) cherry gelatin
- ○ 1 box (15.2 oz) white cake mix

MEAT
- ○ 3 to 4 lbs. boneless pork shoulder butt roast

DAIRY
- ○ Butter
- ○ 1 package (8 oz.) cream cheese

OTHER
- ○ 6 ciabatta rolls
- ○ 1 lb. coleslaw
- ○ 1 carton (8 oz.) frozen whipped topping

MEAL PLANNER

PORK, HAM ♥ MORE
DIG INTO HEARTY FLAVOR WITH THESE MUST-TRY MEALS!

SLOW & EASY

ENTREE:
Slow-Cooked Pork Stew
page 100

SIDES:
Olive & Onion Quick Bread
page 240

DESSERT:
Caramel Fluff
& Toffee Trifle
page 265

TAG YOUR MEAL
MEMORIES WITH
#100 FAMILYMEALS

GROCERY LIST

KITCHEN STAPLES
- ○ Canola oil
- ○ All-purpose flour
- ○ Baking soda
- ○ Brown sugar
- ○ Bay leaves
- ○ Vanilla extract
- ○ Salt
- ○ Pepper

PRODUCE
- ○ 2 large carrots
- ○ 2 celery ribs
- ○ 2 medium onions
- ○ Potatoes for mashing
- ○ 1 bunch fresh rosemary

- ○ 1 bunch fresh thyme
- ○ 1 bunch fresh parsley
- ○ 1 head of garlic

PANTRY
- ○ 1 container (32 oz.) beef broth
- ○ 1 package (6 oz.) pitted dried plums
- ○ 1 can (6 oz.) tomato paste

MEAT
- ○ 2 pork tenderloins (1 lb. each)

DAIRY
- ○ Butter
- ○ 1 quart (32 oz.) buttermilk
- ○ 2 large eggs

- ○ 1 package (8 oz.) shredded sharp cheddar cheese
- ○ 1 pint heavy whipping cream

OTHER
- ○ 1 jar (6.7 oz.) Greek olives
- ○ 1 jar (7 oz.) pitted green olives
- ○ 1 can (2.5 oz.) ripe olives
- ○ 1 bag (8 oz.) milk chocolate English toffee bits
- ○ 1 prepared angel food cake (8-10 oz.)

✂ -

TACO NIGHT

ENTREE:
Barbecue Pork Tacos
with Apple Slaw
page 105

SALAD:
Chipotle Lime
Avocado Salad
page 170

DESSERT:
Blond Butterscotch
Brownies
page 274

TAG YOUR MEAL
MEMORIES WITH
#100 FAMILYMEALS

GROCERY LIST

KITCHEN STAPLES
- ○ All-purpose flour
- ○ Baking powder
- ○ Sugar
- ○ Brown sugar
- ○ Cayenne pepper
- ○ Vanilla extract
- ○ Salt
- ○ Pepper

PRODUCE
- ○ 2 medium ripe avocados
- ○ 2 medium Granny Smith apples
- ○ 1 medium cucumber
- ○ 2 large tomatoes

- ○ 1 medium head red cabbage
- ○ 1 bunch fresh chives
- ○ 1 bunch fresh cilantro

PANTRY
- ○ 1 bottle (16 oz.) cider vinegar
- ○ 1 bottle (18 oz.) barbecue sauce
- ○ 1 bottle (8.5 oz.) maple syrup
- ○ 1 box (6.89 oz.) 18-count taco shells

MEAT
- ○ 2 pork tenderloins (1 lb. each)

DAIRY
- ○ Butter
- ○ 2 large eggs

OTHER
- ○ 1 can (12 oz.) root beer
- ○ 1 bottle (8 oz.) lime juice
- ○ Ground chipotle pepper
- ○ 1 bag (10 oz.) semisweet chocolate chunks
- ○ 4 Heath candy bars (1.4 oz. each)

Pizza Squared

FAMILY QUILT PIZZA

Fill bowls with colorful veggies and favorite meats. Next, let the kids pile on tasty toppings in their personal pizza squares. They can even make designs or write their names in veggie bits!
—Marie Louise Ludwig, Phoenixville, PA

Prep: 30 min. • **Bake:** 20 min.
Makes: 6 servings

1 tube (13.8 oz.) refrigerated pizza crust
1 can (8 oz.) pizza sauce
4 cups (16 oz.) shredded part-skim mozzarella cheese
2 oz. sliced deli ham, cut into ½-in. strips
   Optional toppings: sweet pepper slices, tomatoes, fully cooked sausage, mushrooms, ripe olives, pineapple, pepperoni, yellow summer squash, red onion, broccoli florets, crumbled feta cheese, minced fresh basil and minced fresh chives

Preheat oven to 425°. Unroll pizza crust and press to fit into a greased 15x10x1-in. baking pan, pinching edges to form a rim. Bake 8-10 minutes or until the edges are lightly browned.

Spread crust with pizza sauce; top with the mozzarella cheese. Using ham strips, outline 12 sections. Arrange the toppings of your choice in each section to create individual designs. Bake 10-15 minutes or until the crust is golden brown and cheese is melted.

Per serving: 2 pieces (calculated without optional toppings) equals 395 cal., 14g fat (8g sat. fat), 48mg chol., 892mg sodium, 40g carb. (5g sugars, 1g fiber), 25g pro.

PIZZA PARTIES RULE, or at least they do when they're at Marie Louise Ludgwig's home. She's found a way for everyone to get in on the fun.

"I created this recipe in college to satisfy everyone's cravings for different toppings," she writes. "Now, I make it with my three kids!

"Not only is it a great way to get everyone into the kitchen, but it might be an easy way to cater to all of the preferences at your table."

Mary Louise explains that it's always interesting to see what the kids set on their pizza squares...from simple to extravagant. "For instance, my daughter, Steph, just loves mushrooms and piles them on her squares," says Mary Louise. "My son Nick always turns to the meat and sausage while his brother, Ryan, sticks to plain cheese."

It's fun to get creative, too. "I fashion flowers from olives with scallion stems," she adds. "The kids love stuff like that. In fact, we all enjoy seeing what one another comes with. It's all up to each person's taste—and imagination!"

"A terrific meal gives me time to enjoy the company of my family."

−Susan Lasken
Woodland Hills, California

SEAFOOD and MEATLESS

MIX THINGS UP with these change-of-pace weeknight favorites.

ONE-DISH SEAFOOD MEAL

I came up with these everything-in-one seafood packets for a family reunion, since the recipe can be increased to feed a bunch. Steam builds up inside the foil, so open carefully.
—Allison Brooks, Fort Collins, CO

Takes: 30 min. • **Makes:** 4 servings

- 1 pkg. (20 oz.) refrigerated red potato wedges
- 2 salmon fillets (6 oz. each), halved
- ¾ lb. uncooked shrimp (31-40 per lb.), peeled and deveined
- ½ lb. summer sausage, cubed
- 2 medium ears sweet corn, halved
- 2 Tbsp. olive oil
- 1 tsp. seafood seasoning
- ½ tsp. salt
- ¼ tsp. pepper
- 1 medium lemon, cut into 4 wedges

1. Divide the potatoes, salmon, shrimp, sausage and corn among four pieces of heavy-duty foil (about 18x12-in. rectangles). Drizzle with oil; sprinkle with seasonings. Squeeze lemon juice over top; place squeezed wedges in packets. Fold foil around mixture, sealing tightly.
2. Grill, covered, over medium heat for 12-15 minutes or until fish just begins to flake easily with a fork, shrimp turn pink and potatoes are tender. Open the foil carefully to allow steam to escape.
Per serving: 1 packet equals 509 cal., 30g fat (7g sat. fat), 181mg chol., 1302mg sodium, 21g carb. (5g sugars, 3g fiber), 40g pro.

GOES **GREAT** WITH

Heat up a can of clam chowder while the packets are on the grill or bake some cheddar biscuits from a boxed mix.

FAST FIX ▶

WHITE BEANS & BOW TIES

When we have fresh veggies, we toss them with pasta shapes like penne or bow tie. What a tasty way to enjoy a fast meatless meal!
—Angela Buchanan, Longmont, CO

Takes: 25 min. • **Makes:** 4 servings

2½ cups uncooked whole wheat bow tie pasta (about 6 oz.)
1 Tbsp. olive oil
1 medium zucchini, sliced
2 garlic cloves, minced
2 large tomatoes, chopped
1 can (15 oz.) white kidney or cannellini beans, rinsed and drained
1 can (2¼ oz.) sliced ripe olives, drained
¾ tsp. freshly ground pepper
½ cup crumbled feta cheese

1. Cook pasta according to the package directions. Drain, reserving ½ cup of the pasta water.
2. In a large skillet, heat oil over medium-high heat. Add zucchini; cook and stir for 2-4 minutes or until crisp-tender. Add the garlic; cook for 30 seconds longer. Stir in tomatoes, beans, olives and pepper; bring to a boil. Reduce heat; simmer, uncovered, for 3-5 minutes or until the tomatoes are softened, stirring occasionally.
3. Add the pasta; toss to combine, adding enough of the pasta water to moisten. Stir in cheese.
Per serving: 1½ cups equals 348 cal., 9g fat (2g sat. fat), 8mg chol., 394mg sodium, 52g carb. (4g sugars, 11g fiber), 15g pro.

GOES GREAT WITH

The rustic texture of seven-grain bread makes it a smart addition to this meatless meal.

LEMON-PARSLEY BAKED COD

This is the first fish recipe that got two thumbs up from all the picky meat-only eaters at my table. Tangy lemon gives the cod some oomph.

—Trisha Kruse, Eagle, ID

....

Takes: 30 min. • **Makes:** 4 servings

3	**Tbsp. lemon juice**
3	**Tbsp. butter, melted**
¼	**cup all-purpose flour**
½	**tsp. salt**
¼	**tsp. paprika**
¼	**tsp. lemon-pepper seasoning**
4	**cod fillets (6 oz. each)**
2	**Tbsp. minced fresh parsley**
2	**tsp. grated lemon peel**

"Oh my goodness, this was excellent. Our family agreed it was a keeper. The sauce could be used for any fish recipe. Delicious!"

—SGNURSE, TASTEOFHOME.COM

1. Preheat oven to 400°. In a shallow bowl, mix lemon juice and butter. In a separate shallow bowl, mix flour and seasonings. Dip fillets in lemon juice mixture, then in flour mixture to coat both sides; shake off the excess.

2. Place in a 13x9-in. baking dish coated with cooking spray. Drizzle with remaining lemon juice mixture. Bake 12-15 minutes or until fish just begins to flake easily with a fork. Mix the parsley and lemon peel; sprinkle over fish.

Per serving: 1 fillet equals 232 cal., 10g fat (6g sat. fat), 87mg chol., 477mg sodium, 7g carb. (trace sugars, trace fiber), 28g pro.
Diabetic Exchanges: ½ starch, 4 lean meat, 2 fat.

GOES GREAT WITH

Stir up some flavor with Tortellini Primavera Soup. Turn to page 238 to see how the mild ingredients complement the lemon fish.

UNDER 250 CALORIES

Herb It Your Way

The recipe calls for fresh parsley but you can jazz up the cod fillets with other herbs, too. Sprinkle on some chopped cilantro, sage, dill or rosemary for a full-flavored twist.

GOES GREAT WITH

Zap a package of white rice in the microwave, and drain and rinse a can of black or red beans. Mix them together for the perfect side dish!

FAMILY-FAVORITE FISH TACOS

I like to serve fish tacos with quinoa and black beans for a complete and satisfying meal. If you've got them, add summer toppings like brightly colored peppers, green onions or purple carrots.
—Camille Parker, Chicago, IL

Prep: 20 min. • **Grill:** 20 min.
Makes: 4 servings

- 1 medium ear sweet corn, husk removed
- 1 poblano pepper, halved and seeds removed
- 4 tilapia fillets (4 oz. each)
- ⅛ tsp. salt
- 1 yellow summer squash, halved lengthwise
- 1 medium heirloom tomato, chopped
- ⅓ cup chopped red onion
- 3 Tbsp. coarsely chopped fresh cilantro
- 1 tsp. grated lime peel
- 3 Tbsp. lime juice
- 8 taco shells, warmed
- ½ medium ripe avocado, peeled and sliced

1. Moisten a paper towel with cooking oil; using long-handled tongs, rub on grill rack to coat lightly. Grill the corn and pepper, covered, over medium heat 10-12 minutes or until tender, turning occasionally. Cool vegetables slightly.

2. Meanwhile, sprinkle fish with salt. Grill fish and squash, covered, over medium heat for 7-9 minutes or until the fish just begins to flake easily with a fork and the squash is tender, turning once.

3. Cut corn from cob and place in a bowl. Chop pepper and squash; add to the corn. Stir in tomato, onion, cilantro, lime peel and lime juice. Serve fish in the taco shells; top with corn mixture.

Note: Wear disposable gloves when cutting hot peppers; the oils can burn skin. Avoid touching your face.

Per serving: 2 tacos equals 278 cal., 10g fat (2g sat. fat), 55mg chol., 214mg sodium, 26g carb. (5g sugars, 5g fiber), 25g pro. **Diabetic Exchanges:** 1½ starch, 3 lean meat, 1 vegetable, ½ fat.

"These were just amazing. I added ancho chili pepper powder to the tilapia. Great recipe!"

—SHEENA_MICHELLE_PEEBLES
TASTEOFHOME.COM

GOES GREAT WITH
Slice a large zucchini and brush it with oil. Grill the slices alongside the fish until they're tender.

SOUTHWESTERN CATFISH

I rub catfish fillets with an easy spice blend and grill them up quickly. Topped with salsa and served with baked sweet potatoes, it's a tasty entree.
—Bruce Crittenden, Clinton, MS

Prep: 15 min. + chilling • **Bake:** 10 min.
Makes: 4 servings

- 3 medium tomatoes, chopped
- ¼ cup chopped onion
- 2 jalapeno peppers, seeded and finely chopped
- 2 Tbsp. white wine vinegar
- 3 tsp. salt, divided
- 3 tsp. paprika
- 3 tsp. chili powder
- 1 to 1½ tsp. ground cumin
- 1 to 1½ tsp. ground coriander
- ¾ to 1 tsp. cayenne pepper
- ½ tsp. garlic powder
- 4 catfish fillets (6 oz. each)

1. For salsa, in a large bowl, combine the tomatoes, onion, jalapenos, vinegar and 1 tsp. salt. Cover and refrigerate for at least 30 minutes.
2. Combine the paprika, chili powder, cumin, coriander, cayenne, garlic powder and remaining salt; rub over catfish. Using long-handled tongs, moisten a paper towel with cooking oil and lightly coat the grill rack.
3. Grill fillets, uncovered, over medium heat or broil 4 in. from the heat for 5 minutes on each side or until fish flakes easily with a fork. Serve with salsa.
Note: Wear disposable gloves when cutting hot peppers; the oils can burn skin. Avoid touching your face.
Per serving: 1 fillet equals 107 cal., 4g fat (1g sat. fat), 20mg chol., 1825mg sodium, 10g carb. (4g sugars, 3g fiber), 9g pro.

Table Talk

Who was your most memorable teacher?

Teachers offer both life lessons and memories. Discuss who your favorite instructor was and why. Was there a particular teacher who intimidated you? Share those stories, too.

GOES **GREAT** WITH

Boil some spaghetti and toss it with the extra spaghetti sauce for a speedy side.

MUFFIN TIN LASAGNAS

This is a super fun way to serve lasagna, and a great way to surprise everyone at the table. Easy and quick, these little cups can also be made with whatever ingredients your family craves most!
—Sally Kilkenny, Granger, IA

Prep: 10 min. • **Bake:** 20 min.
Makes: 6 servings

- 1 **large egg, lightly beaten**
- 1 **carton (15 oz.) part-skim ricotta cheese**
- 2 **cups (8 oz.) shredded Italian cheese blend, divided**
- 1 **Tbsp. olive oil**
- 24 **wonton wrappers**
- 1 **jar (24 oz.) garden-style pasta sauce**
   Minced fresh parsley, optional

1. Preheat oven to 375°. In a bowl, mix egg, ricotta cheese and 1¼ cups Italian cheese blend.

2. Generously grease 12 muffin cups with oil; line each with a wonton wrapper. Fill each with 1 Tbsp. ricotta mixture and 1½ Tbsp. pasta sauce. Top each with a second wrapper, rotating corners and pressing down centers. Repeat ricotta and sauce layers. Sprinkle with remaining cheese blend.

3. Bake 20-25 minutes or until cheese is melted. If desired, sprinkle with parsley.

Per serving: 2 muffin tin lasagnas equals 431 cal., 20g fat (9g sat. fat), 83mg chol., 979mg sodium, 38g carb. (10g sugars, 2g fiber), 22g pro.

FISH & CHIPS WITH DIPPING SAUCE

I don't care for all the grease that typically comes along with such a meal. I decided to give the classic dinner a makeover, and it turns out the pickle dip, which we like a lot better than tartar sauce, is healthier.
—Michelle Lucas, Cold Spring, KY

Prep: 30 min. • **Bake:** 30 min.
Makes: 4 servings

½	cup reduced-fat sour cream
2	Tbsp. chopped dill pickle
1	Tbsp. dill pickle juice
⅛	tsp. pepper

FRIES

4	large potatoes (about 2 lbs.)
2	Tbsp. olive oil
½	tsp. salt
¼	tsp. pepper

FISH

1½	cups panko (Japanese) bread crumbs
1	tsp. garlic powder
1	tsp. onion powder
½	tsp. salt
½	tsp. pepper
2	large egg whites, beaten
4	cod fillets (4 oz. each)
	Cooking spray
	Lemon wedges

1. Arrange one oven rack at lowest rack setting; place second rack in middle of oven. Preheat oven to 425°. In a small bowl, mix sour cream, chopped pickle, pickle juice and pepper. Refrigerate, covered, until serving.

2. Cut potatoes into ¼-in. julienne strips. Rinse well and pat dry. In a large bowl, toss with the oil, salt and pepper; transfer to a baking sheet coated with cooking spray. Bake on bottom oven rack 30-35 minutes or until golden brown and tender, turning pieces once.

3. For fish, in a shallow bowl, mix the bread crumbs, garlic powder, onion powder, salt and pepper. Place egg whites in a separate shallow bowl. Dip fish in egg whites, then in the crumb mixture, patting to help the coating adhere.

4. Transfer to a baking sheet coated with cooking spray. Spritz fish with cooking spray. Bake on the top oven rack for 14-16 minutes or until fish just begins to flake easily with a fork. Serve with fries, sour cream mixture and lemon wedges.

Per serving: 1 serving equals 402 cal., 11g fat (3g sat. fat), 53mg chol., 667mg sodium, 48g carb. (6g sugars, 4g fiber), 27g pro. **Diabetic Exchanges:** 3 starch, 3 lean meat, 2 fat.

GOES GREAT WITH

Honey jazzes up an all-time classic in this version of peas and carrots. See page 199 for the easy slow-cooked recipe.

"Love this recipe! It's very easy, and my son likes to make the dipping sauce. My whole family eats this!"

—MELGOODY03, TASTEOFHOME.COM

FAMILY
FAVORITE
♥

GARDEN VEGETABLE GNOCCHI

When we go meatless, we toss gnocchi (my husband's favorite) with veggies and a dab of prepared pesto. I use zucchini in this 30-minute dish, too.
—Elisabeth Larsen, Pleasant Grove, UT

Takes: 30 min. • **Makes:** 4 servings

- 2 medium yellow summer squash, sliced
- 1 medium sweet red pepper, chopped
- 8 oz. sliced fresh mushrooms
- 1 Tbsp. olive oil
- ¼ tsp. salt
- ¼ tsp. pepper
- 1 pkg. (16 oz.) potato gnocchi
- ½ cup Alfredo sauce
- ¼ cup prepared pesto
  Chopped fresh basil, optional

1. Preheat the oven to 450°. In a greased 15x10x1-in. baking pan, toss vegetables with oil, salt and pepper. Roast for 18-22 minutes or until tender, stirring once.
2. Meanwhile, in a large saucepan, cook gnocchi according to package directions. Drain and return to pan.
3. Stir in roasted vegetables, Alfredo sauce and pesto. If desired, sprinkle with basil.
Per serving: 1½ cups equals 402 cal., 14g fat (4g sat. fat), 17mg chol., 955mg sodium, 57g carb. (12g sugars, 5g fiber), 13g pro.

EAT SMART ⑤INGREDIENTS FAST FIX ▶

OVEN-ROASTED SALMON

When I'm starving after work, I want a fast meal with no-fail technique. Roasted salmon is extra tender and has a delicate sweetness. It's always an easy wowza for company.
—Jeanne Ambrose, Milwaukee, WI

Takes: 20 min. • **Makes:** 4 servings

- 1 center-cut salmon fillet (1½ lbs.)
- 1 Tbsp. olive oil
- ½ tsp. salt
- ¼ tsp. pepper

1. Place a large oven-safe skillet in a cold oven. Preheat oven to 450°. Meanwhile, brush salmon with oil and sprinkle with salt and pepper.

2. Carefully remove skillet from the oven. Place fish, skin side down, in skillet. Return to oven; bake uncovered for 14-18 minutes or until the salmon flakes easily and a thermometer reads 125°. Cut salmon into four equal portions.
Per serving: ¼ fillet equals 95 cal., 19g fat (4g sat. fat), 85mg chol., 380mg sodium, 0 carb. (0 sugars, 0 fiber), 29g pro. **Diabetic Exchanges:** 4 lean meat, ½ fat.

GOES GREAT WITH

Loaded with flavor, Tzatziki Potato Salad on page 286 pairs nicely with the mild salmon.

GOES GREAT WITH

Don't have a loaf of bread? Don't worry! Bagels cut into pieces make tasty additions to saucy dinners like this one.

MAKE IT SERVE IT **SHARE IT**

Post photos of your special meals as well as weeknight staples today! Be sure to use **#100FamilyMeals**.

THAI LIME SHRIMP & NOODLES

The flavors just pop in this quick dinner. My family likes spicy foods, but I kept the heat moderate in this version. Adjust it to your liking.
—Teri Rasey, Cadillac, MI

....

Takes: 25 min. • **Makes:** 6 servings

1	cup minced fresh basil
3	Tbsp. lime juice
4	tsp. Thai red chili paste
1	garlic clove, minced
1	tsp. minced fresh gingerroot
1½	lbs. uncooked shrimp (26-30 per lb.), peeled and deveined
12	oz. cooked angel hair pasta
4	tsp. olive oil, divided
1	can (14½ oz.) chicken broth
1	can (13.66 oz.) coconut milk
1	tsp. salt
1	Tbsp. cornstarch
2	Tbsp. cold water
2	Tbsp. grated lime peel

1. Place the first five ingredients in a blender; cover and process until blended. Remove 1 Tbsp. mixture; toss with shrimp.
2. Cook pasta according to the package directions. Meanwhile, in a large nonstick skillet, heat 2 tsp. oil over medium-high heat. Add half of the shrimp mixture; stir-fry 2-4 minutes or until shrimp turn pink. Remove from the pan; keep warm. Repeat with the remaining oil and shrimp mixture.
3. Add the broth, coconut milk, salt and remaining basil mixture to same pan. In a small bowl, mix cornstarch and water until smooth. Stir into the broth mixture. Bring to a boil; cook and stir 1-2 minutes or until slightly thickened. Stir in lime peel.
4. Drain pasta; add pasta and shrimp to sauce, tossing to coat.
Per serving: 1 serving equals 320 cal., 19g fat (13g sat. fat), 141mg chol., 862mg sodium, 15g carb. (1g sugars, 1g fiber), 22g pro.

GOES **GREAT** WITH

Keep citrus the star of your meal when you top off dinner with the orange cookies on page 270!

GOES GREAT WITH

Warm up the family with bowls of this meatless stew. Serve grilled cheese sandwiches on the side.

UNDER 300 CALORIES

LENTIL & CHICKPEA STEW

I got this recipe from a friend at a health food store. I made a few changes until I found a version that my family loves. My husband works outdoors for long hours at a time, and this soup is hearty enough to keep him satisfied.
—Melanie MacFarlane, Bedeque, PE

Prep: 25 min. • **Cook:** 8 hours
Makes: 8 servings (2¾ qt.)

- 2   tsp. olive oil
- 1   medium onion, thinly sliced
- 1   tsp. dried oregano
- ½   tsp. crushed red pepper flakes
- 2   cans (15 oz. each) chickpeas or garbanzo beans, rinsed and drained
- 1   cup dried lentils, rinsed
- 1   can (2¼ oz.) sliced ripe olives, drained
- 3   tsp. smoked paprika
- 4   cups vegetable broth
- 4   cans (8 oz. each) no-salt-added tomato sauce
- 4   cups fresh baby spinach
- ¾   cup fat-free plain yogurt

1. In a small skillet, heat oil over medium-high heat. Add onion, oregano and pepper flakes; cook and stir 8-10 minutes or until onion is tender. Transfer to a 5- or 6-qt. slow cooker.
2. Add the chickpeas, lentils, olives and paprika; stir in broth and tomato sauce. Cook, covered, on low 8-10 hours or until lentils are tender. Stir in the spinach. Top servings with yogurt.
Per serving: 1⅓ cups equals 266 cal., 4g fat (0 sat. fat), 0 chol., 712mg sodium, 45g carb. (11g sugars, 10g fiber), 14g pro.

BUFFALO SHRIMP MAC & CHEESE

For a rich, creamy and slightly spicy shrimp and pasta recipe, you can't beat this crowd-pleasing slow cooker dish. It's a nice twist on the always popular macaroni and cheese.
—Robin Haas, Cranston, RI

Prep: 15 min. • **Cook:** 3½ hours
Makes: 6 servings

- 2   cups 2% milk
- 1   cup half-and-half cream
- 2   Tbsp. Louisiana-style hot sauce
- 1   Tbsp. butter
- 1   tsp. ground mustard
- ½   tsp. onion powder
- ¼   tsp. white pepper
- ¼   tsp. ground nutmeg
- 2   cups (8 oz.) finely shredded cheddar cheese
- 1   cup (4 oz.) shredded Gouda or Swiss cheese
- 1½ cups uncooked elbow macaroni
- ¾   lb. frozen cooked salad shrimp, thawed
- 1   cup (4 oz.) crumbled blue cheese
- 2   Tbsp. minced fresh chives
- 2   Tbsp. minced fresh parsley
       Additional Louisiana-style hot sauce, optional

1. In a 3-qt. slow cooker, combine the first eight ingredients; stir in shredded cheeses and macaroni. Cook, covered, on low for 3 to 3½ hours or until the macaroni is almost tender.
2. Stir in shrimp and blue cheese; cook, covered, 30-35 minutes longer or until heated through. Just before serving, stir in the chives, parsley and, if desired, additional hot sauce.
Per serving: 1 cup equals 551 cal., 34g fat (20g sat. fat), 228mg chol., 1269mg sodium, 22g carb. (7g sugars, 1g fiber), 38g pro.

GOES GREAT WITH

Hawaiian dinner rolls lend sweet flair to this robust main course.

PINEAPPLE SHRIMP STIR-FRY

I came up with this recipe for a luau-themed party and served it with sliced papaya, mango and avocado. My family loved it! If you don't care for coconut, you can sprinkle the dish with chopped macadamia nuts instead.
—Trisha Kruse, Eagle, ID

Takes: 30 min. • **Makes:** 4 servings

- 1   can (20 oz.) unsweetened pineapple tidbits
- 2   Tbsp. cornstarch
- 1   cup chicken broth
- 1   Tbsp. brown sugar
- 1   Tbsp. orange juice
- 1   Tbsp. reduced-sodium soy sauce
- 1   Tbsp. sesame or canola oil
- 1   medium sweet red pepper, thinly sliced
- 1   medium green pepper, thinly sliced
- 1   medium sweet onion, thinly sliced
- 1   lb. uncooked shrimp (31-40 per lb.), peeled and deveined
- ¼   cup flaked coconut, toasted
     Hot cooked rice

1. Drain pineapple, reserving juice. In a small bowl, mix cornstarch, broth, brown sugar, orange juice, soy sauce and the reserved pineapple juice until smooth.
2. In a large skillet, heat oil over medium-high heat. Add peppers and onion; stir-fry 1-2 minutes or just until crisp-tender. Add shrimp; stir-fry 2-3 minutes longer or until shrimp turn pink. Remove from pan.
3. Place pineapple in skillet. Stir cornstarch mixture and add to the pan. Bring to a boil; cook and stir 4-5 minutes or until sauce is thickened. Return shrimp mixture to pan; heat through, stirring to combine. Sprinkle with coconut; serve with rice.
Per serving: 1 cup (calculated without rice) equals 301 cal., 7g fat (3g sat. fat), 139mg chol., 568mg sodium, 38g carb. (27g sugars, 3g fiber), 20g pro.

GOES GREAT WITH
It's hard to believe Tender Whole Wheat Muffins come together in 30 minutes. See page 239 to learn how.

Prepping Peppers

• Cut the top and bottom off the pepper and discard. Cut each side from the pepper by slicing close to the center and then down. Scrape out and discard the seeds.

• Cut away any ribs.

• Place cut side down on the work surface and flatten slightly with your hand. Cut lengthwise into strips.

SALMON WRAPS

My kids love these wraps. I love them, too, because they contain all four food groups right in one handheld meal. We eat fish on Fridays, so these are a staple in my house.
—Jennifer Krey, Clarence, NY

....

Takes: 25 min. • **Makes:** 4 servings

1   **lb. salmon fillet (about 1 in. thick)**
½   **tsp. salt**
¼   **tsp. pepper**

½   **cup salsa verde**
4   **whole wheat tortillas (8 in.), warmed**
1   **cup chopped fresh spinach**
1   **medium tomato, seeded and chopped**
½   **cup shredded Monterey Jack cheese**
½   **medium ripe avocado, peeled and thinly sliced**

1. Sprinkle salmon with salt and pepper; place on an oiled grill rack over medium heat, skin side down. Grill, covered, for 8-10 minutes or until fish just begins to flake easily with a fork.

2. Remove from grill. Break salmon into bite-size pieces, removing skin if desired. Toss gently with salsa; serve in tortillas. Top with remaining ingredients.

Per serving: 1 wrap equals 380 cal. 18g fat (5g sat. fat), 69mg chol., 745mg sodium, 27g carb. (2g sugars, 5g fiber), 27g pro. **Diabetic Exchanges:** 2 starch, 3 lean meat, 2 fat.

GOES **GREAT** WITH

Toss some salad shrimp with salsa and cubed avocado for a quick seafood salad.

Beef It Up!

This pizza makes a great meatless meal, but feel free to add last night's taco meat, cooked chicken or even barbecued shredded pork if you'd like.

MOZZARELLA CORN BREAD PIZZA

My sons like pizza but not takeout, so I pull out my trusty baking pan to make a corn bread pizza with veggies in the crust. Adjust the toppings to your liking.
—Mary Marlowe Leverette, Columbia, SC

Prep: 15 min. + standing • **Bake:** 20 min.
Makes: 10 servings

- 3 cups shredded zucchini
- 1 tsp. salt, divided
- 2 pkg. (8½ oz. each) corn bread/muffin mix
- 3 large eggs, lightly beaten
- ¼ tsp. pepper

TOPPINGS
- 1 jar (14 oz.) pizza sauce
- ¾ cup chopped sweet red or green pepper
- 1 can (2¼ oz.) sliced ripe olives, drained
- 4 green onions, chopped
- ⅓ cup coarsely chopped fresh basil
- 1 Tbsp. minced fresh oregano or 1 tsp. dried oregano
- 3 cups (12 oz.) shredded part-skim mozzarella cheese

1. Preheat oven to 450°. Place zucchini in a colander over a bowl; sprinkle with ¾ tsp. salt and toss. Let stand 15 minutes.
2. Press zucchini and blot dry with paper towels; transfer to a large bowl. Add the muffin mixes, eggs, pepper and remaining salt; stir until blended. Spread evenly into a greased 15x10x1-in. baking pan. Bake for 8-10 minutes or until lightly browned. Reduce oven setting to 350°.
3. Spread pizza sauce over crust. Top with the red pepper, olives and green onions. Sprinkle with herbs and cheese. Bake for 12-15 minutes or until cheese is melted.
Per serving: 1 serving equals 366 cal., 15g fat (6g sat. fat), 79mg chol., 912mg sodium, 42g carb. (14g sugars, 5g fiber), 15g pro.

GOES GREAT WITH
For a fun side, try Easy Peasy Slaw on page 187. It's ready in just 5 minutes!

GOES GREAT WITH

Pick up yellow, red, green and orange pepper strips from the salad bar. Stir-fry them with butter and chopped cilantro for a savory side dish.

NO-FRY BLACK BEAN CHIMICHANGAS

My chimichangas get lovin' from the oven so they're a bit healthier. Black beans and corn keep them meatless, and they're a great use for leftover rice.
—Kimberly Hammond, Kingwood, TX

....

Takes: 25 min. • **Makes:** 6 servings

- 2 cans (15 oz. each) black beans, rinsed and drained
- 1 pkg. (8.8 oz.) ready-to-serve brown rice
- ⅔ cup frozen corn
- ⅔ cup minced fresh cilantro
- ⅔ cup chopped green onions
- ½ tsp. salt
- 6 whole wheat tortillas (8 in.), warmed if necessary
- 4 tsp. olive oil, divided
  Guacamole and salsa, optional

1. Preheat broiler. In a large microwave-safe bowl, mix the beans, rice and corn; microwave, covered, 4-5 minutes or until heated through, stirring halfway. Stir in cilantro, green onions and salt.
2. To assemble, spoon ¾ cup of bean mixture across the center of each tortilla. Fold the bottom and sides of tortilla over filling and roll up. Place on a greased baking sheet, seam side down.
3. Brush tops with 2 tsp. oil. Broil 3-4 in. from heat 45-60 seconds or until golden brown. Turn over; brush the tops with remaining oil. Broil 45-60 seconds longer or until golden brown. If desired, serve with guacamole and salsa.

Per serving: 1 chimichanga (calculated without guacamole and salsa) equals 337 cal., 5g fat (trace sat. fat), 0 chol., 602mg sodium, 58g carb. (2g sugars, 10g fiber), 13g pro.

NOTES

_____
_____
_____
_____
_____
_____
_____
_____
_____

SHRIMP & CORN STIR-FRY

I make this seafood stir-fry at summer's end when my garden is full of tomatoes, squash, garlic and corn.

—Lindsay Honn, Huntingdon, PA

Takes: 20 min. • **Makes:** 4 servings

- 2   Tbsp. olive oil
- 2   small yellow summer squash, sliced
- 1   small onion, chopped
- 1   lb. uncooked shrimp (26-30 per lb.), peeled and deveined
- 1½ cups fresh or frozen corn, thawed
- 1   cup chopped tomatoes
- 4   garlic cloves, minced
- ½   tsp. salt
- ¼   tsp. pepper
- ¼   tsp. crushed red pepper flakes, optional
- ¼   cup chopped fresh basil
     Hot cooked brown rice

1. In a large skillet, heat oil over medium-high heat. Add squash and onion; stir-fry until squash is crisp-tender, 2-3 minutes.
2. Add next six ingredients and, if desired, pepper flakes; stir-fry until shrimp turn pink, 3-4 minutes longer. Top with basil. Serve with rice.

Per serving: 1 serving (calculated without rice) equals: 239 cal., 9g fat (1g sat. fat), 138mg chol., 443mg sodium, 19g carb. (8g sugars, 3g fiber), 22g pro. **Diabetic Exchanges:** 1 starch, 3 lean meat, 1 vegetable, 1½ fat.

GOES GREAT WITH

Add iced tea and sugar cookies to this menu for a super supper lineup.

SUN-DRIED TOMATO PASTA

At my house, this dish is known as Gus's Special Pasta. My oldest child claimed it as his own when he was 8, and I'm always happy to oblige his desire for this cheesy, garlicky, pungent dish.

—Courtney Gaylord, Columbus, IN

Takes: 25 min. • **Makes:** 6 servings

- 1 pkg. (16 oz.) linguine
- 1 jar (7 oz.) julienned oil-packed sun-dried tomatoes
- 6 garlic cloves, minced
- 1 Tbsp. lemon juice
- ½ cup minced fresh parsley
- 1½ cups (6 oz.) crumbled feta cheese
- 1½ cups grated Parmesan cheese

1. In a 6-qt. stockpot, cook the linguine according to the package directions for al dente. Drain, reserving ½ cup pasta water; return linguine to pot.

2. Meanwhile, drain tomatoes, reserving 2 Tbsp. oil. In a small microwave-safe bowl, combine garlic and reserved oil; microwave on high 45 seconds. Stir in drained tomatoes and lemon juice.

3. Add tomato mixture to linguine. Toss with parsley, cheeses and enough pasta water to moisten.

Per serving: 1⅓ cups equals 542 cal., 21g fat (8g sat. fat), 32mg chol., 726mg sodium, 68g carb. (3g sugars, 6g fiber), 23g pro.

GOES **GREAT** WITH

Slices of Italian bread served with oil for dipping make this easy meal special.

SLOW COOKER TUNA NOODLE CASSEROLE

Heres's a take on a family-friendly classic that utilizes the slow cooker. It's easy, wholesome and totally homemade!
—*Taste of Home* Test Kitchen

....

Prep: 25 min. • **Cook:** 4 hours + standing
Makes: 10 servings

¼	**cup butter, cubed**
½	**lb. sliced fresh mushrooms**
1	**medium onion, chopped**
1	**medium sweet pepper, chopped**
1	**tsp. salt, divided**
1	**tsp. pepper, divided**
2	**garlic cloves, minced**
¼	**cup all-purpose flour**
2	**cups reduced-sodium chicken broth**
2	**cups half-and-half cream**
4	**cups uncooked egg noodles (about 6 oz.)**
3	**cans (5 oz. each) light tuna in water, drained**
2	**Tbsp. lemon juice**
2	**cups (8 oz.) shredded Monterey Jack cheese**
2	**cups frozen peas, thawed**
2	**cups crushed potato chips**

1. In a large skillet, melt the butter over medium-high heat. Add the mushrooms, onion, sweet pepper, ½ tsp. salt and ½ tsp. pepper; cook and stir 6-8 minutes or until tender. Add garlic; cook 1 minute longer. Stir in the flour until blended. Gradually whisk in broth. Bring to a boil, stirring constantly; cook and stir mixture 1-2 minutes or until thickened.

2. Transfer to a 5-qt. slow cooker. Stir in cream and noodles. Cook, covered, on low 4-5 hours or until noodles are tender. Meanwhile, in a small bowl, combine tuna, lemon juice and the remaining salt and pepper.

3. Remove insert from slow cooker. Stir cheese, tuna mixture and peas into the noodle mixture. Let stand, uncovered, 20 minutes. Just before serving, sprinkle with potato chips.

Per serving: 1 cup equals 393 cal., 21g fat (12g sat. fat), 84mg chol., 752mg sodium, 28g carb. (5g sugars, 3g fiber), 22g pro.

GOES GREAT WITH

Michigan Cherry Salad (page 178) is the perfect add-on to nearly any meal.

FAMILY FAVORITE ♥

MEATLESS **MEAL**

QUINOA & BLACK BEAN-STUFFED PEPPERS

If you're thinking about a meatless meal, give these no-fuss peppers a try. They come together with a just few ingredients and put a tasty spin on a low-fat meal!
—Cindy Reams, Philipsburg, PA

Takes: 30 min. • **Makes:** 4 servings

- 1½ **cups water**
- 1 **cup quinoa, rinsed**
- 4 **large green peppers**
- 1 **jar (16 oz.) chunky salsa, divided**
- 1 **can (15 oz.) black beans, rinsed and drained**
- ½ **cup reduced-fat ricotta cheese**
- ½ **cup shredded Monterey Jack cheese, divided**

1. Preheat the oven to 400°. In a small saucepan, bring water to a boil. Add the quinoa. Reduce heat; simmer, covered, 10-12 minutes or until water is absorbed.
2. Meanwhile, cut and discard tops from peppers; remove the seeds. Place in a greased 8-in. square baking dish, cut side down. Microwave, uncovered, on high 3-4 minutes or until crisp-tender. Turn peppers cut side up.
3. Reserve ⅓ cup salsa; add the remaining salsa to quinoa. Stir in the beans, ricotta cheese and ¼ cup Monterey Jack cheese. Spoon mixture into peppers; sprinkle with remaining cheese. Bake, uncovered, for 10-15 minutes or until the filling is heated through. Top with reserved salsa.
Per serving: 1 stuffed pepper equals 393 cal., 8g fat (4g sat. fat), 20mg chol., 774mg sodium, 59g carb. (10g sugars, 10g fiber), 18g pro.

Deli coleslaw turns the fish sticks into an easy weeknight meal.

EAT SMART **FAST FIX**

PARMESAN FISH STICKS

I wanted a healthier approach to fish sticks and developed a baked tilapia with a slightly peppery bite. My husband and sons love the crispy coating.
—Candy Summerhill, Alexander, AR

Takes: 25 min. • **Makes:** 4 servings

⅓ cup all-purpose flour
½ tsp. salt
⅛ to ¼ tsp. pepper

2 large eggs
1 cup panko (Japanese) bread crumbs
⅓ cup grated Parmesan cheese
2 Tbsp. garlic-herb seasoning blend
1 lb. tilapia fillets
Cooking spray

1. Preheat oven to 450°. In a shallow bowl, mix flour, salt and pepper. In another bowl, whisk eggs. In a third bowl, toss bread crumbs with cheese and seasoning blend.

2. Cut fillets into 1-in.-wide strips. Dip fish in flour mixture to coat both sides; shake off excess. Dip in eggs, then in crumb mixture, patting to help coating adhere.

3. Place on a foil-lined baking sheet coated with cooking spray. Spritz tops with the spray until crumbs appear moistened. Bake 10-12 minutes or until golden brown and fish begins to flake easily with a fork.

Per serving: 1 serving equals 281 cal., 11g fat (3g sat. fat), 154mg chol., 641mg sodium, 16g carb. (1g sugars, 1g fiber), 28g pro. **Diabetic Exchanges:** 1 starch, 3 lean meat, 1 fat.

CHEESY SUMMER SQUASH FLATBREADS

My family-friendly meatless meal with Mediterranean flair features flatbreads smothered with squash, hummus and just enough mozzarella.
—Matthew Hass, Franklin, WI

Takes: 30 min. • **Makes:** 4 servings

- 3 small yellow summer squash, sliced ¼-in. thick
- 1 Tbsp. olive oil
- ½ tsp. salt
- 2 cups fresh baby spinach, coarsely chopped
- 2 naan flatbreads
- ⅓ cup roasted red pepper hummus
- 1 carton (8 oz.) fresh mozzarella cheese pearls
  Pepper

1. Preheat oven to 425°. Toss squash with oil and salt; spread evenly in a 15x10x1-in. baking pan. Roast 8-10 minutes or until tender. Transfer to a bowl; stir in spinach.
2. Place naan on a baking sheet; spread with hummus. Top with squash mixture and cheese. Bake on a lower oven rack 4-6 minutes or just until cheese is melted. Sprinkle with pepper.
Per serving: ½ topped flatbread equals 332 cal., 20g fat (9g sat. fat), 47mg chol., 737mg sodium, 24g carb. (7g sugars, 3g fiber), 15g pro.

SPEEDY SWAPS!

These flatbreads are easy to customize to your family's tastes.

DON'T LIKE YELLOW SQUASH?
Try green zucchini instead.

WANT TO SPEED UP COOKING TIME?
Set the flatbreads over medium-hot heat on the grill.

GOES GREAT WITH

You can't go wrong with flatbreads and pasta! Toss together Vermicelli Pasta Salad (page 175) ahead of time and beat the kitchen timer.

GINGER SALMON WITH BROWN RICE

What fun it is to prepare heavenly salmon with only a few ingredients! The sesame ginger dressing serves as a glaze and also boosts the flavor of the rice.
—Naylet LaRochelle, Miami, FL

....

Takes: 25 min. • **Makes:** 4 servings

- 4 **salmon fillets (6 oz. each)**
- 5 **Tbsp. reduced-fat sesame ginger salad dressing, divided**

RICE
- ⅓ **cup shredded carrot**
- 4 **green onions, chopped, divided**
- 1½ **cups instant brown rice**
- 1½ **cups water**
- ⅓ **cup reduced-fat sesame ginger salad dressing**

1. Preheat oven to 400°. Place fillets on a foil-lined baking sheet; brush with 3 Tbsp. of the salad dressing. Bake, uncovered, for 10-12 minutes or until the fish just begins to flake easily with a fork. Brush fillets with remaining salad dressing.

2. Meanwhile, place a large saucepan coated with cooking spray over medium heat. Add the carrot and half of the green onion; cook and stir 2-3 minutes or until crisp-tender. Add rice and water; bring to a boil. Reduce heat; simmer, covered, for 5 minutes.

3. Remove from heat; stir in the salad dressing. Let stand, covered, 5 minutes or until liquid is absorbed and rice is tender. Fluff with a fork; serve with the salmon. Sprinkle with remaining green onions.

Per serving: 1 fillet with ½ cup rice mixture equals 446 cal., 19g fat (3g sat. fat), 85mg chol., 605mg sodium, 34g carb. (6g sugars, 2g fiber), 32g pro. **Diabetic Exchanges:** 2 starch, 5 lean meat, 2 fat.

GOES **GREAT** WITH

Turn to page 173 for the recipe for Apple Maple Pecan Salad—a tasty addition to this salmon entree.

Protein
POWERHOUSE

Stick It To 'Em

Overcooked fish
can lose its flavor
and become tough.
Check for doneness
by sticking a fork,
at an angle, into
the thickest portion
of the fish and gently
parting the meat.
When it's opaque
and flakes into
sections, it's
done cooking.

CHIPOTLE MANICOTTI BAKE

I found this recipe while searching for a vegetarian dish that I could use as a main course. This rich manicotti is always a hit.
—Julie Peterson, Crofton, MD

Prep: 30 min. • **Bake:** 30 min. + standing
Makes: 8 servings

- 14 uncooked manicotti shells
- 2 cartons (15 oz. each) part-skim ricotta cheese
- 2 cups (8 oz.) shredded part-skim mozzarella cheese
- 4 green onions, chopped
- 2 large eggs, lightly beaten
- ¼ cup chopped fresh cilantro
- 2 cups chipotle salsa
- 2 cups (8 oz.) shredded pepper jack cheese

1. Preheat oven to 350°. Cook manicotti according to the package directions for al dente. Drain.
2. In a large bowl, mix the ricotta cheese, mozzarella cheese, green onions, eggs and cilantro. Spoon into manicotti. Spread ½ cup salsa into a greased 13x9-in. baking dish. Top with the stuffed manicotti. Pour remaining salsa over top. Bake, uncovered, 20 minutes.
3. Sprinkle with pepper jack cheese. Bake, uncovered, for 10 minutes longer or until cheese is melted. Let stand for 10 minutes before serving.
Per serving: 2 stuffed manicotti equals 597 cal., 34g fat (19g sat. fat), 158mg chol., 899mg sodium, 35g carb. (4g sugars,1g fiber), 39g pro.

GOES GREAT WITH

Steamed broccoli makes a fine complement to this entree.

Table Talk

What might be the headline of a newspaper 100 years from now?

Fast-forward a century from today. What do you think will be the front-page story in the newspaper? Consider what other families will be talking about 100 years from now.

MEAL PLANNER

SEAFOOD ♥ MEATLESS

YOU'RE ONLY MOMENTS AWAY FROM MEALTIME SUCCESS!

CATCH OF THE DAY

ENTREE:
Lemon-Parsley Baked Cod
page 134

SIDE:
Tortellini Primavera Soup
page 238

DESSERT:
Toffee Pecan Bars
page 252

TAG YOUR MEAL
MEMORIES WITH
#100 **FAMILYMEALS**

GROCERY LIST

KITCHEN STAPLES
- ○ All-purpose flour
- ○ Confectioners' sugar
- ○ Paprika
- ○ Vanilla extract
- ○ Salt
- ○ Pepper

PRODUCE
- ○ 1 lemon
- ○ 1 package (10 oz.) julienned carrots
- ○ 1 bunch fresh parsley
- ○ 1 bunch fresh basil leaves

PANTRY
- ○ 2 cartons (32 oz. each) reduced-sodium chicken broth
- ○ 1 can (14 oz.) sweetened condensed milk

MEAT/SEAFOOD
- ○ 4 cod fillets (6 oz. each)

DAIRY
- ○ Butter
- ○ 1 large egg

REFRIGERATED/ FREEZER SECTION
- ○ 1 package. (9 oz.) refrigerated cheese tortellini
- ○ 1 package (12 oz.) frozen peas

OTHER
- ○ Lemon-pepper seasoning
- ○ 1 package (10 oz.) English toffee bits
- ○ 2 bags (2.25 oz each) chopped pecans

✂ -

FISH & CHIPS

ENTREE:
Fish & Chips
with Dipping Sauce
page 140

SIDE:
Honey Butter
Peas and Carrots
page 198

DESSERT:
Chocolaty S'mores Bars
page 264

TAG YOUR MEAL
MEMORIES WITH
#100 **FAMILYMEALS**

GROCERY LIST

KITCHEN STAPLES
- ○ Olive oil
- ○ Garlic powder
- ○ Onion powder
- ○ Dried marjoram
- ○ Salt
- ○ Pepper
- ○ White pepper

PRODUCE
- ○ 1 lemon
- ○ 4 large potatoes (about 2 lbs.)
- ○ 1 lb. carrots
- ○ 1 large onion
- ○ 1 head of garlic

PANTRY
- ○ 1 bottle (12 oz.) honey
- ○ 1 can (8 oz.) panko (Japanese) bread crumbs
- ○ 1 box (12 oz.) Golden Grahams cereal

MEATS/SEAFOOD
- ○ 4 cod fillets (4 oz. each)

DAIRY
- ○ Butter
- ○ 2 large eggs
- ○ 1 container (8 oz.) reduced-fat sour cream

OTHER
- ○ 1 jar (16 oz.) dill pickles
- ○ 1 package (10 oz.) large marshmallows
- ○ ⅓ cup milk chocolate chips

FREEZER SECTION
- ○ 1 package (16 oz.) frozen peas

MEAL PLANNER

SEEAFOOD ♥ MEATLESS

YOU'RE ONLY MOMENTS AWAY FROM MEALTIME SUCCESS!

STOVETOP SUPPER

ENTREE:
Thai Lime Shrimp
& Noodles
page 145

SIDE:
Great Garlic Bread
page 230

DESSERT:
Grandma Brubaker's
Orange Cookies
page 270

TAG YOUR MEAL
MEMORIES WITH
#100 FAMILYMEALS

GROCERY LIST

KITCHEN STAPLES
- ○ Olive oil
- ○ All-purpose flour
- ○ Baking powder
- ○ Baking soda
- ○ Cornstarch
- ○ Confectioners' sugar
- ○ Sugar
- ○ Salt

PRODUCE
- ○ 1 lime
- ○ 3 medium navel oranges
- ○ Fresh gingerroot

- ○ 1 bunch fresh basil
- ○ 1 bunch fresh parsley
- ○ 1 head of garlic

PANTRY
- ○ 1 can (14½ oz.) chicken broth
- ○ 1 box (16 oz.) angel hair pasta
- ○ 1 can (13.66 oz.) coconut milk

MEAT/SEAFOOD
- ○ 1½ lbs. uncooked shrimp (26-30 per lb.)

DAIRY
- ○ Butter
- ○ 2 large eggs
- ○ 1 quart (32 oz.) buttermilk
- ○ 1 container (5 oz.) grated Romano cheese

OTHER
- ○ 1 bottle (4 oz.) Thai red chili paste
- ○ 1 can (16 oz.) shortening
- ○ 1 loaf (1 lb.) French bread

GO MEATLESS

ENTREE:
Mozzarella
Corn Bread Pizza
page 151

SIDE:
Easy Peasy Slaw
page 187

DESSERT:
Loaded M&M
Oreo Cookie Bars
page 265

TAG YOUR MEAL
MEMORIES WITH
#100 FAMILYMEALS

GROCERY LIST

KITCHEN STAPLES
- ○ Light brown sugar
- ○ Vanilla extract
- ○ All-purpose flour
- ○ Baking soda
- ○ Salt
- ○ Pepper

PRODUCE
- ○ 1 large sweet red or green pepper
- ○ Bunch green onions
- ○ 1 package (14 oz.) coleslaw mix
- ○ 2 large zucchini
- ○ 1 bunch green onions

- ○ 1 bunch fresh basil
- ○ 1 sprig fresh oregano

PANTRY
- ○ 2 pkg. (8½ oz. each) corn bread/muffin mix
- ○ 1 jar (14 oz.) pizza sauce
- ○ 1 can (2¼ oz.) sliced ripe olives, drained

DAIRY
- ○ Unsalted butter
- ○ 4 large eggs

- ○ 1 package (16 oz.) shredded part-skim mozzarella cheese

FREEZER SECTION
- ○ 1 bag (16 oz.) frozen peas

OTHER
- ○ 1 bottle (12 oz.) poppy seed salad dressing
- ○ 1 package (14.3 oz.) Oreo cookies
- ○ 1 package (11 oz.) milk chocolate M&M's
- ○ 1 cup sweet and crunchy peanuts

Family Makes a Dream Team

The Robles family (at left) got their kids into the kitchen at an early age (above).

EVER SINCE THESE KIDS COULD SEE OVER THE KITCHEN COUNTER they wanted to lend a helping hand. "It didn't matter if we were cooking or baking, they wanted to be involved," says Edwin Robles, Jr. "As a father of three, I cherish those moments—and any spent with my family in the kitchen."

Edwin happily points out that the kitchen is the one place where many of his family's interactions take place. "Between the chitter-chatter early in the morning and the summaries of everyone's day at night, it's no wonder

our kitchen is the hub of activity at our house," he adds. "Even someone's quick 'drive-thru' to snatch a snack can turn into a memorable moment."

No matter how busy everyone's schedule, Edwin and his wife, Evelyn, make time for family meals. "We turn off our digital devices, and we make it a habit to eat together at the dinner table," says Edwin.

Meals at this household start with everyone pitching in to help. For instance, daughter Nailah, 12, gathers the utensils and preps all the

ingredients. Elijah, 14, sets the table and keeps an eye on the kitchen timer. Even little Myah, 7, lends a hand, gathering all the produce, pots and pans.

"I tell the kids if they can work together on a recipe, an awesome dessert will be their reward," says Edwin. "It's amazing how much they put into helping when they know their efforts pay off with ice cream. Best of all, it's incredible to see the joy in their eyes when they realize how much they've impressed Mom and Dad. That makes a great ending to any meal!"

"Even though things can get hectic, I'm committed to having family dinners nearly every night of the week."

–Kristine Marrar
Clifton Park, New York

NO-FUSS SALADS

LIGHTEN UP with these refreshing additions to family-friendly menus.

CHIPOTLE LIME AVOCADO SALAD

I'm a real believer in clean eating and a healthy lifestyle, which includes eating your veggies. Serve summer's best over tomato slices for a cool salad with just a little bit of heat.
—DJ Cavem, Denver, CO

Takes: 15 min. • **Makes:** 4 servings

- ¼ cup lime juice
- ¼ cup maple syrup
- ½ tsp. ground chipotle pepper
- ¼ tsp. cayenne pepper, optional
- 2 medium ripe avocados, peeled and sliced
- ½ medium cucumber, peeled and chopped
- 1 Tbsp. minced fresh chives
- 2 large tomatoes, cut into ½-in. slices

In a small bowl, whisk lime juice, maple syrup, chipotle pepper and, if desired, cayenne until blended. In another bowl, combine avocados, cucumber and chives. Drizzle with dressing; toss gently to coat. Serve over tomatoes.

Per Serving: 1 serving equals 191 cal., 11g fat (1g sat. fat), 0 chol., 26mg sodium, 25g carb. (17g sugars, 6g fiber), 3g pro.

EAT SMART

GARDEN BOUNTY SALAD

Prepared salad dressing makes this colorful dinner addition a snap. Save even more time by picking up sliced veggies at the grocery store salad bar.
—Jannine Fisk, Malden, MA

Prep: 15 min. • **Cook:** 20 min.
Makes: 16 servings

- ¼ cup olive oil
- 12 cups French or ciabatta bread (about 12 oz.), cut into 1-in. cubes
- 4 large tomatoes, coarsely chopped
- 1 large English cucumber, coarsely chopped
- 1 medium green pepper, cut into 1-in. pieces
- 1 medium sweet yellow pepper, cut into 1-in. pieces
- 1 small red onion, halved and thinly sliced
- ½ cup coarsely chopped fresh basil
- ¼ cup grated Parmesan cheese
- ¾ tsp. kosher salt
- ¼ tsp. coarsely ground pepper
- ½ cup Italian salad dressing

1. In a large skillet, heat 2 Tbsp. of oil over medium heat. Add half of the bread cubes; cook and stir until toasted, about 8 minutes. Remove from pan. Repeat with remaining oil and bread cubes.
2. Combine the bread cubes, tomatoes, cucumber, peppers, onion, basil, cheese, salt and pepper. Drizzle with the salad dressing; toss.
Per Serving: 1 cup equals 131 cal., 6g fat (1g sat. fat), 1mg chol., 310mg sodium, 18g carb. (3g sugars, 2g fiber), 3g pro. **Diabetic Exchanges:** 1 starch, 1 vegetable, 1 fat.

GRILLED MANGO & AVOCADO SALAD

A big hit with my family, this light salad is so easy to make! The healthy option of mango and avocado is about the best combination you could serve.
—Amy Liesemeyer, Tucson, AZ

Takes: 25 min. • **Makes:** 8 servings

- 4 medium firm mangoes, peeled
- 1 Tbsp. canola oil
- ¼ cup lime juice
- ¼ cup olive oil
- 1 Tbsp. black sesame seeds
- ½ tsp. salt
- 2 Tbsp. minced fresh cilantro, optional
- 1 Tbsp. minced fresh mint, optional
- 2 medium cucumbers, peeled, seeded and coarsely chopped
- 2 medium ripe avocados, peeled and coarsely chopped

1. Cut a thin slice off the bottom of each mango. Standing mango upright, slice off a large section of flesh, cutting close to the pit. Rotate and repeat until all the flesh is removed.

2. Brush mangoes with canola oil; place on greased grill rack. Cook, covered, over medium heat or boil 4 in. from the heat for 6-8 minutes or until lightly browned, turning once. Remove from heat; cool slightly. Cut into ¾-in. cubes.

3. Meanwhile, in a large bowl, whisk lime juice, olive oil, sesame seeds, salt and, if desired, cilantro and mint. Add mangoes, cucumbers and avocados; toss to coat. Refrigerate until serving.

Per Serving: ¾ cup equals 249 cal., 15g fat (2g sat. fat), 0 chol., 152mg sodium, 31g carb. (24g sugars, 6g fiber), 3g pro.

Table Talk

If you could be an animal, what would you be?

It's fun to imagine! Take turns around the table, asking everyone why they'd like to be a certain animal. Talk about what would be the best part about being that animal.

APPLE MAPLE PECAN SALAD

A well-made salad has good taste and pleasing crunch. With cabbage, apples and pecans, this one gets high marks in both areas—with extra points for color.
—Emily Tyra, Milwaukee, WI

Prep: 15 min. + standing
Makes: 12 servings

- ¼ cup lemon juice
- ¼ cup canola oil
- ¼ cup maple syrup
- 1½ tsp. Dijon mustard
- ½ tsp. coarsely ground pepper
- 4 cups shredded cabbage
- 3 large Granny Smith apples, julienned
- ½ cup crumbled Gorgonzola cheese
- 1 cup chopped pecans, toasted

Whisk the first five ingredients until blended. Combine cabbage, apples and Gorgonzola; toss with dressing to coat. Let stand 30 minutes before serving. Sprinkle with the pecans.

Note: To toast nuts, bake in a shallow pan in a 350° oven for 5-10 minutes or cook in a skillet over low heat until lightly browned, stirring nuts occasionally.

Per Serving: ¾ cup equals 169 cal., 13g fat (2g sat. fat), 4mg chol., 84mg sodium, 14g carb. (9g sugars, 3g fiber), 2g pro. **Diabetic Exchanges:** 1 starch, 2½ fat.

Mix It Up!

It's easy to change this recipe to suit your family's tastes. Don't like green onions? Leave them out! Love melon? Add some cubed cantaloupe to the salad.

MINTY WATERMELON-CUCUMBER SALAD

Capture fantastic flavors of summer in a refreshing, beautiful salad that will be the talk of the table! It's also perfect to share at potlucks and other get-togethers.
—Roblynn Hunnisett, Guelph, ON

Takes: 20 min. • **Makes:** 16 servings

- 8 cups cubed seedless watermelon
- 2 English cucumbers, halved lengthwise and sliced
- 6 green onions, chopped
- ¼ cup minced fresh mint
- ¼ cup balsamic vinegar
- ¼ cup olive oil
- ½ tsp. salt
- ½ tsp. pepper

In a large bowl, combine watermelon, cucumbers, green onions and mint. In a small bowl, whisk remaining ingredients. Pour over salad and toss to coat. Serve immediately or refrigerate, covered, up to 2 hours before serving.
Per Serving: ¾ cup equals 60 cal., 3g fat (trace sat. fat), 0 chol., 78mg sodium, 9g carb. (8g sugars, 1g fiber), 1g pro. **Diabetic Exchanges:** ½ fruit, ½ fat.

"This is delicious. I will be making it again and again. I did not have fresh mint, so I substituted fresh basil out of my garden. Yum!"

—SCHAEFERSMITH, TOH.COM

VERMICELLI PASTA SALAD

I started making this salad because it's loaded with peppers—my husband's favorite. Don't be surprised when there are no leftovers to take home after the family reunion, picnic or church potluck.
—Janie Colle, Hutchinson, KS

Prep: 20 min. + chilling
Makes: 10 servings

- 12 oz. uncooked vermicelli
- 1 bottle (16 oz.) creamy Italian salad dressing
- 1 small green pepper, chopped
- 1 small sweet red pepper, chopped
- 6 green onions, chopped
- 1 tsp. dill seed
- 1 tsp. caraway seeds
- 1 tsp. poppy seeds

Cook vermicelli according to package directions. Drain; transfer to a large bowl. Add remaining ingredients; toss to coat. Refrigerate until cold.
Per Serving: ¾ cup equals 309 cal., 18g fat (3g sat. fat), 0 chol., 404mg sodium, 30g carb. (5g sugars, 2g fiber), 5g pro.

EAT SMART
EDAMAME CORN CARROT SALAD

I created my salad recipe by trying to think of a dish that was protein-packed, nutritious and light. The result is super easy and visually appealing.
—Maiah Miller, Monterey, CA

....

Prep: 25 min + chilling
Makes: 8 servings

2½ cups frozen shelled edamame
3 cups julienned carrots
1½ cups frozen corn, thawed
4 green onions, chopped
2 Tbsp. minced fresh cilantro
VINAIGRETTE
3 Tbsp. rice vinegar
3 Tbsp. lemon juice
4 tsp. canola oil
2 garlic cloves, minced
½ tsp. salt
½ tsp. pepper

1. Place edamame in a small saucepan; add water to cover. Bring to a boil; cook 4-5 minutes or until tender. Drain; cool edamame slightly.

2. In a large bowl, combine carrots, corn, green onions, cilantro and edamame. In a small bowl, whisk vinaigrette ingredients until blended. Pour over the salad; toss to coat. Refrigerate salad for at least 2 hours before serving.
Per Serving: ⅔ cup equals 111 cal., 5g fat (trace sat. fat), 0 chol., 135mg sodium, 14g carb. (4g sugars, 3g fiber), 5g pro. **Diabetic Exchanges:** 1 starch, ½ fat.

....

EAT SMART FAST FIX
SUMMER BUZZ FRUIT SALAD

For picnics, cookouts and showers, we make a sweet salad of watermelon, cherries, blueberries and microgreens. No matter where I take it, it always delivers the wow factor.
—Kaliska Russell, Talkeetna, AK

....

Takes: 15 min • **Makes:** 6 servings

2 cups watermelon balls
2 cups fresh sweet cherries, pitted and halved
1 cup fresh blueberries
½ cup cubed English cucumber
½ cup microgreens or torn mixed salad greens
½ cup crumbled feta cheese
3 fresh mint leaves, thinly sliced
¼ cup honey
1 Tbsp. lemon juice
1 tsp. grated lemon peel

Combine the first seven ingredients. In a small bowl, whisk together remaining ingredients. Drizzle over salad; toss.
Per Serving: ¾ cup equals 131 cal., 2g fat (1g sat. fat), 5mg chol., 94mg sodium, 28g carb. (24g sugars, 2g fiber), 3g pro. **Diabetic Exchanges:** 1 starch, 1 fruit.

EAT SMART FAST FIX
BROCCOLI SLAW WITH LEMON DRESSING

Our family absolutely loves broccoli, so I'm happy there's finally a slaw mix in stores that uses broccoli stems. I like this slaw best after it sits 20 minutes or so for the flavors to meld.
—Donna Marie Ryan, Topsfield, MA

....

Takes: 15 min. • **Makes:** 10 servings

½ cup sour cream
3 Tbsp. lemon juice
2 Tbsp. mayonnaise
1 Tbsp. white wine vinegar
2 tsp. grated lemon peel
1 tsp. Dijon mustard
½ tsp. salt
¼ tsp. freshly ground pepper
1 pkg. (12 oz.) broccoli coleslaw mix
2 large red apples, juliennned

In a large bowl, mix the first eight ingredients. Add coleslaw mix and apples; toss to coat. Refrigerate, covered, until serving.
Per Serving: ¾ cup equals 79 cal., 4g fat (2g sat. fat), 9mg chol., 152mg sodium, 9g carb. (6g sugars, 2g fiber), 1g pro. **Diabetic Exchanges:** ½ starch, 1 fat.

COLORFUL QUINOA SALAD

My youngest daughter recently learned she has to avoid gluten, dairy and eggs, which gave me a new challenge in the kitchen. I put together a side everyone could share at the dinner table. We love it the next day, too.
—Catherine Turnbull, Burlington, ON

Prep: 30 min. + cooling
Makes: 8 servings

- 2 cups water
- 1 cup quinoa, rinsed
- 2 cups fresh baby spinach, thinly sliced
- 1 cup grape tomatoes, halved
- 1 medium cucumber, seeded and chopped
- 1 medium sweet orange pepper, chopped
- 1 medium sweet yellow pepper, chopped
- 2 green onions, chopped

DRESSING

- 3 Tbsp. lime juice
- 2 Tbsp. olive oil
- 4 tsp. honey
- 1 Tbsp. grated lime peel
- 2 tsp. minced fresh gingerroot
- ¼ tsp. salt

1. In a large saucepan, bring water to a boil. Add quinoa. Reduce heat; simmer, covered, 12-15 minutes or until liquid is absorbed. Remove from heat; fluff with a fork. Transfer to a large bowl; cool quinoa completely.
2. Stir the spinach, tomatoes, cucumber, peppers and green onions into quinoa. In a small bowl, whisk dressing ingredients until blended. Drizzle over quinoa mixture; toss to coat. Refrigerate until serving.
Per Serving: ¾ cup equals 143 cal., 5g fat (1g sat. fat), 0 chol., 88mg sodium, 23g carb. (6g sugars, 3g fiber), 4g pro. **Diabetic Exchanges:** 1 starch, 1 vegetable, 1 fat.

SICILIAN SALAD

Loaded with family-friendly flavor, this hearty salad comes together in no time. Chop the tomatoes and celery and cube the mozzarella a day early, and you'll have this ready in moments. Best of all, it goes with just about anything.
—Beth Burgmeier, East Dubuque, IL

Takes: 15 min. • **Makes:** 10 servings

- 1 pkg. (12 oz.) iceberg lettuce blend
- 1 jar (16 oz.) pickled banana peppers, drained and sliced
- 1 jar (5¾ oz.) sliced green olives with pimientos, drained
- 3 plum tomatoes, chopped
- 4 celery ribs, chopped
- 1 cup chopped pepperoni
- ½ cup cubed part-skim mozzarella cheese
- ½ cup Italian salad dressing

In a large bowl, combine the first seven ingredients. Drizzle with dressing and toss to coat.
Per Serving: ¾ cup equals 229 cal., 11 fat (3g sat. fat), 9mg chol., 606mg sodium, 25g carb. (4g sugars, 2g fiber), 8g pro.

APPLE-PECAN SALAD WITH HONEY VINAIGRETTE

Sweet-tart apples such as Braeburn or Empire pair well with Parmesan cheese. You can also try this salad with a Bartlett or Bosc pear and blue cheese.
—Anna Russell, Peterborough, ON

Takes: 15 min. • **Makes:** 10 servings

- 7 cups torn Bibb or Boston lettuce
- 1 medium apple, sliced
- ⅓ cup pecan halves, toasted
- ¼ cup cider vinegar
- 3 Tbsp. honey
- 2 Tbsp. olive oil
- ½ tsp. honey mustard
- ⅛ tsp. salt
- ⅛ tsp. pepper
- 1 cup shredded Parmesan cheese

In a serving bowl, combine the lettuce, apple and pecans. In a small bowl, whisk the vinegar, honey, oil, mustard, salt and pepper. Pour over salad; toss to coat. Sprinkle with cheese.
Per Serving: ¾ cup equals 115 cal., 8g fat (2g sat. fat), 6mg chol., 170mg sodium, 9g carb. (7g sugars, 1g fiber), 4g pro. **Diabetic Exchanges:** ½ starch, 1 fat.

JAZZED-UP SLAW

I wanted to rev up coleslaw to serve with pulled-pork barbecue. Nothing adds zip like a squirt of Sriracha and a shower of chopped cilantro.

—Julie Peterson, Crofton, MD

Takes: 10 min. • **Makes:** 6 servings

- 1 cup mayonnaise
- 3 garlic cloves, minced
- 1 tsp. Sriracha Asian hot chili sauce
- ¼ tsp. salt
- ⅛ tsp. cayenne pepper
- 1 pkg. (14 oz.) coleslaw mix
- ½ cup minced fresh cilantro
- 1 medium ripe avocado, peeled and cubed, optional

In a small bowl, mix first five ingredients. Place coleslaw mix and cilantro in a large bowl. Add the dressing and toss to coat. Refrigerate until serving. If desired, top with avocado.

Per Serving: ⅔ cup (calculated without avocado) equals 286 cal., 29g fat (4g sat. fat), 13mg chol., 341mg sodium, 5g carb. (3g sugars, 2g fiber), 1g pro.

"I am a from-scratch cook. To streamline preparation, I create meal plans and rely on recipes that come together without much fuss."

—CHRISTI ROSS, GUTHRIE, TX

EAT SMART **FAST FIX** ▶

MICHIGAN CHERRY SALAD

This recipe reminds me of what I love about my home state: apple picking with my children, buying greens at the farmer's market and tasting cherries on vacations. What a great way to enjoy our family meals together.

—Jennifer Gilbert, Brighton, MI

Takes: 15 min. • **Makes:** 8 servings

- 7 oz. fresh baby spinach (about 9 cups)
- 3 oz. spring mix salad greens (about 5 cups)
- 1 large apple, chopped
- ½ cup coarsely chopped pecans, toasted
- ½ cup dried cherries
- ¼ cup crumbled Gorgonzola cheese

DRESSING
- ¼ cup fresh raspberries
- ¼ cup red wine vinegar
- 3 Tbsp. cider vinegar
- 3 Tbsp. cherry preserves
- 1 Tbsp. sugar
- 2 Tbsp. olive oil

1. In a large bowl, combine the first six ingredients.

2. Place raspberries, vinegars, preserves and sugar in a blender. While processing, gradually add the oil in a steady stream. Drizzle over salad; toss to coat.

Note To toast nuts, bake in a pan in a 350° oven for 5-10 minutes or cook in a skillet over low heat until browned, stirring occasionally.

Per Serving: 1½ cups equals 172 cal., 10g fat (2g sat. fat), 3mg chol., 78mg sodium, 21g carb. (16g sugars, 3g fiber), 3g pro. **Diabetic Exchanges:** 1 starch, 2 vegetable, 2 fat.

How to
Slice Avocados

- Cut into the ripe avocado from stem to stern until you hit the seed. Repeat to cut the avocado into quarters.

- Twist to separate.

- Pull out the seed.

- Pull the skin back like a banana peel. Slice as you like.

UNDER
200
CALORIES

GARDEN CUCUMBER SALAD

If you like cucumber salad as I do, this one's a cool pick. With a mix of fresh veggies, feta and Greek seasoning, it's a refreshing addition to summer meals.
—Katie Stanczak, Hoover, AL

Takes: 10 min. + chilling
Makes: 12 servings

- 4 medium cucumbers, cut into ½-in. pieces (about 7 cups)
- 2 medium sweet red peppers, chopped
- 1 cup cherry tomatoes, halved
- 1 cup (4 oz.) crumbled feta cheese
- ½ cup finely chopped red onion
- ½ cup olive oil
- ¼ cup lemon juice
- 1 Tbsp. Greek seasoning
- ½ tsp. salt

Place all ingredients in a large bowl; toss gently to combine. Refrigerate, covered, at least 30 minutes before serving.

Per Serving: ¾ cup equals 125 cal., 11g fat (2g sat. fat), 5mg chol., 431mg sodium, 5g carb. (3g sugars, 2g fiber), 3g pro. **Diabetic Exchanges:** 1 vegetable, 2 fat.

GREEN SALAD WITH TANGY BASIL VINAIGRETTE

A tart and tangy dressing turns a basic salad into something special. It's good enough for company as well as weeknight dining, and it pairs perfectly with just about anything.
—Kristin Rimkus, Snohomish, WA

Takes: 15 min. • **Makes:** 4 servings

- 3 Tbsp. white wine vinegar
- 4½ tsp. minced fresh basil
- 4½ tsp. olive oil
- 1½ tsp. honey
- ¼ tsp. salt
- ⅛ tsp. pepper
- 6 cups torn mixed salad greens
- 1 cup cherry tomatoes, halved
- 2 Tbsp. shredded Parmesan cheese

In a small bowl, whisk first six ingredients until blended. In a large bowl, combine salad greens and tomatoes. Drizzle with vinaigrette; toss to coat. Sprinkle with Parmesan cheese.

Per Serving: 1 cup equals 89 cal., 6g fat (1g sat. fat), 2mg chol., 214mg sodium, 7g carb. (4g sugars, 2g fiber), 3g pro. **Diabetic Exchanges:** 1 vegetable, 1 fat.

NOTES

_____
_____
_____
_____
_____
_____
_____
_____
_____

SWEET POTATO & CHICKPEA SALAD

Set this satisfying salad on the family table and watch it disappear! It's also great to double for parties.
—Brenda Gleason, Hartland, WI

Prep: 15 min. • **Bake:** 20 min.
Makes: 8 servings

- 2 medium sweet potatoes (about 1 lb.), peeled and cubed
- 1 Tbsp. olive oil
- ½ tsp. salt
- ¼ tsp. pepper
- 1 can (15 oz.) garbanzo beans or chickpeas, rinsed and drained

DRESSING

- 2 Tbsp. seasoned rice vinegar
- 4 tsp. olive oil
- 1 Tbsp. minced fresh gingerroot
- 1 garlic clove, minced
- ¼ tsp. salt
- ¼ tsp. pepper

SALAD

- 4 cups spring mix salad greens
- ¼ cup crumbled feta cheese

1. In a bowl, combine the sweet potatoes, oil, salt and pepper; toss to coat. Transfer to a 15x10x1-in. baking pan coated with cooking spray. Roast at 425° for 20-25 minutes or until tender, stirring once.

2. In a large bowl, combine the garbanzo beans and sweet potatoes. In a small bowl, whisk the dressing ingredients. Add to the sweet potato mixture; toss to coat. Serve over salad greens; top with cheese.

Per Serving: ½ cup sweet potato mixture with ½ cup salad equals 134 cal., 6g fat (1g sat. fat), 2mg chol., 466mg sodium, 18g carb. (6g sugars, 4g fiber), 4g pro. **Diabetic Exchanges:** 1 starch, 1 fat.

READY IN 15 MINUTES

BACON-TOMATO SALAD

We love this wonderful salad that tastes like a piled-high BLT but with less time, effort and carbs. Plus, you can make it hours ahead and keep it in the fridge until dinner is ready.
—Denise Thurman, Columbia, MO

Takes: 15 min. • **Makes:** 6 servings

- 1 pkg. (12 oz.) iceberg lettuce blend
- 2 cups grape tomatoes, halved
- ¾ cup coleslaw salad dressing
- ¾ cup shredded cheddar cheese
- 12 bacon strips, cooked and crumbled

In a large bowl, combine lettuce blend and tomatoes. Drizzle with dressing; sprinkle with cheese and bacon.

Per Serving: 1¼ cups equals 268 cal., 20g fat (6g sat. fat), 41mg chol., 621mg sodium, 11g carb. (9g sugars, 1g fiber), 10g pro.

CITRUS AVOCADO SPINACH SALAD

Tossing this salad together with creamy avocado and tangy citrus is so simple. You don't even need to peel the oranges.
—Karole Friemann, Kimberling City, MO

Prep: 15 min. • **Makes:** 8 servings

- 8 cups fresh baby spinach (about 6 oz.)
- 1 jar (24 oz.) refrigerated citrus salad, drained
- 2 medium ripe avocados, peeled and sliced
- 1 cup (4 oz.) crumbled blue cheese
  Sliced almonds, toasted, optional
  Salad dressing of your choice

Divide spinach among eight plates; top with citrus salad and avocados. Sprinkle with cheese and, if desired, almonds; drizzle with dressing. Serve immediately.

Note: To toast nuts, bake in a shallow pan in a 350° oven for 5-10 minutes or cook in a skillet over low heat until lightly browned, stirring nuts occasionally.

Per Serving: 1 serving (calculated without almonds and dressing) equals 168 cal., 10g fat (4g sat. fat), 13mg chol., 231mg sodium, 16g carb. (10g sugars, 3g fiber), 5g pro.

"Involving kids in meal prep is a good chance to talk. You never know what interesting stories your teens may have to share."
—NANCY BROWN, DAHINDA, IL

Leftovers to "Planned-Overs"

Wrap any leftover Garden Tomato Salad in tortillas with cooked, sliced chicken or lamb for a zesty lunch. You can also use leftover dressing to fry up fresh, sliced mushrooms for a quick side dish to serve alongside beef entrees.

FAST FIX

SPINACH SALAD WITH POPPY SEED DRESSING

I love to serve this salad as part of a healthy meal. It's simple and fast, and my family can't get enough of it.
—Nikki Barton, Chef-In-Training.com

Takes: 25 min. • **Makes:** 6 servings

- 4 cups fresh baby spinach
- 4 cups torn iceberg lettuce
- 1½ cups sliced fresh mushrooms
- ½ lb. bacon strips, cooked and crumbled

DRESSING
- ¼ cup red wine vinegar
- ¼ cup chopped red onion
- 3 Tbsp. sugar
- ¾ tsp. salt
- ¼ tsp. ground mustard
- ½ cup canola oil
- 1½ tsp. poppy seeds

1. In a large bowl, combine the spinach, lettuce, mushrooms and bacon. Place vinegar, onion, sugar, salt and mustard in blender. While processing, gradually add oil in a steady stream. Transfer to a bowl; stir in poppy seeds.
2. Divide salad among six plates; drizzle with dressing.
Per serving: 1½ cups with 2 tablespoons dressing equals 280 cal., 24g fat (3g sat. fat), 14mg chol., 557mg sodium., 10g carb. (8g sugars, 1g fiber), 6g pro.

EAT SMART **FAST FIX**

GARDEN TOMATO SALAD

For as long as I can remember, my mom made a colorful salad of tomatoes and cucumbers. Now I make it whenever tomatoes are in season. What a lovely way to celebrate the best of summer's fresh flavors!
—Shannon Copley, Pickerington, OH

Takes: 15 min. • **Makes:** 8 servings

- 3 large tomatoes, cut into wedges
- 1 large sweet onion, cut into thin wedges
- 1 large cucumber, sliced

DRESSING
- ¼ cup olive oil
- 2 Tbsp. cider vinegar
- 1 garlic clove, minced
- 1 tsp. minced fresh basil
- 1 tsp. minced chives
- ½ tsp. salt

In a bowl, combine tomatoes, onion and cucumber. In a small bowl, whisk dressing ingredients until blended. Drizzle over salad; gently toss to coat. Serve immediately.
Per Serving: 1 cup equals 92 cal., 7g fat (1g sat. fat), 0 chol., 155mg sodium, 7g carb. (5g sugars, 1g fiber), 1g pro. **Diabetic Exchanges:** 1 vegetable, 1½ fat.

SNAP PEA SALAD

A quick and easy dressing amps up the flavor of sugar snap peas in my change-of-pace salad. Crunchy, colorful and unique, the snappy salad adds a bit of fun to our family dinners.
—Jean Ecos, Hartland, WI

....

Takes: 20 min. • **Makes:** 12 servings

- ¼ cup white wine vinegar
- ¼ cup Dijon mustard
- 2 Tbsp. minced fresh parsley
- 2 Tbsp. olive oil
- 2 Tbsp. honey
- 1 Tbsp. lemon juice
- 1 tsp. salt
- ½ tsp. pepper
- 3 lbs. fresh sugar snap peas
  Grated lemon peel, optional

1. For vinaigrette, in a small bowl, whisk the first eight ingredients until blended. In a 6-qt. stockpot, bring 16 cups water to a boil. Add snap peas; cook, uncovered, 2-3 minutes or just until peas turn bright green. Remove the peas and immediately drop into ice water. Drain and pat dry; place in a large bowl.

2. Drizzle with vinaigrette and toss to coat. Serve immediately or refrigerate, covered, up to 4 hours before serving. If desired, sprinkle with lemon peel.

Per Serving: ¾ cup equals 84 cal., 3g fat (trace sat. fat), 0 chol., 322mg sodium, 12g carb. (7g sugars, 3g fiber), 4g pro. **Diabetic Exchanges:** ½ starch, 1 vegetable, ½ fat.

BLUE CHEESE & GRAPE COLESLAW

Dishes like coleslaw beg for a fresh approach. I update mine with almonds, grapes, blue cheese and bacon for a bowl of color and crunch.
—Jeannine Bunge, Hartley, IA

....

Prep: 10 min. + chilling
Makes: 8 servings

- 1 pkg. (14 oz.) coleslaw mix
- ¾ cup sliced almonds, toasted
- ¾ cup quartered green grapes
- ¾ cup quartered seedless red grapes
- ½ cup crumbled blue cheese
- 3 bacon strips, cooked and crumbled
- ¼ tsp. pepper
- ¾ cup coleslaw salad dressing

Combine the first seven ingredients. Pour dressing over salad; toss to coat. Refrigerate 1 hour.

Note: To toast nuts, bake in a shallow pan in a 350° oven for 5-10 minutes or cook in a skillet over low heat until lightly browned, stirring nuts occasionally.

Per Serving: ¾ cup equals 212 cal., 15g fat (3g sat. fat), 17mg chol., 339mg sodium, 16g carb. (12g sugars, 3g fiber), 5g pro.

COLOR IT RUBY SALAD

Just looking at this bright red salad cheers me up—and then I get to taste it! For garnish, sprinkle on fresh chives and mild white cheese.
—Lorraine Caland, Shuniah, ON

Prep: 15 min. • **Makes:** 12 servings

- 2 Tbsp. red wine vinegar
- 1 Tbsp. Dijon mustard
- ½ tsp. kosher salt
- ¼ tsp. pepper
- ⅓ cup extra virgin olive oil
- 1 lb. small tomatoes, quartered
- ¾ lb. cherry tomatoes, halved
- ¾ lb. fresh strawberries, hulled and sliced
- 2 cans (15 oz. each) beets, drained and chopped

Mix vinegar, mustard, salt and pepper; gradually whisk in oil until blended. Toss with tomatoes, strawberries and beets. Serve immediately.

Per Serving: 1 cup equals 98 cal., 6g fat (1g sat. fat), 0 chol., 251mg sodium, 10g carb. (7g sugars, 3g fiber), 1g pro. **Diabetic Exchanges:** ½ starch, 1 fat.

MIXED GREEN SALAD WITH CRANBERRY VINAIGRETTE

Dried cranberries, tart apples, glazed walnuts and rich blue cheese add interest to this tasty introduction to any meal. The cranberry dressing is a standout.
—Gretchen Farr, Port Orford, OR

Takes: 25 min. • **Makes:** 8 servings

- 1 cup fresh or frozen cranberries
- ⅓ cup sugar
- ⅓ cup water
- ½ cup cider vinegar
- 1½ tsp. Dijon mustard
- 3 Tbsp. olive oil

SALAD

- 2 pkg. (5 oz. each) spring mix salad greens
- 1 medium tart apple, chopped
- ⅔ cup dried cranberries
- ⅔ cup glazed walnuts
- ⅔ cup crumbled blue cheese

1. In a small saucepan, combine the cranberries, sugar and water. Cook over medium heat until berries pop, about 10 minutes.

2. Cool slightly. Place cranberry mixture, vinegar and mustard in a blender; cover, processing until pureed. While processing, gradually add the oil in a steady stream. Refrigerate until serving.

3. Just before serving, in a large bowl, combine salad greens, apple, cranberries and walnuts. Drizzle with 1 cup of the vinaigrette and toss to coat. Sprinkle with the blue cheese. Serve with the remaining vinaigrette.

Per Serving: 1½ cups equals 230 cal., 12g fat (3g sat. fat), 8mg chol., 224mg sodium, 30g carb. (22g sugars, 3g fiber), 4g pro.

KALE SALAD

I love to make meals that wow everyone at the table. The flavor in this kale dish sets it apart from other salads.
—Gina Myers, Spokane, WA

Takes: 15 min. • **Makes:** 8 servings

- 10 cups sliced kale (about 1 bunch)
- 1 medium apple, thinly sliced
- 3 Tbsp. olive oil
- 2 Tbsp. lemon juice
- 1 tsp. salt
- ½ tsp. pepper
- ¼ cup crumbled feta cheese
- ¼ cup salted pumpkin seeds or pepitas

1. Place kale in a large bowl. With clean hands, massage kale until leaves become soft and darkened, about 2-3 minutes; stir in apple.

2. In a small bowl, whisk oil, lemon juice, salt and pepper until blended. Drizzle over salad; toss to coat. Sprinkle with cheese and pumpkin seeds.

Per serving: 1¼ cup equals 113 cal., 9g fat (2g sat. fat), 2mg chol., 381mg sod., 6g carb. (2g sugars, 1g fiber), 4g pro. **Diabetic Exchanges:** ½ starch, 2 fat.

GRILLED ROMAINE WITH CHIVE-BUTTERMILK DRESSING

I was grilling steak one night and wanted to make a special side dish. I'd seen a grilled Caesar salad recipe and decided to create my own version. It couldn't be easier to make, and it's a treat alongside whatever else you're grilling.
—Crystal Schlueter, Northglenn, CO

Takes: 25 min. • **Makes:** 4 servings

- 2 romaine hearts, halved lengthwise
- 3 Tbsp. olive oil
- 3 Tbsp. buttermilk
- 3 Tbsp. reduced-fat plain Greek yogurt
- 4 tsp. minced fresh chives
- 2 tsp. lemon juice
- ½ tsp. minced garlic
   Dash salt
   Dash pepper
- ¼ cup shredded Parmesan cheese
- 4 bacon strips, cooked and crumbled

1. Brush the romaine halves with oil. Grill romaine, uncovered, over medium-high heat 6-8 minutes or until the leaves begin to wilt and color, turning once.
2. Meanwhile, in a small bowl, whisk the buttermilk, yogurt, chives, lemon juice, garlic, salt and pepper until blended; drizzle over cut sides of romaine. Top with cheese and bacon.
Per Serving: ½ romaine heart equals 76 cal., 15g fat (4g sat. fat), 13mg chol., 299mg sodium, 3g carb. (1g sugars, 1g fiber), 7g pro.

PINA COLADA CARROT SALAD

Looking for something tropical? Just mix up a carrot salad with pina colada yogurt, green grapes and macadamia nuts.
—Emily Tyra, Milwaukee, WI

Takes: 10 min. • **Makes:** 4 servings

- 1 pkg. (10 oz.) julienned carrots
- 1 cup green grapes, halved
- ¾ cup (6 oz.) pina colada yogurt
- ⅓ cup salted dry roasted macadamia nuts, chopped
   Lemon wedges

In a large bowl, combine carrots, grapes, yogurt and macadamia nuts; toss to coat. Squeeze lemon wedges over salad before serving.
Per Serving: ¾ cup equals 184 cal., 9g fat (2g sat. fat), 2mg chol., 157mg sodium, 24g carb. (19g sugars, 3g fiber), 3g pro. **Diabetic Exchanges:** 1 starch, 1 vegetable, 1½ fat.

EASY PEASY SLAW

Eyes light up when I bring out this slaw jazzed up with peas, peanuts and poppy seed dressing. It's a fast and fresh way to dress up meals.
—Sue Ort, Des Moines, IA

Takes: 5 min. • **Makes:** 12 servings

- 4 cups frozen peas (about 16 oz.), thawed
- 1 pkg. (14 oz.) coleslaw mix
- 4 green onions, chopped
- 1 cup poppy seed salad dressing
- 1 cup sweet and crunchy peanuts or honey-roasted peanuts

Place peas, coleslaw mix and green onions in a large bowl. Pour dressing over salad and toss to coat. Stir in peanuts just before serving.
Per Serving: ⅔ cup equals 202 cal., 12g fat (2g sat. fat), 7mg chol., 178mg sodium, 20g carb. (14g sugars, 4g fiber), 4g pro. **Diabetic Exchanges:** 1 starch, 1 vegetable, 2 fat.

EAT SMART `FAST FIX`

HONEY-YOGURT BERRY SALAD

I wanted my family to eat more fruit without more sugary ingredients. Play with different low-fat yogurts and fruits to make your very own berry salad.
—Betsy King, Duluth, MN

Takes: 10 min. • **Makes:** 8 servings

- 1½ cups sliced fresh strawberries
- 1½ cups fresh raspberries
- 1½ cups fresh blueberries
- 1½ cups fresh blackberries
- 1 cup (8 oz.) reduced-fat plain yogurt
- 1 Tbsp. honey
- ¼ tsp. grated orange peel
- 1 Tbsp. orange juice

Place the berries in a glass bowl; toss to combine. In a small bowl, mix remaining ingredients. Spoon over berries.

Per Serving: ¾ cup fruit with 2 Tbsp. yogurt mixture equals 76 cal., 1g fat (trace sat. fat), 2mg chol., 23mg sodium, 16g carb. (11g sugars, 4g fiber), 3g pro. **Diabetic Exchange:** 1 fruit.

FETA GARBANZO BEAN SALAD

This super-quick chickpea salad is a hit with my gang. If there are any leftovers, which rarely happens, I pile them into pitas for lunches the next day!
—Judy Doepel, Charlton, NY

Takes: 15 min. • **Makes:** 4 servings

- 1 can (15 oz.) garbanzo beans, rinsed and drained
- 1½ cups coarsely chopped English cucumber (about ½ medium)
- 1 can (2¼ oz.) sliced ripe olives, drained
- 1 medium tomato, seeded and chopped
- ¼ cup thinly sliced red onion
- ¼ cup chopped fresh parsley
- 3 Tbsp. olive oil
- 1 Tbsp. lemon juice
- ¼ tsp. salt
- ⅛ tsp. pepper
- 5 cups torn mixed salad greens
- ½ cup crumbled feta cheese

Place the first 11 ingredients in a large bowl; toss to combine. Sprinkle salad with cheese.

Per Serving: 2 cups equals 268 cal., 16g fat (3g sat. fat), 8mg chol., 586mg sodium, 24g carb. (4g sugars, 7g fiber), 9g pro. **Diabetic Exchanges:** 1 starch, 1 lean meat, 1 vegetable, 3 fat.

CRAZY-QUICK CORN & BLACK BEAN SALAD

This colorful, crunchy salad is chock-full of nutrition and taste that all ages will love. Try it with a variety of entrees, or even as a wholesome salsa!
—Krista Frank, Rhododendron, OR

Prep: 15 min. + chilling
Makes: 8 servings

- 1 can (15¼ oz.) whole kernel corn, drained
- 1 can (15 oz.) black beans, rinsed and drained
- 2 large tomatoes, finely chopped
- 1 large red onion, finely chopped
- ¼ cup minced fresh cilantro
- 2 garlic cloves, minced

DRESSING
- 2 Tbsp. sugar
- 2 Tbsp. white vinegar
- 2 Tbsp. canola oil
- 1½ tsp. lime juice
- ¼ tsp. salt
- ¼ tsp. ground cumin
- ¼ tsp. pepper

In a large bowl, combine the first six ingredients. In a small bowl, whisk the dressing ingredients; pour over corn mixture and toss to coat. Cover and refrigerate for at least 1 hour. Stir before serving. Serve with a slotted spoon.
Per Serving: ⅔ cup equals 128 cal., 4g fat (0 sat. fat), 0 chol., 351mg sodium, 19g carb. (9g sugars, 4g fiber), 4g pro. **Diabetic Exchanges:** 1 starch, 1 vegetable, 1 fat.

DILL GARDEN SALAD

I love to cut up whatever vegetables are on hand and toss them with the delicious dressing and fresh dill. This salad shows up on our table several times a week.
—Bethany Martin, Milton, PA

Takes: 15 min. • **Makes:** 6 servings

- 3 cups chopped English cucumbers
- 1 large tomato, seeded and cut into ½-in. pieces
- 1 small sweet red pepper, chopped
- 2 Tbsp. chopped sweet onion
- 3 Tbsp. reduced-fat mayonnaise
- 4 tsp. olive oil
- 2 tsp. sugar
- 2 tsp. rice vinegar
- ½ tsp. salt
- ¼ tsp. garlic powder
- ¼ tsp. pepper
- 2½ tsp. snipped fresh dill

In a large bowl, combine the cucumbers, tomato, red pepper and onion. In a small bowl, whisk the mayonnaise, oil, sugar, vinegar, salt, garlic powder and pepper until blended. Stir in dill. Spoon dressing over salad; toss to coat.
Per Serving: 1 cup equals 75 cal., 6g fat (1g sat. fat), 3mg chol., 260mg sodium, 6g carb. (4g sugars, 1g fiber), 1g pro. **Diabetic Exchanges:** 1 vegetable, 1 fat.

MEAL PLANNER

NO-FUSS 💙 SALADS

ADD GREENS TO ANY MENU AND A GREAT DINNER AWAITS.

SPECIAL MENU

ENTREE:
Beef Brisket
page 22

SALAD:
Sweet Potato &
Chickpea Salad
page 182

DESSERT:
Almond-Vanilla
Yogurt Parfaits
page 287

TAG YOUR MEAL
MEMORIES WITH
#100 FAMILYMEALS

GROCERY LIST

KITCHEN STAPLES
- ○ Olive oil
- ○ Cornstarch
- ○ Liquid smoke
- ○ Celery salt
- ○ Worcestershire sauce
- ○ Salt
- ○ Pepper

PRODUCE
- ○ 1 large onion
- ○ 2 medium sweet potatoes (about 1 lb.)
- ○ 1 small piece gingerroot

- ○ 1 head of garlic
- ○ 1 package (5 oz.) spring mix salad greens

PANTRY
- ○ 1 can (15 oz.) garbanzo beans or chickpeas
- ○ 1 jar (16 oz.) almond butter
- ○ 1 package (3.4 oz.) instant vanilla or cheesecake pudding mix

MEAT
- ○ 1 fresh beef brisket (2½ to 3 lbs.)

DAIRY
- ○ 1 package (4 oz.) crumbled feta cheese
- ○ 1 container (32 oz.) reduced-fat plain Greek yogurt

OTHER
- ○ 1 can (12 oz.) beer or nonalcoholic beer
- ○ 1 bottle (12 oz.) seasoned rice vinegar
- ○ 1 bag (12 oz.) granola with fruit and nuts
- ○ 1 bag (2.25 oz.) sliced almonds

ALL-TIME FAVS

ENTREE:
Slow Cooker
Tuna Noodle Casserole
page 156

SALAD:
Michigan Cherry Salad
page 178

DESSERT:
Texas Tumbleweeds
page 268

TAG YOUR MEAL
MEMORIES WITH
#100 FAMILYMEALS

GROCERY LIST

KITCHEN STAPLES
- ○ Olive oil
- ○ All-purpose flour
- ○ Sugar
- ○ Salt
- ○ Pepper

PRODUCE
- ○ 1 large apple
- ○ 1 pint fresh raspberries
- ○ 1 package (8 oz.) sliced mushrooms
- ○ 1 medium onion
- ○ 1 medium sweet pepper
- ○ 2 packages (5 oz. each) baby spinach
- ○ 1 package (5 oz.) spring mix salad greens
- ○ 1 head of garlic

PANTRY
- ○ 3 cans (5 oz. each) light tuna in water
- ○ 1 jar (16 oz.) creamy peanut butter
- ○ 1 can (14.5 oz.) reduced-sodium chicken broth
- ○ 1 package (12 oz.) egg noodles
- ○ 1 jar (12 oz.) cherry preserves
- ○ 1 bottle (16 oz.) red wine vinegar
- ○ 1 bottle (16 oz.) cider vinegar

DAIRY
- ○ Butter
- ○ 1 package (8 oz.) shredded Monterey Jack cheese

- ○ 1 package (4 oz.) crumbled Gorgonzola cheese
- ○ 1 carton (16 oz.) half-and-half cream

OTHER
- ○ 1 bottle (8 oz.) lemon juice
- ○ 1 package (16 oz.) frozen peas
- ○ 1 package (5 oz.) dried cherries
- ○ 1 package (6 oz.) pecans
- ○ 1 package (11 oz.) butterscotch chips
- ○ 1 can (9 oz.) potato sticks
- ○ 1 bag (10 oz.) potato chips

MEAL PLANNER

NO-FUSS ♥ SALADS

ADD GREENS TO ANY MENU AND A GREAT DINNER AWAITS.

MOM'S BEST

ENTREE:
Mom's Chicken Tetrazzini
page 74

SALAD:
Apple-Pecan Salad with
Honey Vinaigrette
page 177

DESSERT:
Lemon Fluff
page 298

TAG YOUR MEAL
MEMORIES WITH
#100 FAMILYMEALS

GROCERY LIST

KITCHEN STAPLES
- ○ Olive oil
- ○ All-purpose flour
- ○ Sugar
- ○ Vanilla extract
- ○ Salt
- ○ Pepper

PRODUCE
- ○ 1 medium apple
- ○ 2 cups sliced fresh mushrooms
- ○ 1 small onion
- ○ 1 small green pepper
- ○ 2 medium heads Bibb lettuce

PANTRY
- ○ 1 box (12 oz.) spaghetti
- ○ 1 carton (32 oz.) chicken broth
- ○ 1 bottle (16 oz.) cider vinegar
- ○ 1 jar (4 oz.) diced pimientos
- ○ 1 package (.3 oz.) sugar-free lemon gelatin
- ○ 1 can (12 oz.) evaporated milk
- ○ 1 box (13.5 oz.) graham cracker crumbs

MEAT
- ○ 1 rotisserie chicken
- ○ 1 package (8 oz.) bacon

DAIRY
- ○ Butter
- ○ 1 brick (8 oz.) reduced-fat cream cheese
- ○ 1 canister (8 oz.) grated Romano
- ○ 1 package (6 oz.) shredded Parmesan cheese

OTHER
- ○ 1 bottle (12 oz.) honey
- ○ 1 bottle (12 oz.) honey mustard
- ○ 1 bottle (2.5 oz.) lemon juice
- ○ 1 package (13 oz.) frozen peas
- ○ 1 package (4.5 oz.) pecan halves

✂ -

GRILLED FEAST

ENTREE:
Citrus-Glazed Pork Chops
page 123

SALAD:
Apple Maple Pecan Salad
page 173

DESSERT:
Pecan Butterscotch
Cookies
page 250

TAG YOUR MEAL
MEMORIES WITH
#100 FAMILYMEALS

GROCERY LIST

KITCHEN STAPLES
- ○ Canola oil
- ○ Pepper

PRODUCE
- ○ 3 large Granny Smith apples
- ○ 2 limes
- ○ 1 jalapeno pepper
- ○ 1 small piece gingerroot
- ○ 1 small head cabbage

PANTRY
- ○ 1 jar (12 oz.) orange marmalade
- ○ 1 box (32 oz.) complete buttermilk pancake mix
- ○ 1 package (3.4 oz.) instant butterscotch pudding mix

MEAT
- ○ 4 bone-in pork loin chops (8 oz. each)

DAIRY
- ○ Butter
- ○ 1 large egg
- ○ 1 container (4 oz.) crumbled Gorgonzola cheese

OTHER
- ○ 1 bottle (2.5 oz.) lemon juice
- ○ 1 bottle (8.5 oz.) maple syrup
- ○ 1 bottle (10 oz.) Dijon mustard
- ○ 1 package (10 oz.) pecans

Bringing the Family Together

Nikki Barton serves up food and fun for husband, Derek, and children (from left) Avrie, Grant and Jace. See page 184 for Nikki's Spinach Salad with Poppy Seed Dressing.

FOR FOOD BLOGGER Nikki Barton, sharing a family meal is a top priority. "We try to sit down to home-cooked meals often," she says. "It's a great time to share our day. Best of all, the kids really open up when we are all together, and a lot of my fondest conversations occurred at our dinner table."

Family meals were key in Nikki's childhood home. "I remember watching Mom cook and thinking, *Cooking is fun, and food brings people together.*"

After Nikki married her husband, Derek, she realized she needed to amp up her cooking skills. "I was overwhelmed with how I was going to cook for him," she explains.

"My grandma gave me collections of family recipes. When I put my own spins on them, they became popular at my home and with friends and extended family. That's when I began my own food blog, *www.chef-in-training.com.*

"It's a spot for anyone who wants to learn how to serve family meals," she adds. "I want people to learn to cook and develop a passion for the kitchen."

Nikki instilled an interest for cooking in her little ones, too. "My kids love helping," she says. "They like eating what they've prepared, making it easier to get them to eat veggies. They also help plan our weekly dinner calendar. This gets them excited about dinner."

The Bartons don't plan on skipping family meals any time soon. "Home-cooked dinners bring us a measure of warmth," Nikki says, "not only to our tummies, but to our hearts as well!"

"The busier we are, the more important sit-down dinners become. It's our time to spend together."

−Susan Lasken
Woodland Hills, California

SIMPLE SIDES

ROUNDOUT meals easily with these best-loved dinner additions.

QUICK BARBECUED BEANS

A simple, classic recipe—but cooking it on the grill introduces a subtle flavor. This dish features a nice blend of beans, and preparation time is minimal. Best of all, it's sized right for family meals!
—Millie Vickery, Lena, IL

Takes: 25 min. • **Makes:** 5 servings

- 1 can (16 oz.) kidney beans, rinsed and drained
- 1 can (15½ oz.) great northern beans, rinsed and drained
- 1 can (15 oz.) pork and beans
- ½ cup barbecue sauce
- 2 Tbsp. brown sugar
- 2 tsp. prepared mustard

1. In an ungreased 8-in. square disposable foil pan, combine all ingredients.
2. Grill beans, covered, over medium heat for 15-20 minutes or until heated through, stirring occasionally.
Per Serving: ¾ cup equals 264 cal., 2g fat (trace sat. fat), 0 chol., 877mg sodium, 51g carb. (15g sugars, 13g fiber), 14g pro.

"Really good, easy. I left it uncovered for half the time to caramel it up. I would make it again."

—DUBLINLAB, TASTEOFHOME.COM

BEST EVER
TASTE OF HOME
TEST KITCHEN

CHEESE TORTELLINI WITH TOMATOES AND CORN

For a taste of summer, add fresh corn and basil plus cherry tomatoes to easy-to-use grocery store tortellini. It's a good dish for picnics , but why not treat yourself at home?
—Sally Maloney, Dallas, GA

Takes: 25 min. • **Makes:** 4 servings

1 pkg. (9 oz.) refrigerated cheese tortellini
3⅓ cups fresh or frozen corn (about 16 oz.)
2 cups cherry tomatoes, quartered
2 green onions, thinly sliced
¼ cup minced fresh basil
2 Tbsp. grated Parmesan cheese
4 tsp. olive oil
¼ tsp. garlic powder
⅛ tsp. pepper

In a 6-qt. stockpot, cook the tortellini according to package directions, adding corn during last 5 minutes of cooking. Drain; transfer to a large bowl. Add the remaining ingredients; toss to coat.

Per Serving: 1¾ cups equals 366 cal., 12g fat (4g sat. fat), 30mg chol., 286mg sodium, 57g carb. (6g sugars, 5g fiber), 14g pro.

LEMONY ZUCCHINI RIBBONS

Fresh zucchini gets a shave and a drizzle of lemony goodness in this fabulous salad. Sprinkle on the goat cheese or feta and dive right in.
—Ellie Martin Cliffe, Milwaukee, WI

Takes: 15 min. • **Makes:** 4 servings

- 1   Tbsp. olive oil
- ½   tsp. grated lemon peel
- 1   Tbsp. lemon juice
- ½   tsp. salt
- ¼   tsp. pepper
- 3   medium zucchini
- ⅓   cup crumbled goat or feta cheese

1. For dressing, in a small bowl, mix the first five ingredients. Using a vegetable peeler, shave zucchini lengthwise into very thin slices; arrange on a serving plate.
2. To serve, drizzle with dressing and toss lightly to coat. Top with cheese.
Per Serving: ¾ cup equals 83 cal., 6g fat (2g sat. fat), 12mg chol., 352mg sodium, 5g carb. (3g sugars, 2g fiber), 3g pro. **Diabetic Exchanges:** 1 vegetable, 1 fat.

Zucchini Ribbons

To make zucchini ribbons, trim the ends from the zucchini. Next, use a vegetable peeler to make long, thin strips from zucchini. Use the ribbons in salads or in place of pasta to cut carbs.

SLOW COOKER DRESSING

Here's an easy dressing that's perfect for weeknight meals and sure to make happy memories. Once everything is in the slow cooker, you're free to turn your attention to the other dishes.
—Rita Nodland, Bismarck, ND

Prep: 15 min. • **Cook:** 3 hours
Makes: 8 servings

- 2   Tbsp. olive oil
- 1   medium celery rib, chopped
- 1   small onion, chopped
- 8   cups unseasoned stuffing cubes
- 1   tsp. poultry seasoning
- ¼   tsp. salt
- ¼   tsp. pepper
- 2   cups reduced-sodium chicken broth

1. In a large skillet, heat oil over medium-high heat. Add celery and onion; cook and stir until tender.
2. In a large bowl, toss bread cubes with poultry seasoning, salt and pepper. Stir in the celery mixture. Add broth to bread mixture and toss to coat. Transfer to a greased 5-qt. slow cooker. Cook, covered, on low 3-4 hours or until heated through.
Per Serving: ½ cup equals 226 cal., 5g fat (trace sat. fat), 0 chol., 635mg sodium, 40g carb. (3g sugars, 3g fiber), 8g pro.

FAMILY FAVORITE

EAT SMART **SLOW COOKER**

HONEY-BUTTER PEAS AND CARROTS

The classic combination of peas and carrots is made even better with a few simple flavor enhancers. Slow cooking allows the ingredients to meld for maximum richness.
—Theresa Kreyche, Tustin, CA

Prep: 15 min. • **Cook:** 5¼ hours
Makes: 12 servings

- 1 lb. carrots, sliced
- 1 large onion, chopped
- ¼ cup water
- ¼ cup butter, cubed
- ¼ cup honey
- 4 garlic cloves, minced
- 1 tsp. salt
- 1 tsp. dried marjoram
- ⅛ tsp. white pepper
- 1 pkg. (16 oz.) frozen peas

In a 3-qt. slow cooker, combine the first nine ingredients. Cook, covered, on low 5 hours. Stir in peas. Cook, covered, on high for 15-25 minutes longer or until vegetables are tender.

Per Serving: ½ cup equals 106 cal., 4g fat (2g sat. fat), 10mg chol., 293mg sodium, 16g carb. (10g sugars, 3g fiber), 3g pro. **Diabetic Exchanges:** 1 starch, 1 fat.

Table Talk

If you could go back in time, what period of history would you revisit?

Learn about your children's favorite history lessons with this Table Talk exercise. Their answers might surprise you, and you'll have a chance to teach a little history yourself!

BAKED PARMESAN BREADED SQUASH

Yellow summer squash crisps beautifully when baked. You don't have to turn the pieces, but do keep an eye on them.
—Debi Mitchell, Flower Mound, TX

Prep: 20 min. • **Bake:** 20 min.
Makes: 6 servings

- 4 cups thinly sliced yellow summer squash (3 medium)
- 3 Tbsp. olive oil
- ½ tsp. salt
- ½ tsp. pepper
- ⅛ tsp. cayenne pepper
- ¾ cup panko (Japanese) bread crumbs
- ¾ cup grated Parmesan cheese

1. Preheat oven to 450°. Place squash in a large bowl. Add oil and seasonings; gently toss to coat.

2. In a shallow bowl, mix bread crumbs and cheese. Dip squash in crumb mixture to coat both sides, patting to help coating adhere. Place on parchment paper-lined baking sheets. Bake for 20-25 minutes or until golden brown, rotating pans halfway through baking.

Per Serving: ⅔ cup equals 137 cal., 10g fat (2g sat. fat), 7mg chol., 346mg sodium, 8g carb. (trace sugars, 2g fiber), 5g pro. **Diabetic Exchanges:** 1 vegetable, 2 fat.

CALIFORNIA QUINOA

I'm always changing up salads. Here I used tomato, zucchini and olives for a Greek-inspired dish. Try adding a few more favorite fresh veggies you know your family will love.
—Elizabeth Lubin, Huntington Beach, CA

Takes: 30 min. • **Makes:** 4 servings

- 1 Tbsp. olive oil
- 1 cup quinoa, rinsed and well drained
- 2 garlic cloves, minced
- 1 medium zucchini, chopped
- 2 cups water
- ¾ cup canned garbanzo beans or chickpeas, rinsed and drained
- 1 medium tomato, finely chopped
- ½ cup crumbled feta cheese
- ¼ cup finely chopped Greek olives
- 2 Tbsp. minced fresh basil
- ¼ tsp. pepper

In a large saucepan, heat the oil over medium-high heat. Add the quinoa and garlic; cook and stir 2-3 minutes or until quinoa is lightly browned. Stir in zucchini and water; bring to a boil. Reduce heat; simmer, covered, 12-15 minutes or until the liquid is absorbed. Stir in remaining ingredients; heat through.

Per Serving: 1 cup equals 310 cal., 11g fat (3g sat. fat), 8mg chol., 353mg sodium, 42g carb. (3g sugars, 6g fiber), 11g pro. **Diabetic Exchanges:** 2 starch, 1 lean meat, 1 vegetable, 1½ fat.

THYME-ROASTED VEGETABLES

The aroma of these roasting vegetables calls everyone to the table. My husband is known for having more than one serving at a time. It's that good.

—Jasmine Rose, Crystal Lake, IL

Prep: 25 min. • **Bake:** 45 min.
Makes: 10 servings

- 2 lbs. red potatoes, cubed (about 9 cups)
- 3 cups sliced sweet onions (about 1½ large)
- 3 medium carrots, sliced
- ½ lb. medium fresh mushrooms, halved
- 1 large sweet red pepper, cut into 1½-in. pieces
- 1 large sweet yellow pepper, cut into 1½-in. pieces
- 2 Tbsp. butter, melted
- 2 Tbsp. olive oil
- 1 Tbsp. minced fresh thyme or 1 tsp. dried thyme
- 1 tsp. salt
- ¼ tsp. pepper

1. Preheat oven to 400°. In a large bowl, combine vegetables. Add remaining ingredients; toss to coat.
2. Transfer to a 15x10x1-in. baking pan. Roast 45-50 minutes or until tender, stirring occasionally.
Per serving: ¾ cup equals 151 cal., 5g fat (2g sat. fat), 6mg chol., 274mg sod., 24g carb. (5g sugars, 4g fiber), 3g pro. **Diabetic Exchanges:** 1 starch, 1 vegetable, 1 fat.

PARMESAN CREAMED SPINACH

Rich and creamy spinach takes only minutes to make. And kids are more likely to eat their spinach when it's this tasty!

—Leann Ross, San Tan Valley, AZ

Takes: 20 min. • **Makes:** 4 servings

- ½ lb. sliced fresh mushrooms
- 1 small onion, chopped
- 2 tsp. butter
- 2 tsp. olive oil
- 1 garlic clove, minced
- ¼ tsp. salt
- ¼ tsp. pepper
- 1 pkg. (9 oz.) fresh spinach
- ½ pkg. (4 oz.) cream cheese, cubed
- ½ cup shredded Parmesan cheese

1. In a large skillet, saute the mushrooms and onion in butter and oil until tender. Add the garlic, salt and pepper; cook for 1 minute longer.
2. Add spinach and cream cheese; cook and stir until cream cheese is smooth and spinach is wilted. Sprinkle with cheese.
Per Serving: ½ cup equals 217 cal., 17g fat (10g sat. fat), 44mg chol., 470mg sodium, 8g carb. (2g sugars, 2g fiber), 10g pro.

MUSHROOM & PEAS RICE PILAF

I give side dishes flair by jazzing up mixes with vegetables. Add peas and baby portobello mushrooms to a rice pilaf mix for a fun burst of color and a variety of textures.

—Stacy Mullens, Gresham, OR

Takes: 25 min. • **Makes:** 6 servings

- 1 pkg. (6.6 oz.) rice pilaf mix with toasted almonds
- 1 Tbsp. butter
- 1½ cups fresh or frozen peas
- 1 cup sliced baby portobello mushrooms

1. Prepare the rice pilaf according to the package directions.
2. In a large skillet, heat the butter over medium heat. Add peas and mushrooms; cook and stir 6-8 minutes or until tender. Stir in the rice.
Per Serving: ⅔ cup equals 177 cal., 6g fat (2g sat. fat), 10mg chol., 352mg sodium, 28g carb. (3g sugars, 3g fiber), 5g pro. **Diabetic Exchanges:** 2 starch, ½ fat.

OVEN-DRIED TOMATOES

EAT SMART (5) INGREDIENTS

OVEN-DRIED TOMATOES

*We owned an organic greenhouse
and business that offered classes. I had
100 tomato varieties to work with, so
I started oven-drying them and taught
my students how to do it, too.*
—Sue Gronholz, Beaver Dam, WI

Prep: 15 min. • **Bake:** 5 hours
Makes: 4 servings

- 8 plum tomatoes
  Ice water
- ¼ cup olive oil
- ¼ cup minced fresh basil
- 4 garlic cloves, minced
- ½ tsp. salt
- ¼ tsp. pepper

1. Preheat the oven to 250°. Fill a large
saucepan two-thirds with water; bring
to a boil. Cut a shallow "X" on the bottom
of each tomato. Place tomatoes, a few
at a time, in boiling water just until skin
at the "X" begins to loosen, about 30
seconds. Remove and immediately drop
into ice water. Pull off and discard skins.
2. Cut the tomatoes in half lengthwise.
Combine all the ingredients; toss to coat.
Transfer the tomatoes, cut side up, to
a greased 15x10x1-in. baking pan. Roast
until the tomatoes are soft and slightly
shriveled, about 5 hours. Cool tomatoes
completely; refrigerate.
Per Serving: 4 tomato halves equals 147 cal.,
14g fat (2g sat. fat), 0 chol., 302mg sodium,
6g carb. (3g sugars, 2g fiber), 1g pro.
Diabetic Exchanges: 1 vegetable, 3 fat.

EAT SMART (5) INGREDIENTS FAST FIX ▶

LEMON-ROASTED ASPARAGUS

*When it comes to fixing asparagus,
it's hard to go wrong. The earthy flavors
in this easy recipe burst with every bite.*
—Jenn Tidwell, Fair Oaks, CA

Takes: 20 min. • **Makes:** 8 servings

- 2 lbs. fresh asparagus, trimmed
- ¼ cup olive oil
- 4 tsp. grated lemon peel
- 2 garlic cloves, minced
- ½ tsp. salt
- ½ tsp. pepper

Preheat oven to 425°. Place asparagus
in a greased 15x10x1-in. baking pan. Mix
the remaining ingredients; drizzle over
the asparagus. Toss to coat. Roast for
8-12 minutes or until crisp-tender.
Per Serving: 1 serving equals 75 cal., 7g fat
(1g sat. fat), 0 chol., 154mg sodium, 3g carb.
(1g sugars, 1g fiber), 2g pro. **Diabetic
Exchanges:** 1 vegetable, 1½ fat.

SLOW COOKER 🍲

ORANGE SPICE CARROTS

*In order to get my son to eat veggies,
I mix and match flavors and spices. My
slow-cooker dish of carrots with orange
and cinnamon has him hooked.*
—Christina Addison, Blanchester, OH

Prep: 10 min. • **Cook:** 4 hours
Makes: 6 servings

- 2 lbs. medium carrots or baby
  carrots, cut into 1-in. pieces
- ½ cup packed brown sugar
- ½ cup orange juice
- 2 Tbsp. butter
- ¾ tsp. ground cinnamon
- ½ tsp. salt
- ¼ tsp. ground nutmeg
- 4 tsp. cornstarch
- ¼ cup cold water

1. In a 3-qt. slow cooker, combine the first
seven ingredients. Cook, covered, on low
4-5 hours or until carrots are tender.
2. In a small bowl, mix the cornstarch and
water until smooth; gradually stir into
carrot mixture until sauce is thickened.
Per Serving: ⅔ cup equals 187 cal., 4g fat (3g
sat. fat), 10mg chol., 339mg sodium, 38g carb.
(27g sugars, 4g fiber), 2g pro.

MOM'S SPANISH RICE

My mom is famous for her Spanish rice. So whenever I want a taste of home, I simply pull out her recipe and make it for my own family.
—Joan Hallford, North Richland Hills, TX

Takes: 20 min. • **Makes:** 4 servings

- 1   lb. lean ground beef (90% lean)
- 1   large onion, chopped
- 1   medium green pepper, chopped
- 1   can (15 oz.) tomato sauce
- 1   can (14½ oz.) no-salt-added diced tomatoes, drained
- 1   tsp. ground cumin
- 1   tsp. chili powder
- ½   tsp. garlic powder
- ¼   tsp. salt
- 2⅔ cups cooked brown rice

1. In a large skillet, cook beef, onion and pepper over medium heat 6-8 minutes or until the beef is no longer pink and the onion is tender, breaking up the beef into crumbles; drain.
2. Stir in the tomato sauce, tomatoes and seasonings; bring to a boil. Add rice; heat through, stirring occasionally.
Per Serving: 1½ cups equals 395 cal., 11g fat (4g sat. fat), 71mg chol., 757mg sodium, 46g carb. (8g sugars, 6g fiber), 29g pro. **Diabetic Exchanges:** 2 starch, 3 lean meat, 2 vegetable.

PESTO PASTA & POTATOES

This healthier pasta recipe is pretty simple to begin with, but the cooking method makes it even simpler. You can throw the green beans and pasta into one big pot.
—Laura Flowers, Moscow, ID

Takes: 30 min. • **Makes:** 12 servings

- 1½ lbs. small red potatoes, halved
- 12   oz. uncooked whole grain spiral pasta
- 3   cups cut fresh or frozen green beans
- 1   jar (6½ oz.) prepared pesto
- 1   cup grated Parmigiano-Reggiano cheese

1. Place the potatoes in a large saucepan; add water to cover. Bring to a boil. Reduce heat; cook, uncovered, for 9-11 minutes or until tender. Drain; transfer to a large serving bowl.
2. Meanwhile, cook the pasta according to package directions, adding the green beans during last 5 minutes of cooking; drain, reserving ¾ cup pasta water.
3. Add the pasta and green beans to the potatoes. Stir in the pesto, cheese and enough reserved pasta water to coat.
Per Serving: ¾ cups equals 261 cal., 10g fat (3g sat. fat), 11mg chol., 233mg sodium, 34g carb. (2g sugars, 5g fiber), 11g pro. **Diabetic Exchanges:** 2 starch, 2 fat.

EASY HOMEMADE CHUNKY APPLESAUCE

This applesauce is so easy, and my family loves when I make it from scratch. And I love knowing what's in it!
—Marilee Cardinal, Burlington, NJ

Takes: 30 min. • **Makes:** 5 cups

- 7   medium McIntosh, Empire or other apples (about 3 lbs.)
- ½   cup sugar
- ½   cup water
- 1   Tbsp. lemon juice
- ¼   tsp. almond or vanilla extract

1. Peel, core and cut each apple into eight wedges. Cut each wedge crosswise in half; place in a large saucepan. Add remaining ingredients.
2. Bring to a boil. Reduce heat; simmer, covered, 15-20 minutes or until desired consistency, stirring occasionally.
Per Serving: ¾ cup equals 139 cal., 0 fat (0 sat. fat), 0 chol., 0 sodium, 36g carb. (33g sugars, 2g fiber), 0 pro.

"My biggest time-saver comes in knowing what we'll have for each meal, so I am not wasting time trying to decide what to make. I plan menus using a 4-week rotation chart."
—ANN WEGENER, SPRINGVILLE, IN

EDDIE'S FAVORITE FIESTA CORN

When fresh sweet corn is available, I love making this splurge of a side dish. Frozen corn works, but taste as you go and add sugar if needed.

—Anthony Bolton, Bellevue, NE

Prep: 15 min. • **Cook:** 25 min.
Makes: 8 servings

- ½ **lb. bacon strips, chopped**
- 5 **cups fresh or frozen super sweet corn**
- 1 **medium sweet red pepper, finely chopped**
- 1 **medium sweet yellow pepper, finely chopped**
- 1 **pkg. (8 oz.) reduced-fat cream cheese**
- ½ **cup half-and-half cream**
- 1 **can (4 oz.) chopped green chilies, optional**
- 2 **tsp. sugar**
- 1 **tsp. pepper**
- ¼ **tsp. salt**

1. In a 6-qt. stockpot, cook the bacon over medium heat until crisp, stirring occasionally. Remove with a slotted spoon; drain on paper towels. Discard drippings, reserving 1 Tbsp. in pan.
2. Add the corn, red pepper and yellow pepper to drippings; cook and stir over medium-high heat 5-6 minutes or until tender. Stir in remaining ingredients until blended; bring to a boil. Reduce heat; simmer, covered, 8-10 minutes or until mixture is thickened.
Per Serving: ⅔ cup equals 249 cal., 14g fat (7g sat. fat), 39mg chol., 399mg sodium, 22g carb. (9g sugars, 2g fiber), 10g pro.

(5) INGREDIENTS
THYME-BAKED APPLE SLICES

My children love baked apple slices along with chicken fingers for lunch. Serve them as a healthy alternative to potatoes with any meat dish.

—Constance Henry, Hibbing, MN

Prep: 15 min. • **Bake:** 25 min.
Makes: 6 servings

- 4 **cups apple cider**
- ¼ **cup butter, cubed**
- 8 **large Braeburn apples (about 4 lbs.)**
- 3½ **tsp. minced fresh thyme, divided**

1. Place cider in a large saucepan. Bring to a boil; cook 18-20 minutes or until liquid is reduced to ⅔ cup. Remove from heat; stir in butter.
2. Peel and cut each apple into eight wedges. In a large bowl, toss apples with ¼ cup of the reduced cider and 3 tsp. thyme. Transfer to a foil-lined 15x10x1-in. baking pan. Bake 10 minutes.
3. Drizzle with remaining reduced cider. Bake 12-15 minutes longer or until tender. Sprinkle with remaining thyme.
Per Serving: ¾ cup equals 264 cal., 8g fat (5g sat. fat), 20mg chol., 78mg sodium, 51g carb. (42g sugars, 3g fiber), 1g pro.

> ### A Perfect Crowd Pleaser
> Don't reserve this corn dish for family dinners. Double the recipe and take it along to large get-togethers. The corn travels well and keeps nicely in a slow cooker for buffets.

QUICK & EASY
AU GRATIN POTATOES

Au gratin potatoes are usually reserved for special occasions, but this speedy version makes them a great addition to casual weeknight meals, too.
—Carol Blue, Barnesville, PA

Prep: 10 min. • **Bake:** 50 min.
Makes: 12 servings

- 2 cups (16 oz.) sour cream
- 1 can (10¾ oz.) condensed cream of chicken soup, undiluted
- ½ tsp. salt
- ¼ tsp. pepper
- 1 pkg. (30 oz.) frozen shredded hash brown potatoes, thawed
- 2 cups (8 oz.) shredded cheddar cheese
- 1 small onion, chopped
- 2 cups crushed cornflakes
- ¼ cup butter, melted

1. Preheat oven to 350°. In a large bowl, mix sour cream, condensed soup, salt and pepper; stir in potatoes, cheese and onion. Transfer the mixture to a greased 13x9-in. baking dish.
2. In a small bowl, mix crushed cornflakes and melted butter; sprinkle over potato mixture. Bake, uncovered, 50-60 minutes or until golden brown.
Per Serving: ¾ cup equals 394 cal., 22g fat (14g sat. fat), 70mg chol., 680mg sodium, 36g carb. (5g sugars, 2g fiber), 11g pro.

EAT SMART **FAST FIX**
TOMATOES WITH
BUTTERMILK VINAIGRETTE

We make the most of tomatoes when they are in season and plentiful, and I love them with an old-fashioned, summery tasting homemade dressing .
—Judith Foreman, Alexandria, VA

Takes: 20 min. • **Makes:** 12 servings

- ¾ cup buttermilk
- ¼ cup minced fresh tarragon
- ¼ cup white wine vinegar
- 3 Tbsp. canola oil
- 1½ tsp. sugar
- ½ tsp. ground mustard
- ¼ tsp. celery salt
- ¼ tsp. pepper
- 4 lbs. cherry tomatoes, halved
- ⅓ cup minced fresh chives

1. In a small bowl, whisk the first eight ingredients until blended. Refrigerate, covered, until serving.
2. Just before serving, arrange tomatoes on a platter; drizzle with the vinaigrette. Sprinkle with chives.
Per Serving: ¾ cup equals 79 cal., 4g fat (trace sat. fat), 1mg chol., 63mg sodium, 10g carb. (6g sugars, 2g fiber), 2g pro. **Diabetic Exchanges:** ½ starch, 1 vegetable, ½ fat.

(5) INGREDIENTS **FAST FIX**

COCONUT ACORN SQUASH

Save yourself some time in the kitchen by tossing squash in the microwave to cook. Then add a little bottled chutney and coconut to take the quick dish from bland to grand.

—Deirdre Cox, Kansas City, MO

Takes: 20 min. • **Makes:** 4 servings

- 2 small acorn squash
- ¼ cup mango chutney
- ¼ cup flaked coconut
- 3 Tbsp. butter, melted
- ¼ tsp. salt
- ⅛ tsp. pepper

1. Cut each squash in half; remove and discard seeds. Place the squash halves in "a microwave-safe dish, cut side down. Microwave squash, covered, on high for 10-12 minutes or until tender.

2. Turn squash cut side up. Mix chutney, coconut and melted butter; spoon into centers of squash. Sprinkle with salt and pepper. Microwave, covered, on high for 2-3 minutes or until heated through.

Note: This recipe was tested in a 1,100-watt microwave.

Per Serving: 1 filled squash half equals 251 cal., 11g fat (7g sat. fat), 23mg chol., 400mg sodium, 39g carb. (16g sugars, 4g fiber), 2g pro.

BRUSSELS SPROUTS WITH GARLIC & GOAT CHEESE

I wanted to up the veggie game in my house, so I smothered Brussels sprouts with garlic and goat cheese. It's really a side dish, but we even eat it for lunch!
—Brenda Williams, Santa Maria, CA

Takes: 30 min.
Makes: 16 servings (⅔ cup each)

- 3 lbs. Brussels sprouts, trimmed and halved
- ¼ cup olive oil
- 8 garlic cloves, minced
- 1 tsp. salt
- ½ tsp. pepper
- 1 pkg. (5.3 oz.) fresh goat cheese, crumbled

Preheat oven to 425°. Toss first five ingredients; spread in a greased 15x10x1-in. pan. Roast until tender, 20-25 minutes, stirring occasionally. Transfer to a bowl; toss with cheese.
Per Serving: ⅔ cup: 81 cal., 5g fat (1g sat. fat), 6mg chol., 205mg sodium, 8g carb. (2g sugars, 3g fiber), 4g pro. **Diabetic Exchanges:** 1 vegetable, 1 fat.

BROWNED BUTTER ROASTED CAULIFLOWER

Growing up, my mother (who insists on loving some of the least popular vegetables) always raved about how deliciously sweet and tender cauliflower can be. The briny capers, lemon juice and sweet raisins together allow the caramelized, nutty cauliflower to shine.
—Gina Myers, Spokane, WA

Prep: 50 min. • **Bake:** 15 min.
Makes: 4 servings

- 6 garlic cloves, unpeeled
- 3 Tbsp. unsalted butter
- 1 medium head cauliflower, broken into florets
- ¼ tsp. salt
- ¼ tsp. pepper
- ¼ cup golden raisins
- ¼ cup chopped fresh parsley
- 1 Tbsp. capers, drained and coarsely chopped
- 2 tsp. lemon juice

1. Preheat oven to 400°. Cut stem ends off unpeeled garlic cloves. Wrap cloves in a piece of foil. Bake 25-30 minutes or until cloves are soft. Unwrap and cool to room temperature. Squeeze garlic from skins. Mash with a fork.
2. Meanwhile, in a small heavy saucepan, melt butter over medium heat. Heat 5-7 minutes or until golden brown, stirring constantly. Remove from heat.
3. Place cauliflower in a greased 15x10x1-in. baking pan. Drizzle with browned butter; sprinkle with salt and pepper. Toss to coat. Roast 15-20 minutes or until cauliflower is golden brown and tender.
4. Transfer to a bowl. Add remaining ingredients and roasted garlic; toss to combine.
Per serving: ¾ cup equals 148 cal., 9g fat (5g sat. fat), 23mg chol., 260mg sod., 17g carb. (10g sugars, 4g fiber), 4g pro.

LEMON DATE COUSCOUS

Couscous is a fast and perfect base for bold flavors, colors and textures—lemon, dates, carrots, spinach and almonds.
—Roxanne Chan, Albany, CA

Takes: 10 min. • **Makes:** 4 servings

- ¾ cup uncooked couscous
- ½ cup fresh baby spinach
- ½ cup shredded carrots
- ¼ cup chopped dates
- 2 Tbsp. sliced almonds
- 1 tsp. lemon juice
- ¼ tsp. grated lemon peel
- ⅛ tsp. salt
- ⅛ tsp. lemon-pepper seasoning
  Thinly sliced green onions

1. Cook the couscous according to the package directions.
2. Meanwhile, in a small bowl, combine spinach, carrots, dates, almonds, lemon juice, peel, salt and lemon-pepper. Stir in couscous. Garnish with green onions.
Per Serving: ¾ cup equals 179 cal., 2g fat (trace sat. fat), 0 chol., 104mg sodium, 37g carb. (9g sugars, 3g fiber), 6g pro. **Diabetic Exchange:** 2½ starch.

TOMATO-ONION GREEN BEANS

Fresh green beans are the star of this healthy side. For a delicious ending to a busy day, serve with grilled chicken, pork tenderloin or seafood.
—David Feder, Buffalo Grove, IL

Takes: 30 min. • **Makes:** 6 servings

- 2 Tbsp. olive oil
- 1 large onion, finely chopped
- 1 lb. fresh green beans, trimmed
- 3 Tbsp. tomato paste
- ½ tsp. salt
- 2 Tbsp. minced fresh parsley

1. In a large skillet, heat oil over medium-high heat. Add onion; cook until tender and lightly browned, stirring occasionally.
2. Meanwhile, place green beans in a large saucepan; add water to cover. Bring to a boil. Cook, covered, 5-7 minutes or until crisp-tender. Drain; add to onion. Stir in the tomato paste and salt; heat through. Sprinkle with parsley.
Per Serving: ⅔ cup equals 81 cal., 5g fat (1g sat. fat), 0 chol., 208mg sodium, 9g carb. (4g sugars, 3g fiber), 2g pro. **Diabetic Exchanges:** 1 vegetable, 1 fat.

NOTES

Seasoned to Perfection

Make Tomato-Onion Green Beans your own by adding whatever herbs and spices your family enjoys. Toss in a dash of basil or oregano. Ground cumin adds easy flair. Or simply stir in a little Italian seasoning mix.

FAMILY *FAVORITE*
♥

OH-SO-GOOD CREAMY MASHED POTATOES

I always use Yukon Golds for mashed potatoes because of their buttery flavor and low moisture content. They easily absorb the warm milk or melted butter you add to your spuds.
—Brittany Jackson, Seymour, WI

Prep: 20 min. • **Cook:** 25 min.
Makes: 18 servings

- 8 large Yukon Gold potatoes, peeled and quartered (about 6 lbs.)
- 2 tsp. salt
- 2½ cups 2% milk
- ½ cup butter, cubed
- 3 tsp. garlic salt
- 1 tsp. pepper
- ¼ cup sour cream
  Additional 2% milk, optional
  Chopped fresh parsley

1. Place potatoes and salt in a stockpot; add water to cover. Bring to a boil. Reduce heat; cook, uncovered, for 20-25 minutes or until potatoes are tender. Meanwhile, in a large saucepan, heat the milk, butter, garlic salt and pepper over medium heat until butter is melted.
2. Drain potatoes, then shake over low heat for 1-2 minutes to dry. Mash the potatoes with a potato masher or beat with a mixer; gradually add milk mixture. Stir in sour cream. Stir in additional milk to thin if desired. Sprinkle with parsley.
Per Serving: ¾ cup equals 204 cal., 7g fat (4g sat. fat), 19mg chol., 237mg sodium, 32g carb. (4g sugars, 3g fiber), 5g pro.

EASY GREEN BEANS WITH MUSHROOMS

My family actually looks forward to veggies made with sliced almonds for crunch and garlic for a little kick.
—Cheryl Wittman, Bergen, NY

Prep: 10 min. • **Cook:** 5 hours
Makes: 10 servings

- 2 lbs. fresh green beans, trimmed
- 1 lb. sliced fresh mushrooms
- 1 large onion, finely chopped
- 2 Tbsp. butter, melted
- 2 Tbsp. olive oil
- 3 garlic cloves, minced
- ½ tsp. salt
- ¼ tsp. pepper
- ½ cup sliced almonds, toasted

In a 6-qt. slow cooker, combine all the ingredients except the almonds. Cook, covered, on low until beans are tender, 5-6 hours. Remove with a slotted spoon. Top with almonds.
Note: To toast nuts, bake in a shallow pan in a 350° oven for 5-10 minutes or cook in a skillet over low heat until lightly browned, stirring nuts occasionally.
Per Serving: 1 serving equals 116 cal., 8g fat (2g sat. fat), 6mg chol., 145mg sodium, 11g carb. (4g sugars, 4g fiber), 4g pro. **Diabetic Exchanges:** 1 vegetable, 1½ fat.

TROPICAL GINGER RICE

This change-of-pace idea comes together in moments and rounds out family meals with a burst of sweet-tart flavor. Try it with dried cherries, too.
—Charlene Chambers, Ormond Beach, FL

Takes: 25 min. • **Makes:** 8 servings

- 2 cups uncooked long grain rice
- 1 Tbsp. minced fresh gingerroot
- 4 cups chicken broth
- ⅔ cup dried tropical fruit
- ⅔ cup chopped pecans, toasted

In a large saucepan, combine rice, ginger and broth; bring to a boil. Reduce heat; simmer, covered, 18-22 minutes or until liquid is absorbed and rice is tender. Stir in dried fruit and pecans.
Per Serving: 1 cup equals 186 cal., 5g fat (trace sat. fat), 2mg chol., 408mg sodium, 32g carb. (5g sugars, 1g fiber), 4g pro.

GARDEN-FRESH RAINBOW CHARD

EAT SMART ⑤ INGREDIENTS FAST FIX

Chard is a member of the beet family, prized for its green leaves and celery-like stalks. Stir up these good-for-you greens with garlic and red onion.
—*Taste of Home* Test Kitchen

Takes: 20 min. • **Makes:** 4 servings

- 2 Tbsp. olive oil
- 1 medium red onion, halved and sliced
- 3 garlic cloves, sliced
- ¼ cup chicken broth
- 2 bunches rainbow Swiss chard, coarsely chopped (about 16 cups)
- 2 Tbsp. lemon juice
- ¼ tsp. salt
- ¼ tsp. pepper

1. In a 6-qt. stockpot, heat the oil over medium-high heat. Add onion; cook and stir for 2-3 minutes or until tender. Add garlic; cook 1 minute longer.
2. Add the broth and chard; cook and stir for 5-6 minutes or until chard is tender. Remove from heat; stir in the lemon juice, salt and pepper.

Per Serving: ½ cup equals 115 cal., 7g fat (1g sat. fat), 0 chol., 631mg sodium, 11g carb. (4g sugars, 4g fiber), 4g pro. **Diabetic Exchanges:** 2 vegetable, 1½ fat.

SLOW COOKER 🍲
SIMPLE VEGETARIAN SLOW-COOKED BEANS

When I know I'll have a hungry family to feed, I go to a tasty veggie delight with beans, spinach, tomatoes and carrots. It's on our table often.
—Jennifer Reid, Farmington, ME

Prep: 15 min. • **Cook:** 4 hours
Makes: 8 servings

- 4 cans (15½ oz. each) great northern beans, rinsed and drained
- 4 medium carrots, finely chopped (about 2 cups)
- 1 cup vegetable stock
- 6 garlic cloves, minced
- 2 tsp. ground cumin
- ¾ tsp. salt
- ⅛ tsp. chili powder
- 4 cups fresh baby spinach, coarsely chopped
- 1 cup oil-packed sun-dried tomatoes, patted dry and chopped
- ⅓ cup minced fresh cilantro
- ⅓ cup minced fresh parsley

In a 3-qt. slow cooker, combine the first seven ingredients. Cook, covered, on low 4-5 hours or until carrots are tender, adding the spinach and tomatoes during the last 10 minutes of cooking. Stir in the cilantro and parsley.
Per Serving: ¾ cup equals 229 cal., 3g fat (trace sat. fat), 0 chol., 672mg sodium, 40g carb. (2g sugars, 13g fiber), 12g pro.

EAT SMART ⑤ INGREDIENTS FAST FIX
SAUTEED SQUASH WITH TOMATOES & ONIONS

My favorite meals show a love of family and food. Zucchini with tomatoes is my family's version of ratatouille.
—Adan Franco, Milwaukee, WI

Takes: 20 min. • **Makes:** 8 servings

- 2 Tbsp. olive oil
- 1 medium onion, finely chopped
- 4 medium zucchini, chopped
- 2 large tomatoes, finely chopped
- 1 tsp. salt
- ¼ tsp. pepper

1. In a large skillet, heat oil over medium-high heat. Add the onion; cook and stir for 2-4 minutes or until tender. Add zucchini; cook and stir 3 minutes.
2. Stir in tomatoes, salt and pepper; cook and stir 4-6 minutes longer or until squash is tender. Serve with a slotted spoon.
Per Serving: ¾ cup equals 60 cal., 4g fat (1g sat. fat), 0 chol., 306mg sodium, 6g carb. (4g sugars, 2g fiber), 2g pro. **Diabetic Exchanges:** 1 vegetable, ½ fat.

ROASTED SWEET POTATO WEDGES

Sweet potatoes roasted with curry and smoked paprika delight everybody at our table. The mango chutney makes a tangy dip without any work on my part.
—Maitreyi Jois, Streamwood, IL

....

Takes: 25 min. • **Makes:** 4 servings

- 2 medium sweet potatoes (about 1 lb.), cut into ½-in. wedges
- 2 Tbsp. olive oil
- 1 tsp. curry powder
- ½ tsp. salt
- ½ tsp. smoked paprika
- ⅛ tsp. coarsely ground pepper
   Minced fresh cilantro
   Mango chutney, optional

1. Preheat oven to 425°. Place the sweet potatoes in a large bowl. Mix the oil and seasonings; drizzle over sweet potatoes and toss to coat. Transfer to an ungreased 15x10x1-in. baking pan.

2. Roast for 15-20 minutes or until tender, turning occasionally. Sprinkle wedges with cilantro. If desired, serve with chutney.

Per Serving: 1 serving (calculated without chutney) equals 159 cal., 7g fat (1g sat. fat), 0 chol., 305mg sodium, 23g carb. (9g sugars, 3g fiber), 2g pro. **Diabetic Exchanges:** 1½ starch, 1½ fat.

BUTTERNUT SQUASH & POTATO MASH

Some people like squash, some people like potatoes. Mash the two together, and you've got true love! This is a smart way to get kids to eat their veggies.
—Jasmine Rose, Crystal Lake, IL

Prep: 25 min. • **Cook:** 20 min.
Makes: 10 servings

- 8 cups cubed peeled butternut squash (about 4 lbs.)
- 4 cups cubed peeled potatoes (about 4 medium)
- 16 garlic cloves, peeled
- 2 Tbsp. sesame seeds
- 1 tsp. ground cumin
- 1 cup (4 oz.) shredded Colby-Monterey Jack cheese
- 2 Tbsp. butter
- 1½ tsp. salt
- ½ tsp. pepper

1. Place squash, potatoes and garlic in a Dutch oven; add water to cover. Bring to a boil. Reduce heat; cook, uncovered, 10-15 minutes or until tender.
2. Meanwhile, in a dry small skillet, toast sesame seeds and cumin over medium-low heat 3-4 minutes or until aromatic, stirring frequently. Remove from heat.
3. Drain squash mixture. Mash vegetables, adding cheese, butter, salt and pepper. Sprinkle with sesame seed mixture.
Per Serving: ¾ cup equals 190 cal., 7g fat (4g sat. fat), 16mg chol., 448mg sod., 31g carb. (4g sugars, 4g fiber), 6g pro. **Diabetic Exchanges:** 2 starch, 1½ fat

UNDER **200** CALORIES

HERBED NOODLES WITH EDAMAME

Here's a side dish to give your meal a pop of flavor. All the fresh herbs make it feel extra-special, and frozen edamame makes it quick and easy.

—Marie Rizzio, Interlochen, MI

Takes: 30 min. • **Makes:** 4 servings

- 3½ cups uncooked egg noodles
- 2 Tbsp. butter
- 1 green onion, sliced
- 1 Tbsp. finely chopped sweet red pepper
- ½ cup frozen shelled edamame, thawed
- ¼ cup reduced-sodium chicken broth
- 1 Tbsp. minced fresh parsley
- 1½ tsp. minced fresh marjoram
- 1½ tsp. minced fresh chives
- 1 Tbsp. olive oil
- ¼ cup grated Romano cheese

1. Cook noodles according to the package directions. Meanwhile, in a large skillet, heat butter over medium-high heat. Add onion and red pepper; cook and stir until tender. Stir in edamame and broth; heat through. Add herbs.

2. Drain noodles and add to skillet; toss to combine. Transfer to a serving plate. Drizzle with oil and sprinkle with cheese.

Per Serving: 1 cup equals 264 cal., 14g fat (6g sat. fat), 50mg chol., 214mg sodium, 26g carb. (1g sugars, 2g fiber), 10g pro.

EAT SMART **FAST FIX ▶**
LEMON MUSHROOM ORZO

Sometimes I serve this lovely dish hot, sometims chilled. It brightens up any meal. Yum!

—Shelly Nelson, Akeley, MN

Takes: 25 min. • **Makes:** 12 servings

- 1 pkg. (16 oz.) orzo pasta
- 3 Tbsp. olive oil, divided
- ¾ lb. sliced fresh mushrooms
- ¾ cup chopped pecans, toasted
- ½ cup minced fresh parsley
- 1 tsp. grated lemon peel
- 3 Tbsp. lemon juice
- 1 tsp. salt
- ½ tsp. pepper

1. Cook orzo according to the package directions. Meanwhile, in a large skillet, heat 2 Tbsp. oil over medium-high heat. Add the mushrooms; cook and stir until tender and lightly browned. Drain orzo.

2. In a large bowl, place orzo, mushroom mixture, pecans, parsley, lemon peel, lemon juice, salt, pepper and remaining oil; toss to combine.

Per Serving: ¾ cup equals 225 cal., 9g fat (1g sat. fat), 0 chol., 202mg sodium, 31g carb. (2g sugars, 2g fiber), 6g pro. **Diabetic Exchanges:** 2 starch, 1 fat.

Easy Edamame

Edamame is quickly becoming popular with today's busy family cooks. Produced from early-harvested soybeans, the veggie is a good source of fiber, protein and calcium. Look for edamame in the freezer section.

"It's always a delight when I find recipes that everyone likes."

—SUSAN LASKEN, WOODLAND HILL, CA

EAT SMART
ROASTED VEGETABLES WITH SAGE

When I can't decide what vegetables to serve, I just roast a mixture. That's how we boost the "veggie love" at our house.
—Betty Fulks, Onia, AR

Prep: 20 min. • **Bake:** 35 min.
Makes: 8 servings

- 5 cups cubed peeled butternut squash
- ½ lb. fingerling potatoes (about 2 cups)
- 1 cup fresh Brussels sprouts, halved
- 1 cup fresh baby carrots
- 3 Tbsp. butter
- 1 Tbsp. minced fresh sage or 1 tsp. dried sage leaves
- 1 garlic clove, minced
- ½ tsp. salt

1. Preheat oven to 425°. Place vegetables in a large bowl. In a microwave, melt the butter; stir in remaining ingredients. Add to vegetables and toss to coat.
2. Transfer to a greased 15x10x1-in. baking pan. Roast 35-45 minutes or until tender, stirring occasionally.
Per Serving: ¾ cup equals 122 cal., 5g fat (3g sat. fat), 11mg chol., 206mg sodium, 20g carb. (4g sugars, 3g fiber), 2g pro. **Diabetic Exchanges:** 1 starch, 1 fat.

EAT SMART **(5)INGREDIENTS FAST FIX**
LEMON PEPPER ROASTED BROCCOLI

Fresh green broccoli turns tangy and tasty when roasted with lemon juice and pepper. Sprinkle with almonds for a happy crunch.
—Liz Bellville, Havelock, NC

Takes: 25 min. • **Makes:** 8 servings

- 1½ lbs. fresh broccoli florets (about 12 cups)
- 2 Tbsp. olive oil
- ½ tsp. lemon juice
- ¼ tsp. salt
- ¼ tsp. coarsely ground pepper, divided
- ¼ cup chopped almonds
- 2 tsp. grated lemon peel

1. Preheat oven to 450°. Place broccoli in a large bowl. Whisk oil, lemon juice, salt and ⅛ tsp. pepper until blended; drizzle over broccoli and toss to coat. Transfer to a 15x10x1-in. baking pan.
2. Roast 10-15 minutes or until tender. Transfer to a serving dish. Sprinkle with the almonds, lemon peel and remaining pepper; toss to combine.
Per Serving: 1 cup equals 84 cal., 6g fat (1g sat. fat), 0 chol., 103mg sodium, 7g carb. (trace sugars, 4g fiber), 4g pro. **Diabetic Exchanges:** 1 vegetable, 1 fat.

MEAL PLANNER

SIMPLE ♥ SIDES

FOUR MORE WAYS TO REACH YOUR 100-MEAL GOAL!

SLOW & SUPER

ENTREE:
Slow Cooker Beef Tips
page 14

SALAD:
Tomato-Onion
Green Beans
page 210

DESSERT:
Panna Cotta with
Papaya Coulis
page 282

TAG YOUR MEAL
MEMORIES WITH
#100 FAMILYMEALS

GROCERY LIST

KITCHEN STAPLES
- ⃝ Olive oil
- ⃝ Worcestershire sauce
- ⃝ Cornstarch
- ⃝ Sugar
- ⃝ Vanilla extract
- ⃝ Salt
- ⃝ Pepper

PRODUCE
- ⃝ 1 pint fresh raspberries
- ⃝ 1 large papaya
- ⃝ 1 lime

- ⃝ 1 small onion
- ⃝ 1 large onion
- ⃝ 2 packages (6 oz. each) sliced baby portobello mushrooms
- ⃝ 1 lb. fresh green beans
- ⃝ Potatoes for mashing
- ⃝ 1 bunch fresh parsley
- ⃝ 1 bunch fresh mint

PANTRY
- ⃝ 1 can (6 oz.) tomato paste
- ⃝ 1 can (14.5 oz.) beef broth

MEAT
- ⃝ 1 beef top sirloin steak (1 lb.)

DAIRY
- ⃝ 1 bottle (32 oz.) 2% milk
- ⃝ 1 pint heavy whipping cream

OTHER
- ⃝ 1 box (1 oz) unflavored gelatin
- ⃝ Dry red wine

SIMPLE SUPPER

ENTREE:
Bacon & Swiss
Chicken Sandwiches
page 56

SIDE:
Tomatoes with
Buttermilk Vinaigrette
page 207

DESSERT:
Lemon-Berry
Ice Cream Pie
page 264

TAG YOUR MEAL
MEMORIES WITH
#100 FAMILYMEALS

GROCERY LIST

KITCHEN STAPLES
- ⃝ Canola oil
- ⃝ Sugar
- ⃝ Celery salt
- ⃝ Ground mustard
- ⃝ 1 bottle (3.4 oz.) Montreal steak seasoning
- ⃝ Pepper

PRODUCE
- ⃝ 1 pint fresh strawberries
- ⃝ 4 lbs. cherry tomatoes
- ⃝ 1 head of lettuce
- ⃝ 1 large tomato
- ⃝ 1 bunch fresh chives

- ⃝ 1 bunch fresh tarragon

PANTRY
- ⃝ 1 Tbsp. honey
- ⃝ 1 bottle (12.7 oz.) white wine vinegar

MEAT
- ⃝ 4 boneless skinless chicken breast halves (4 oz. each)
- ⃝ 1 package (8 oz.) bacon

DAIRY
- ⃝ 1 bottle (32 oz.) buttermilk
- ⃝ 1 package (7 oz.) sliced Swiss cheese

FREEZER SECTION
- ⃝ 1 pint strawberry ice cream
- ⃝ 1 container frozen whipped topping

OTHER
- ⃝ 4 whole wheat hamburger buns
- ⃝ 1 bottle (12 oz.) Dijon mustard
- ⃝ 1 jar (15 oz.) reduced-fat mayonnaise
- ⃝ 1 graham cracker crust (9 in.)
- ⃝ 1 jar (10 oz.) lemon curd

MEAL PLANNER

SIMPLE ♥ SIDES

FOUR MORE WAYS TO REACH YOUR 100-MEAL GOAL!

SOUTHERN TREAT

ENTREE:
Crispy Fried Chicken
page 64

SIDE:
Butternut Squash &
Potato Mash
page 215

DESSERT:
Apple Pie
Oatmeal Dessert
page 261

TAG YOUR MEAL
MEMORIES WITH
#100 FAMILYMEALS

GROCERY LIST

KITCHEN STAPLES
- ○ Oil for deep-fat frying
- ○ All-purpose flour
- ○ Baking powder
- ○ Brown sugar
- ○ Garlic salt
- ○ Paprika
- ○ Poultry seasoning
- ○ Sesame seeds
- ○ Ground cumin
- ○ Vanilla extract
- ○ Salt
- ○ Pepper

PRODUCE
- ○ 3 medium apples
- ○ 4 lbs. butternut squash
- ○ 4 medium potatoes
- ○ 2 heads of garlic

PANTRY
- ○ 1 canister (18 oz.) quick-cooking oats

MEAT
- ○ 2 broiler/fryer chickens (3½ to 4 lbs. each)

DAIRY
- ○ 1 quart (32 oz.) 2% milk
- ○ Butter
- ○ 5 large eggs
- ○ 1 package (8 oz.) shredded Colby-Monterey Jack cheese

OTHER
- ○ 1 bottle (1.12 oz.) apple pie spice
- ○ 1.5 quarts vanilla ice cream

✂ -

EASY TO IMPRESS

ENTREE:
Busy-Day Pork Chops
page 109

SIDE:
Thyme-Roasted
Vegetables
page 202

DESSERT:
Coconut Brownies
page 259

TAG YOUR MEAL
MEMORIES WITH
#100 FAMILYMEALS

GROCERY LIST

KITCHEN STAPLES
- ○ Olive oil
- ○ Cooking spray
- ○ Garlic powder
- ○ Salt
- ○ Pepper

PRODUCE
- ○ 2 lbs. red potatoes
- ○ 2 large onions
- ○ 3 medium carrots
- ○ ½ lb. fresh mushrooms
- ○ 1 large sweet red pepper
- ○ 1 large sweet yellow pepper
- ○ 1 bunch fresh thyme

PANTRY
- ○ 1 canister (8 oz.) seasoned bread crumbs
- ○ 1 box (18.3 oz.) fudge brownie mix (13x9-in. pan size)

MEAT
- ○ 4 boneless pork loin chops (4 oz. each)

DAIRY
- ○ Butter
- ○ 1 quart (32 oz.) fat-free milk
- ○ 2 large eggs

- ○ 1 canister (8 oz.) grated Parmesan cheese
- ○ 1 tub (8 oz.) sour cream

OTHER
- ○ 1 can (15 oz.) coconut-pecan frosting
- ○ 1 bag (12 oz.) semisweet chocolate chips

Sides to Celebrate

Jasmine Rose cooks up Butternut Squash & Potato Mash (*p.215*) and Thyme-Roasted Vegetables (*p. 202*) for her extended family (at left).

For Jasmine Rose, there's always time for a hearty meal. "We try to eat at least one meal together each day," she says.

"While we eat, we really talk with each other. It's a value I learned from my grandmothers, Elsie and Hattie, and something I continue teaching my family today," she adds.

Jasmine plans her menus around lots of good vegetables and wholesome ingredients. "My kids were raised picking berries on farms, and I've always tried to cook with fresh, seasonal foods

because they taste so good—even in the dead of winter. Root vegetables, squash, mushrooms and home-dried herbs are so satisfying, we don't mind waiting for spring as much."

Jasmine has a large extended family with many nephews and nieces, and her vegetable side dishes prove quite popular at family gatherings. "I have a big family to celebrate with," Jasmine writes. "Our get-togethers are always eclectic, thanks to the dozens of people gathered around the table."

No matter who sits at Jasmine's table, she says there's lots of fun and plenty of belly laughs to go around. " I truly believe that food and sharing meals can bring people together," she adds. "Come to the table with kindness, and there will be abundance for all."

"We should remember this all year long, not just during holidays or special celebrations," she says. "Food makes people feel good. After all, the world needs more hugs—and bowls brimming with tasty veggies!"

"I like to think our children will recall moments enjoying food together. That's why we have sit-down meals."

-Sarah Burks, Wathena, Kansas

EASY SOUPS *and* BREADS

CREATE heartwarming moments when these classics are on the menu.

CHEESEBURGER SOUP

My mother-in-law gave me her recipe for cheeseburger soup, but I changed it a bit to make it my own. It's the perfect comfort food for a cozy night.
—Christina Addison, Blanchester, OH

Prep: 20 min. • **Cook:** 7 hours
Makes: 6 servings (2¼ qt.)

- 1 lb. lean ground beef (90% lean)
- 1 small onion, chopped
- 1¾ lbs. potatoes (about 3-4 medium), peeled and cut into ½-in. pieces
- 3 cups chicken broth
- 1½ cups whole milk
- 2 medium carrots, shredded
- 1 celery rib, finely chopped
- 1 Tbsp. dried parsley flakes
- ½ tsp. salt
- ½ tsp. dried basil
- ¼ tsp. pepper
- 1 pkg. (8 oz.) process cheese (Velveeta), cubed
- ¼ cup sour cream
  Chopped fresh parsley, optional

1. In a large skillet, cook beef and onion over medium heat 6-8 minutes or until beef is no longer pink, breaking up beef into crumbles; drain. Transfer to a 4- or 5-qt. slow cooker. Add potatoes, broth, milk, carrots, celery and the seasonings. Cook, covered, on low 7-9 hours or until vegetables are tender.
2. Stir in cheese until melted. Stir in sour cream. If desired, sprinkle with parsley.
Per Serving: 1½ cups equals 300 cal., 15g fat (8g sat. fat), 75mg chol., 949mg sodium, 21g carb. (7g sugars, 2g fiber), 19g pro.

MONKEY BREAD BISCUITS

Classic monkey bread is a sweetly spiced breakfast treat. I came up with a quick and easy savory version that nearly any family will simply love for dinner.
—Dana Johnson, Scottsdale, AZ

Takes: 20 min. • **Makes:** 1 dozen

- 1   tube (16.3 oz.) large refrigerated flaky biscuits
- 3   Tbsp. butter, melted
- 1   garlic clove, minced
- ½   tsp. Italian seasoning
- ¼   cup grated Parmesan cheese
  Additional Italian seasoning

1. Preheat oven to 425°. Separate the biscuits; cut each into six pieces. In a large bowl, combine butter, garlic and Italian seasoning; add biscuit pieces and toss to coat pieces.

2. Place four pieces of biscuit in each of twelve greased muffin cups. Sprinkle with cheese and additional Italian seasoning. Bake 8-10 minutes or until golden brown. Serve warm.

Per Serving: 1 biscuit equals 159 cal., 9g fat (3g sat. fat), 9mg chol., 418mg sodium, 16g carb. (3g sugars, 1g fiber), 3g pro.

FAMILY FAVORITE

SPEEDY CHICKEN CHOWDER

Gently spiced chowder is always good for kids, but adults can rev up their servings with hot pepper sauce. It's my go-to on busy nights.

—Andrea Early, MS, RD, Harrisonburg, VA

Prep: 15 min. • **Cook:** 25 min.
Makes: 8 servings

¼ cup butter
1 large onion, chopped
1 medium green pepper, chopped
¼ cup all-purpose flour
1 Tbsp. paprika
2 medium potatoes, peeled and chopped
1 carton (32 oz.) chicken broth
1 skinned rotisserie chicken, shredded
6 cups fresh or frozen corn
1 Tbsp. Worcestershire sauce
½ to 1 tsp. hot pepper sauce
1 tsp. salt
1 cup 2% milk

1. In a stockpot, heat the butter over medium-high heat. Add the onion and pepper; cook, stirring, until vegetables are crisp-tender, 3-4 minutes. Stir in flour and paprika until blended.
2. Add potatoes; stir in broth. Bring to a boil; reduce the heat and simmer, covered, until tender, 12-15 minutes.
3. Stir in chicken, corn, sauces and salt; bring to a boil. Reduce heat and cook, uncovered, until the corn is tender, 4-6 minutes. Add milk; heat through (do not boil).
Per Serving: 1½ cups equals 351 cal., 12g fat (5g sat. fat), 75mg chol., 920mg sodium, 39g carb. (7g sugars, 4g fiber), 25g pro.

FAST FIX
SPICY SAUSAGE SOUP WITH TORTELLINI

This soup is such a family treasure; both my daughters asked for the recipe when they moved out on their own. I cook the tortellini separately, but if you prefer you can let them plump up in the soup broth.

—Cynthia Krakowiak, Langhorne, PA

Takes: 30 min. • **Makes:** 8 servings

2 cartons (32 oz. each) chicken broth
1 lb. bulk hot or mild Italian sausage
1 pkg. (9 oz.) refrigerated cheese tortellini
1 can (14½ oz.) fire-roasted or Italian diced tomatoes
1 tsp. Italian seasoning
3 cups fresh spinach, thinly sliced

1. In a 6-qt. stockpot, bring broth to a boil. Carefully drop the sausage by heaping teaspoonfuls into the boiling broth. Add tortellini, tomatoes and Italian seasoning; return to a boil.
2. Reduce the heat; simmer, uncovered, 8-10 minutes or until sausage is cooked through and pasta is tender. Add spinach; stir until wilted.
Freeze option: Freeze the cooled soup in freezer containers. To use, partially thaw in refrigerator overnight. Heat through in a saucepan, stirring soup occasionally and adding a little broth if necessary.
Per Serving: 1½ cups equals 304 cal., 19g fat (6g sat. fat), 57mg chol., 1696mg sodium, 20g carb. (3g sugars, 2g fiber), 14g pro.

BROCCOLI-MUSHROOM BUBBLE BAKE

I got bored with the same old breakfast casseroles served at our monthly moms' meeting, so I decided to create a new version. Judging by the reactions of the other moms, this one's a keeper.
—Shannon Koene, Blacksburg, VA

....

Prep: 20 min. • **Bake:** 25 min.
Makes: 12 servings

- 1   tsp. canola oil
- ½   lb. fresh mushrooms, finely chopped
- 1   medium onion, finely chopped
- 1   tube (16.3 oz.) large refrigerated flaky biscuits
- 1   pkg. (10 oz.) frozen broccoli with cheese sauce
- 3   large eggs
- 1   can (5 oz.) evaporated milk
- 1   tsp. Italian seasoning
- ½   tsp. garlic powder
- ½   tsp. salt
- ¼   tsp. pepper
- 1½ cups (6 oz.) shredded Colby-Monterey Jack cheese

1. Preheat oven to 350°. In a large skillet, heat the oil over medium-high heat. Add the mushrooms and onion; cook and stir 4-6 minutes or until tender.

2. Cut each biscuit into eight pieces; place in a greased 13x9-in. baking dish. Top with mushroom mixture.

3. Cook the broccoli with cheese sauce according to package directions. Spoon over mushroom mixture.

4. In a large bowl, whisk eggs, milk and seasonings; pour over top. Sprinkle with cheese. Bake for 25-30 minutes or until golden brown.

Per Serving: 1 piece equals 233 cal., 13g fat (6g sat. fat), 64mg chol., 648mg sodium, 21g carb. (6g sugars, 1g fiber), 9g pro.

EASY CHEESY BISCUITS

I'm a big fan of homemade biscuits but not the rolling and cutting that goes into making them. The drop biscuit method solves everything.

—Christina Addison, Blanchester, OH

Takes: 30 min. • **Makes:** 1 dozen

- 3 cups all-purpose flour
- 3 tsp. baking powder
- 1 Tbsp. sugar
- 1 tsp. salt
- ¾ tsp. cream of tartar
- ½ cup cold butter
- 1 cup (4 oz.) shredded sharp cheddar cheese
- 1 garlic clove, minced
- ¼ to ½ tsp. crushed red pepper flakes
- 1¼ cups 2% milk

1. Preheat oven to 450°. In a large bowl, whisk flour, baking powder, sugar, salt and cream of tartar. Cut in butter until mixture resembles coarse crumbs. Stir in cheese, garlic and pepper flakes. Add milk; stir just until moistened.

2. Drop dough by heaping ¼ cupfuls 2 in. apart onto a greased baking sheet. Bake for 18-20 minutes or until golden brown. Serve warm.

Per Serving: 1 biscuit equals 237 cal., 12g fat (7g sat. fat), 32mg chol., 429mg sodium, 26g carb. (2g sugars, 1g fiber), 7g pro.

SLOW COOKER 🍲

HAM & CORN CHOWDER

When the day calls for a warm bowl of chunky soup, we haul out the slow cooker and whip up a big batch of this satisfying favorite.

—Andrea Laidlaw, Shady Side, MD

Prep: 25 min. • **Cook:** 8½ hours
Makes: 12 servings

- 1½ lbs. potatoes (about 3 medium), peeled and cut into ½-in. cubes
- 4 cups fresh or frozen corn, thawed (about 20 oz.)
- 4 cups cubed deli ham
- 2 small onions, chopped
- 4 celery ribs, chopped
- 4 garlic cloves, minced
- ¼ tsp. pepper
- 3 cups chicken broth
- 2 Tbsp. cornstarch
- 2 cups whole milk
- 2 cups (8 oz.) shredded sharp cheddar cheese
- 1 cup sour cream
- 3 Tbsp. minced fresh parsley

1. Place the first eight ingredients in a 6-qt. slow cooker. Cook, covered, on low 8-10 hours or until potatoes are tender.

2. In a small bowl, mix the cornstarch and milk until smooth; stir into soup. Cook, covered, on high 20-30 minutes or until thickened, stirring occasionally. Stir in cheese, sour cream and parsley until cheese is melted.

Per Serving: 1¼ cups equals 291 cal., 14g fat (8g sat. fat), 65mg chol., 974mg sodium, 23g carb. (7g sugars, 2g fiber), 19g pro.

HEARTY MACARONI VEGETABLE SOUP

Requiring just a few minutes of prep, this delightful soup truly couldn't be easier to make. Simply open up the containers, pour the ingredients into a pot and the soup is practically done!
—Metzel Turley, South Charleston, WV

Takes: 25 min. • **Makes:** 7 servings

- 1 pkg. (1.4 oz.) vegetable soup mix
- 1 envelope (.6 oz.) cream of chicken soup mix
- 2 cans (5½ oz. each) spicy tomato juice
- 4 cups water
- 2 cans (15 oz. each) mixed vegetables, drained
  Dash crushed red pepper flakes
  Dash dried minced garlic
- ½ cup uncooked elbow macaroni

In a Dutch oven, combine soup mixes and tomato juice. Stir in water, mixed vegetables, pepper flakes and garlic; bring to a boil. Add macaroni. Reduce heat; cook, uncovered, 10-15 minutes or until the macaroni is tender, stirring soup occasionally.
Per Serving: 1 cup equals 94 cal., 1g fat (trace sat. fat), trace chol., 944mg sodium, 19g carb. (6g sugars, 3g fiber), 4g pro.

KiDS in the KiTCHeN

Preparing Cheddar Corn Dog Muffins? Let little ones line the muffin cups and stir the batter. Older kids can fill the cups.

⑤INGREDIENTS FAST FIX

CHEDDAR CORN DOG MUFFINS

I wanted a change from hot dogs, so I made corn dog muffins. Adding some jalapenos to this kid-friendly recipe won over my husband, too.
—Becky Tarala, Palm Coast, FL

Takes: 25 min. • **Makes:** 9 muffins

- 1 pkg. (8½ oz.) corn bread/muffin mix
- ⅔ cup 2% milk
- 1 large egg, lightly beaten
- 5 turkey hot dogs, sliced
- ½ cup shredded sharp cheddar cheese
- 2 Tbsp. finely chopped pickled jalapeno, optional

1. Preheat the oven to 400°. Line nine muffin cups with foil liners or grease nine nonstick muffin cups.
2. In a small bowl, combine muffin mix, milk and egg; stir in hot dogs, cheese and, if desired, jalapeno. Fill the prepared cups three-fourths full.
3. Bake 14-18 minutes or until a toothpick inserted in center comes out clean. Cool for 5 minutes before removing from pan to a wire rack. Serve warm. Refrigerate any leftovers.
Freeze option: Freeze the cooled muffins in resealable plastic freezer bags. To use, microwave each muffin on high for 30-60 seconds or until heated through.
Per Serving: 1 muffin equals 216 cal., 10g fat (4g sat. fat), 46mg chol., 619mg sodium, 23g carb. (7g sugars, 2g fiber), 8g pro.

GREAT GARLIC BREAD

This tasty garlic bread topped with flavor makes a great side for any pasta dish.
—*Taste of Home* Test Kitchen

Takes: 15 min. • **Makes:** 8 servings

½ cup butter, melted
¼ cup grated Romano cheese
4 garlic cloves, minced
1 loaf (1 lb.) French bread, halved lengthwise
2 Tbsp. minced fresh parsley

1. Preheat oven to 350°. In a small bowl, mix butter, cheese and garlic; brush over cut sides of bread. Place on a baking sheet, cut side up. Sprinkle with parsley.
2. Bake 7-9 minutes or until light golden brown. Cut into slices; serve warm.
Per Serving: 1 slice equals 283 cal., 14g fat (8g sat. fat), 34mg chol., 457mg sodium, 33g carb. (1g sugars, 1g fiber), 8g pro.

THE ULTIMATE CHICKEN NOODLE SOUP

Our first Wisconsin winter was so cold, all I wanted to eat was soup. This recipe is in heavy rotation from November to April at our house.
—Gina Nistico, Milwaukee, WI

Prep: 15 min. • **Cook:** 45 min. + standing
Makes: 10 servings

2½ lbs. bone-in chicken thighs
1¼ tsp. pepper, divided
½ tsp. salt
1 Tbsp. canola oil
1 large onion, chopped (about 2 cups)
1 garlic clove, minced
10 cups chicken broth
4 celery ribs, chopped (about 2 cups)
4 medium carrots, chopped (about 2 cups)
2 bay leaves
1 tsp. minced fresh thyme or ¼ tsp. dried thyme
3 cups uncooked kluski or other egg noodles (about 8 oz.)
1 Tbsp. chopped fresh parsley
1 Tbsp. lemon juice

1. Pat the chicken dry with paper towels; sprinkle with ½ tsp. pepper and salt. In a 6-qt. stockpot, heat oil over medium-high heat. Add chicken in batches, skin side down; cook for 3-4 minutes or until dark golden brown. Remove chicken from pot; remove and discard the skin. Discard the drippings, reserving 2 Tbsp.
2. Add onion to drippings; cook and stir over medium-high heat 4-5 minutes or until tender. Add garlic; cook 1 minute longer. Add broth, stirring to loosen browned bits from pan. Bring to a boil. Return chicken to the pot. Add celery, carrots, bay leaves and thyme. Reduce heat; simmer, covered, 25-30 minutes or until chicken is tender.
3. Transfer chicken to a plate. Remove soup from heat. Add noodles; let stand, covered, 20-22 minutes or until noodles are tender.
4. Meanwhile, when the chicken is cool enough to handle, remove meat from bones; discard bones. Shred meat into bite-size pieces. Return meat to pot. Stir in parsley and lemon juice. Adjust the seasoning with salt and remaining ¾ tsp. pepper. Remove bay leaves.
Per Serving: 1⅓ cups equals 239 cal., 12g fat (3g sat. fat), 68mg chol., 1176mg sodium, 14g carb. (3g sugars, 2g fiber), 18g pro.

Get to Know Kluski Noodles

Kluski is a generic name for Polish egg noodles. They combine the best of Old and New Worlds: the tender texture of a handmade noodle in a go-to pantry item. Try them when you want to add "homemade flair" to your next batch of soup or to your favorite noodle casserole.

HAM & GREEN ONION BISCUITS

I started with my grandmother's biscuits and added a few of my own ingredients. When I make them with my kids, it feels like she's with us.
—Amy Chase, Vanderhoof, BC

Prep: 20 min. • **Bake:** 10 min.
Makes: about 1 dozen

- 2 cups all-purpose flour
- 3 tsp. baking powder
- 1 tsp. sugar
- ¼ tsp. garlic salt
  Dash pepper
- 6 Tbsp. cold butter, cubed
- 1 cup finely chopped fully cooked ham
- 2 green onions, chopped
- ¾ cup 2% milk

1. Preheat oven to 450°. In a large bowl, whisk the first five ingredients. Cut in butter until mixture resembles coarse crumbs. Stir in ham and green onions. Add milk; stir just until moistened.
2. Turn the dough onto a lightly floured surface; knead gently 8-10 times. Pat or roll dough to ½-in. thickness; cut with a floured 2½-in. biscuit cutter. Place 2 in. apart on an ungreased baking sheet. Bake for 10-12 minutes or until golden brown. Serve warm.
Per Serving: 1 biscuit equals 151 cal., 7g fat (4g sat. fat), 23mg chol., 315mg sodium, 17g carb. (1g sugars, 1g fiber), 5g pro.

TASTE OF HOME
BEST EVER
TEST KITCHEN

CHIMICHURRI MONKEY BREAD

The herby goodness of my favorite sauce shines in this nostalgic bread recipe that comes together quickly, thanks to refrigerated biscuits. Serve warm alongside Italian entrees or, with marinara for dipping, as an appetizer.
—Eden Dranger, Los Angeles, CA

Prep: 20 min. • **Bake:** 20 min.
Makes: 12 servings

- ¼ cup minced fresh parsley
- ¼ cup olive oil
- 2 Tbsp. minced fresh oregano
- 1 Tbsp. white wine vinegar
- 2 garlic cloves
- ¾ tsp. kosher salt
- ¼ tsp. ground cumin
- ¼ tsp. pepper
- ⅛ tsp. crushed red pepper flakes
- 2 tubes (12 oz. each) refrigerated buttermilk biscuits

1. In a shallow bowl, combine first nine ingredients. Cut each biscuit in half and shape into a ball. Roll in herb mixture.
2. Place biscuit pieces in a greased 10-in. fluted tube pan. Bake bread at 375° for 18-22 minutes or until golden brown. Cool for 5 minutes before inverting onto a serving plate.
Per Serving: 1 serving equals 179 cal., 6g fat (1g sat. fat), 0 chol., 603mg sodium, 27g carb. (trace sugars, trace fiber), 5g pro.

HERBY PARMESAN BREAD

I've been making my Parmesan bread for so many years, I can no longer recall where I got the recipe! But thanks to the convenient baking mix, you can get this loaf into the oven fast.

—Lesley Archer, Chapala, Mexico

Prep: 10 min. • **Bake:** 35 min. + cooling
Makes: 1 loaf (12 slices)

- 3¾ cups biscuit/baking mix
- 1 cup plus 2 Tbsp. grated Parmesan cheese, divided
- 1 tsp. Italian seasoning
- ½ tsp. salt
- 1 large egg
- 1 can (5 oz.) evaporated milk
- ¾ cup water

1. Preheat oven to 350°. In a large bowl, combine biscuit mix, 1 cup cheese, Italian seasoning and salt. In a small bowl, whisk the egg, milk and water. Stir into the dry ingredients just until moistened. Transfer to a greased 8x4-in. loaf pan. Sprinkle with remaining cheese.
2. Bake 35-40 minutes or until a toothpick inserted in center comes out clean. Cool 10 minutes before removing from pan to a wire rack.
Per Serving: 1 slice equals 207 cal., 9g fat (4g sat. fat), 28mg chol., 702mg sodium, 25g carb. (2g sugars, 1g fiber), 7g pro.

BASIL TOMATO SOUP WITH ORZO

The soup is so scrumptious that it's worth the little time it takes to chop up fresh onion, garlic and basil. It's even better the next day after all the flavors have had a chance to blend together.

—Tonia Billbe, Elmira, NY

Prep: 15 min. • **Cook:** 25 min.
Makes: 16 servings

- 1 large onion, chopped
- ¼ cup butter, cubed
- 2 garlic cloves, minced
- 3 cans (28 oz. each) crushed tomatoes
- 1 carton (32 oz.) chicken broth
- 1 cup loosely packed basil leaves, chopped
- 1 Tbsp. sugar
- ½ tsp. pepper
- 1¼ cups uncooked orzo pasta
- 1 cup heavy whipping cream
- ½ cup grated Romano cheese

1. In a Dutch oven, saute onion in butter for 3 minutes. Add the garlic; cook for 1-2 minutes longer or until onion is tender. Stir in the tomatoes, broth, basil, sugar and pepper. Bring to a boil. Reduce heat; cover and simmer for 15 minutes.
2. Meanwhile, cook the orzo according to package directions; drain. Add the orzo and cream to soup; heat through (do not boil). Sprinkle servings with cheese.
Per Serving: 1 cup equals 204 cal., 10g fat (6g sat. fat), 33mg chol., 533mg sodium, 24g carb. (2g sugars, 3g fiber), 7g pro.

SPINACH & TORTELLINI SOUP

My tomato broth is perfect for cheese tortellini and fresh spinach in this fast fix. Add extra garlic, oregano and basil to suit your taste.
—Debbie Wilson, Burlington, NC

Takes: 20 min. • **Makes:** 6 servings

- 1 tsp. olive oil
- 2 garlic cloves, minced
- 1 can (14½ oz.) no-salt-added diced tomatoes, undrained
- 3 cans (14½ oz. each) vegetable broth
- 2 tsp. Italian seasoning
- 1 pkg. (9 oz.) refrigerated cheese tortellini
- 4 cups fresh baby spinach
  Shredded Parmesan cheese and freshly ground pepper

1. In a large saucepan, heat the oil over medium heat. Add garlic; cook and stir for 1 minute. Stir in tomatoes, broth and Italian seasoning; bring to a boil. Add the tortellini; bring to a gentle boil. Cook, uncovered, 7-9 minutes or just until the tortellini are tender.

2. Stir in spinach. Sprinkle servings with cheese and pepper.

Per Serving: 1⅓ cups (calculated without cheese) equals 162 cal., 5g fat (2g sat. fat), 18mg chol., 998mg sodium, 25g carb. (4g sugars, 2g fiber), 6g pro.

GRANDMA'S BISCUITS

Homemade biscuits add a warm, comforting touch to any meal. My grandmother makes these tender biscuits to go with chowder.
—Melissa Obernesser, Utica, NY

Takes: 25 min. • **Makes:** 10 biscuits

- 2 cups all-purpose flour
- 3 tsp. baking powder
- 1 tsp. salt
- ⅓ cup shortening
- ⅔ cup 2% milk
- 1 large egg, lightly beaten

1. Preheat oven to 450°. In a large bowl, whisk flour, baking powder and salt. Cut in shortening until the mixture resembles coarse crumbs. Add milk; stir just until mixture is moistened.

2. Turn onto a lightly floured surface; knead gently 8-10 times. Pat dough into a 10x4-in. rectangle. Cut the rectangle lengthwise in half; cut crosswise to make 10 squares.

3. Place 1 in. apart on ungreased baking sheet; brush tops with egg. Bake biscuits for 8-10 minutes or until golden brown. Serve warm.

Per Serving: 1 biscuit equals 165 cal., 7g fat (2g sat. fat), 20mg chol., 371mg sodium, 20g carb. (1g sugars, 1g fiber), 4g pro.

PEPPERONI PIZZA SOUP

Once upon a time, my husband and I owned a pizzeria where this dish was always popular. We've since sold the restaurant, but I still make the soup pretty regularly.
—Estella Peterson, Madras, OR

Prep: 20 min. • **Cook:** 8¼ hours
Makes: 6 servings

- 2 cans (14½ oz. each) Italian stewed tomatoes, undrained
- 2 cans (14½ oz. each) reduced-sodium beef broth
- 1 small onion, chopped
- 1 small green pepper, chopped
- ½ cup sliced fresh mushrooms
- ½ cup sliced pepperoni, halved
- 1½ tsp. dried oregano
- ⅛ tsp. pepper
- 1 pkg. (9 oz.) refrigerated cheese ravioli
  Shredded part-skim mozzarella cheese and sliced ripe olives

1. In a 4-qt. slow cooker, combine the first eight ingredients. Cook mixture, covered, on low 8-9 hours.

2. Stir in the ravioli; cook, covered, on low 15-30 minutes or until pasta is tender. Top servings with cheese and olives.

Per Serving: 1½ cups (calculated without cheese and olives) equals 203 cal., 6g fat (3g sat. fat), 26mg chol., 1008mg sodium, 28g carb. (8g sugars, 4g fiber), 10g pro.

"Picking up fast food would be an easy solution, but it doesn't feed the soul like serving something you prepared yourself."
—BECKY LOHMILLER, MONTICELLO, IN

HERB QUICK BREAD

This simple loaf is especially good with soups and stews, but slices are also tasty alongside fresh green salads. The herbs make it a flavorful addition to dinner any time of the year.

—Donna Roberts, Manhattan, KS

Prep: 15 min. • **Bake:** 40 min. + cooling
Makes: 1 loaf (16 slices)

- 3 cups all-purpose flour
- 3 Tbsp. sugar
- 1 Tbsp. baking powder
- 3 tsp. caraway seeds
- ½ tsp. salt
- ½ tsp. ground nutmeg
- ½ tsp. dried thyme
- 1 large egg
- 1 cup fat-free milk
- ⅓ cup canola oil

1. Preheat oven to 350°. In a large bowl, whisk first seven ingredients. In another bowl, whisk egg, milk and oil until blended. Add to flour mixture; stir just until mixture is moistened.

2. Transfer the dough to a 9x5-in. loaf pan coated with cooking spray. Bake the bread for 40-50 minutes or until a toothpick inserted in center comes out clean. Cool in pan 10 minutes before removing to a wire rack to cool.

Per Serving: 1 slice equals 147 cal., 5g fat (1g sat. fat), 12mg chol., 160mg sodium, 21g carb. (3g sugars, 1g fiber), 3g pro. **Diabetic Exchanges:** 1½ starch, 1 fat.

PESTO BREADSTICKS

Calling for only a handful of ingredients, these savory bites are the perfect additions to quick weeknight menus.
—*Taste of Home* Test Kitchen

....

Takes: 20 min. • **Makes:** 1 dozen

- 1 tube (11 oz.) refrigerated breadsticks
- 2 Tbsp. prepared pesto
- ¼ tsp. garlic pepper blend
- 1 Tbsp. butter, melted
- 2 Tbsp. shredded Parmesan cheese

1. Unroll and separate breadsticks; place on an ungreased baking sheet. Combine the pesto and garlic pepper; brush over the breadsticks. Twist each breadstick three times.
2. Brush with butter; sprinkle with cheese. Bake at 375° for 10-13 minutes or until golden brown. Serve warm.

Per Serving: 1 breadstick equals 95 cal., 4g fat (2g sat. fat), 4mg chol., 231mg sodium, 13g carb. (1g sugars, trace fiber), 3g pro. **Diabetic Exchanges:** 1 starch, ½ fat.

CHICKEN BARLEY CHOWDER

My kids always ask for leftovers of this 30-minute soup for their lunches. It's my favorite way to get barley on the family table. The mashed squash helps make it creamy but not heavy.
—Pamela Cleghorn, Campbellsburg, IN

....

Takes: 30 min.
Makes: 8 servings

- 2 Tbsp. olive oil
- 1 lb. boneless skinless chicken breasts, cut into ¾-in. pieces
- 1 small onion, finely chopped

- 1 pkg. (12 oz.) frozen mashed winter squash, thawed (about 1⅓ cups)
- ¾ cup quick-cooking barley
- 2 tsp. reduced-sodium taco seasoning
- ½ tsp. salt
- ¼ tsp. pepper
- 1 carton (32 oz.) reduced-sodium chicken broth
- 1 can (15 oz.) black beans, rinsed and drained
- 2 cups frozen corn
- 1 cup half-and-half cream
- ½ cup salsa
- ½ cup chopped fresh cilantro
  Diced avocado and chopped tomatoes, optional

1. In a 6-qt. stockpot, heat the oil over medium-high heat. Add chicken and onion; cook and stir 2-3 minutes or just until onion is tender.
2. Stir in the squash, barley, seasonings and broth; bring to a boil. Reduce heat; simmer, covered, 10-12 minutes or until barley is tender.
3. Add beans, corn, cream, salsa and cilantro; heat mixture through, stirring occasionally. If desired, serve soup with avocado and tomatoes.

Freeze option: Freeze the cooled soup in freezer containers. To use, partially thaw in refrigerator overnight. Heat through in a saucepan, stirring occasionally and adding a little broth or milk if necessary.

Per Serving: 1¼ cups (calculated without avocado and tomatoes) equals 298 cal., 8g fat (3g sat. fat), 46mg chol., 681mg sodium, 35g carb. (4g sugars, 7g fiber), 20g pro. **Diabetic Exchanges:** 2 starch, 2 lean meat, 1 fat.

TORTELLINI PRIMAVERA SOUP

Years ago, I ran across an idea for combining tortellini with peas and carrots, and I added my own touch. Skip the basil if you don't have any .
—Kari George, Ellicott City, MD

Takes: 25 min. •**Makes:** 4 servings

- 2 **cartons (32 oz. each) reduced-sodium chicken broth**
- 1 **pkg. (10 oz.) julienned carrots**
- 1 **pkg. (9 oz.) refrigerated cheese tortellini**
- 1 **cup frozen peas (about 4 oz.)**
- ¼ **tsp. pepper**
  Thinly sliced fresh basil leaves

1. In a large saucepan, bring the broth to a boil. Add the carrots, tortellini, peas and pepper; return to a boil. Cook, uncovered, 7-9 minutes or until pasta is tender. Top individual servings with basil.
Freeze option: Freeze the cooled soup in freezer containers. To use, partially thaw soup in the refrigerator overnight. Heat through in a saucepan, stirring occasionally.
Per Serving: 2¼ cups equals 282 cal., 6g fat (3g sat. fat), 28mg chol., 1461mg sodium, 43g carb. (9g sugars, 5g fiber), 17g pro.

MARINA'S GOLDEN CORN FRITTERS

Just one bite of these fritters takes me back to when my children were young. They're all grown up now, but the happy tradition lives on at get-togethers. Serve the fritters with maple syrup for dipping.
—Marina Castle, Canyon Country, CA

Takes: 30 min. •**Makes:** 32 fritters

- 2½ **cups all-purpose flour**
- 3 **tsp. baking powder**
- 2 **tsp. dried parsley flakes**
- 1 **tsp. salt**
- 2 **large eggs**
- ¾ **cup 2% milk**
- 2 **Tbsp. butter, melted**
- 2 **tsp. grated onion**
- 1 **can (15¼ oz.) whole kernel corn, drained**
  Oil for deep-fat frying

1. In a large bowl, whisk the flour, baking powder, parsley and salt. In another bowl, whisk eggs, milk, melted butter and onion until blended. Add to the dry ingredients, stirring just until moistened. Fold in corn.
2. In an electric skillet or deep fryer, heat oil to 375°. Drop batter by tablespoonfuls, several at a time, into hot oil. Fry fritters 2-3 minutes on each side or until golden brown. Drain on paper towels.
Per Serving: 2 fritters equals 162 cal., 8g fat (2g sat. fat), 28mg chol., 327mg sodium, 18g carb. (2g sugars, 1g fiber), 4g pro.

HONEY BEER BREAD

It's true. This yummy bread requires only four ingredients! Just mix them up, pour the batter into the pan and bake.
—Cak Marshall, Salem, OR

Prep: 5 min. • **Bake:** 45 min. + cooling
Makes: 1 loaf (12 slices)

- 3 **cups self-rising flour**
- 3 **Tbsp. sugar**
- ⅓ **cup honey**
- 1 **bottle (12 oz.) beer**

1. Preheat oven to 350°. In a large bowl, whisk flour and sugar. Stir in honey and beer just until moistened.
2. Transfer to a greased 8x4-in. loaf pan. Bake 45-50 minutes or until a toothpick inserted in center comes out clean. Cool in pan for10 minutes before removing to a wire rack to cool.
Per Serving: 1 slice equals 163 cal., 0 fat (0 sat. fat), 0 chol., 374mg sodium, 35g carb. (12g sugars, 1g fiber), 3g pro.

TENDER WHOLE WHEAT MUFFINS

Want light and nourishing oven-baked treats? Simple whole wheat muffins are wonderful paired with just about any meal or as an after-school snack.
—Kristine Chayes Smithtown, NY

Takes: 30 min. • **Makes:** 10 muffins

- 1 cup all-purpose flour
- 1 cup whole wheat flour
- 2 Tbsp. sugar
- 2½ tsp. baking powder
- 1 tsp. salt
- 1 large egg
- 1¼ cups milk
- 3 Tbsp. butter, melted

1. Preheat oven to 400°. In a large bowl, whisk flours, sugar, baking powder and salt. In another bowl, whisk egg, milk and melted butter until blended. Add to flour mixture; stir just until moistened.

2. Fill greased muffin cups three-fourths full. Bake muffins 15-17 minutes or until a toothpick inserted in center comes out clean. Cool 5 minutes before removing from pan to a wire rack. Serve warm.

Per Serving: 1 muffin equals 152 cal., 5g fat (3g sat. fat), 35mg chol., 393mg sodium, 22g carb. (4g sugars, 2g fiber), 5g pro. **Diabetic Exchanges:** 1½ starch, 1 fat.

TUSCAN CHICKEN SOUP

Change up your traditional chicken soup by adding healthy white kidney beans and some greens. This dish is a great way to use up any leftover chicken.
—Rosemary Goetz, Hudson, NY

Prep: 15 min. • **Cook:** 20 min.
Makes: 4 servings

- 1 small onion, chopped
- 1 small carrot, sliced
- 1 Tbsp. olive oil
- 2 cans (14½ oz. each) chicken broth
- 1 cup water
- ¾ tsp. salt
- ¼ tsp. pepper
- 1 can (15 oz.) white kidney or cannellini beans, rinsed and drained
- ⅔ cup uncooked small spiral pasta
- 3 cups thinly sliced fresh escarole or spinach
- 2 cups shredded cooked chicken

1. In a large saucepan, saute the onion and carrot in oil until onion is tender. Add the broth, water, salt and pepper; bring to a boil. Stir in the beans and pasta; return to a boil.

2. Reduce heat; cover and simmer soup 15 minutes or until pasta and vegetables are tender, stirring occasionally. Add the escarole and chicken; heat through.

Per Serving: 1½ cup equals 329 cal., 10g fat (2g sat. fat), 67mg chol., 1542mg sodium, 30g carb. (3g sugars, 6g fiber), 28g pro.

SAVORY CORN BREAD

When you want to serve up some corn bread, look no further than this recipe. It's the best—on the table at home and at potlucks.
—Krista Klaus, Round Rock, TX

Prep/Total: 30 min. • **Makes:** 9 servings

- 1 cup yellow cornmeal
- ½ cup all-purpose flour
- 3 tsp. baking powder
- 1 tsp. salt
- ½ tsp. baking soda
- 1 large egg
- 1 cup buttermilk
- ½ cup 2% milk
- ¼ cup canola oil

1. Preheat oven to 450°. In a small bowl, whisk cornmeal, flour, baking powder, salt and baking soda. In another bowl, whisk egg, buttermilk, milk and oil until blended. Add liquids to the flour mixture; stir just until moistened.

2. Transfer to a greased 8-in. square baking pan. Bake 15-18 minutes or until a toothpick inserted in center comes out clean. Serve warm.

Per Serving: 1 piece equals 170 cal., 8g fat (1g sat. fat), 23mg chol., 533mg sodium, 21g carb. (2g sugars, 1g fiber), 4g pro.

OLIVE & ONION QUICK BREAD

I've been baking for more than 50 years, and I still feel like I'm an artist creating a masterpiece of love. Make extra loaves of this olive bread to give away.
—Paula Marchesi, Lenhartsville, PA

Prep: 15 min. • **Bake:** 45 min. + cooling
Makes: 1 loaf (12 slices)

- 1 Tbsp. canola oil
- 1 medium onion, finely chopped
- 2 cups all-purpose flour
- 1 Tbsp. minced fresh rosemary
- 1 tsp. baking soda
- ½ tsp. salt
- 2 large eggs
- 1 cup buttermilk
- 2 Tbsp. butter, melted
- ¼ cup plus 2 Tbsp. sharp cheddar cheese, divided
- ¼ cup each chopped pitted green and ripe olives

1. Preheat oven to 350°. In a skillet, heat oil over medium-high heat. Add onion; cook and stir 2-3 minutes or until tender. Remove from heat.

2. In a large bowl, whisk flour, rosemary, baking soda and salt. In another bowl, whisk eggs, buttermilk and melted butter until blended. Add to the flour mixture; stir just until moistened. Fold in ¼ cup cheese, olives and onion.

3. Transfer to a greased 8x4-in. loaf pan. Bake for 40 minutes. Sprinkle remaining cheese over top. Bake 5-10 minutes longer or until a toothpick inserted in the center comes out clean. Cool in pan 10 minutes before removing to a wire rack to cool.

Per Serving: 1 slice equals 150 cal., 6g fat (2g sat. fat), 41mg chol., 373mg sodium, 18g carb. (1g sugars, 1g fiber), 5g pro.

EASY CHICKEN CORN CHOWDER

I often play around with ingredients already in my pantry instead of running to the store when I haven't planned for dinner. This was the happy result of one experiment! Omit the bacon to cut fat.
—Barbara Banski, Fenton, MI

Takes: 30 min. • **Makes:** 4 servings

- 2 Tbsp. butter
- 1 small onion, finely chopped
- 1 celery rib, finely chopped
- 1 small sweet red pepper, finely chopped
- 2 cans (14¾ oz. each) cream-style corn
- 1½ cups chopped cooked chicken
- 1 can (12 oz.) reduced-fat evaporated milk
- 1 tsp. chicken bouillon granules
- ½ tsp. pepper
- 8 bacon strips, cooked and crumbled

1. In a large saucepan, heat the butter over medium-high heat. Add onion, celery and red pepper; cook and stir 6-8 minutes or until tender.

2. Stir in corn, chicken, milk, bouillon and pepper; heat through, stirring occasionally (do not boil). Top servings with bacon.

Per Serving: 1½ cups equal 474 cal., 18g fat (7g sat. fat), 94mg chol., 1252mg sodium, 51g carb. (18g sugars, 3g fiber), 31g pro.

3. Remove from grill. Spoon plum tomato mixture over crust; top with cheese and cherry tomatoes. Return flatbread to grill. Grill, covered, 2-4 minutes or until crust is golden brown and cheese is melted.

To bake flatbread: Preheat oven to 425°. Unroll and press the dough onto bottom of a 15x10x1-in. baking pan coated with cooking spray. Bake for 6-8 minutes or until lightly browned. Assemble the flatbread as directed. Bake 8-10 minutes longer or until the crust is golden and cheese is melted.

Per Serving: 1 piece equals 235 cal., 9g fat (3g sat. fat), 12mg chol., 476mg sodium, 29g carb. (7g sugars, 3g fiber), 8g pro. **Diabetic Exchanges:** 1½ starch, 1 vegetable, 1½ fat.

⑤INGREDIENTS FAST FIX

CREAMY CHICKEN SOUP

Kids won't think twice about eating vegetables once they're mixed into a creamy, cheesy soup.
—LaVonne Lundgren, Sioux City, IA

Takes: 30 min. • **Makes:** 7 servings

- 4 cups cubed cooked chicken breast
- 3½ cups water
- 2 cans (10¾ oz. each) condensed cream of chicken soup, undiluted
- 1 pkg. (16 oz.) frozen mixed vegetables, thawed
- 1 can (14½ oz.) diced potatoes, drained
- 1 pkg. (16 oz.) process cheese (Velveeta), cubed

In a Dutch oven, combine the first five ingredients. Bring to a boil. Reduce heat; cover and simmer for 8-10 minutes or until vegetables are tender. Stir in cheese just until melted (do not boil).

Per Serving: 1½ cups equals 481 cal., 24g fat (12g sat. fat), 121mg chol., 1650mg sodium, 26g carb. (8g sugars, 4g fiber), 39g pro.

EAT SMART FAST FIX

TRIPLE TOMATO FLATBREAD

Tomatoes are the main reason I have a vegetable garden. I developed this dish to show off my plum, sun-dried and cherry tomatoes. Always a welcome sight on the table, it's also easy to make.
—Rachel Kimbrow, Portland, OR

Takes: 20 min. • **Makes:** 8 pieces

- 1 tube (13.8 oz.) refrigerated pizza crust
  Cooking spray
- 3 plum tomatoes, finely chopped (about 2 cups)
- ½ cup soft sun-dried tomato halves (not packed in oil), julienned
- 2 Tbsp. olive oil
- 1 Tbsp. dried basil
- ¼ tsp. salt
- ¼ tsp. pepper
- 1 cup shredded Asiago cheese
- 2 cups yellow and/or red cherry tomatoes, halved

1. Unroll and press the pizza dough into a 15x10-in. rectangle. Transfer dough to an 18x12-in. piece of heavy-duty foil coated with cooking spray; spritz dough with cooking spray. In a large bowl, toss plum tomatoes and sun-dried tomatoes with oil and seasonings.

2. Carefully invert dough onto grill rack; remove foil. Grill, covered, over medium heat 2-3 minutes or until bottom is golden brown. Turn; grill for 1-2 minutes longer or until second side begins to brown.

CHEESE & PESTO BISCUITS

Biscuits always liven up a meal, especially when they're golden brown and filled with pesto, garlic and cheese for a little extra zip.
—Liz Bellville, Havelock, NC

Takes: 25 min. • **Makes:** 1 dozen

2 cups all-purpose flour
2 tsp. baking powder
½ tsp. salt
¼ tsp. baking soda
⅓ cup cold butter, cubed
1 cup (4 oz.) shredded Italian cheese blend
1¼ cups buttermilk
1 Tbsp. prepared pesto
1 Tbsp. butter, melted
1 garlic clove, minced

1. Preheat oven to 450°. In a large bowl, whisk the flour, baking powder, salt and baking soda. Cut in the butter until the mixture resembles coarse crumbs. Stir in cheese. In a small bowl, whisk the buttermilk and pesto until blended; stir into flour mixture just until moistened.
2. Drop dough by ¼ cupfuls 2 in. apart onto an ungreased baking sheet. Bake 10-12 minutes or until golden brown.
3. Mix melted butter and garlic; brush over biscuits. Serve warm.
Per Serving: 1 biscuit equals 175 cal., 9g fat (5g sat. fat), 24mg chol., 357mg sodium, 18g carb. (1g sugars, 1g fiber), 5g pro.

SHORTCUT SAUSAGE MINESTRONE

I call this surprisingly good soup my magic soup for its soothing powers. When she needs a healing touch, my daughter-in-law always asks for it.
—Marta Smith, Claremont, PA

Takes: 25 min. • **Makes:** 6 servings

¾ lb. Italian turkey sausage links, casings removed
1 small green pepper, chopped
1 small onion, chopped
2 cups cut fresh green beans or frozen cut green beans
2 cups water
1 can (16 oz.) kidney beans, rinsed and drained
1 can (14½ oz.) diced tomatoes with basil, oregano and garlic, undrained
1 can (14½ oz.) reduced-sodium chicken broth
¾ cup uncooked ditalini or other small pasta

1. In a 6-qt. stockpot, cook the sausage, pepper and onion over medium heat for 5-7 minutes or until the sausage is no longer pink, breaking up sausage into crumbles; drain.
2. Add green beans, water, kidney beans, tomatoes and broth; bring to a boil. Stir in ditalini; cook, uncovered, 10-11 minutes or until pasta is tender, stirring occasionally.
Per Serving: 1⅓ cups equals 232 cal., 4g fat (1g sat. fat), 21mg chol., 773mg sodium, 34g carb. (6g sugars, 7g fiber), 16g pro.

READY IN
25
MINUTES

FAST FIX ▶
HERBED CHEESE STICKS

We love the breadsticks we get at our local pizza parlor, but now I make the same wonderful cheesy sticks at home.
—Heather Bates, Athens, ME

Takes: 30 min. • **Makes:** 16 cheese sticks

- 1 pkg. (6½ oz.) pizza crust mix
- 1½ tsp. garlic powder
- 1 Tbsp. olive oil
- 1 cup (4 oz.) shredded part-skim mozzarella cheese
- ¼ cup shredded Parmesan cheese
- 1 tsp. Italian seasoning
  Pizza sauce

1. Preheat oven to 450°. Mix the pizza dough according to package directions, adding garlic powder to dry mix. Cover; let rest 5 minutes.
2. Knead dough 4-5 times or until easy to handle. On a greased baking sheet, press dough into an 8-in. square. Brush top with oil; sprinkle with cheeses and Italian seasoning.
3. Bake 6-8 minutes or until cheese is lightly browned. Cut in half; cut each half crosswise into eight strips. Serve with pizza sauce.
Per Serving: 1 cheese stick (calculated without pizza sauce) equals 72 cal., 3g fat (1g sat. fat), 5mg chol., 117mg sodium, 8g carb. (1g sugars, trace fiber), 3g pro.

Some Like It Spicy

The starches in this chowder make it the perfect dish to spice up with hot pepper sauce, sliced jalapenos, red pepper flakes or simply additional black pepper.

---

(5) INGREDIENTS FAST FIX ▶
BACON-POTATO CORN CHOWDER

On the farm where I was raised, a warm soup with homey ingredients was always a treat after a chilly day outside.
—Katie Lillo, Big Lake, MN

Takes: 30 min. • **Makes:** 6 servings

- ½ lb. bacon strips, chopped
- ¼ cup chopped onion
- 1½ lbs. Yukon Gold potatoes (about 5 medium), peeled and cubed
- 1 can (14¾ oz.) cream-style corn
- 1 can (12 oz.) evaporated milk
- ¼ tsp. salt
- ¼ tsp. pepper

1. In a large skillet, cook bacon over medium heat until crisp, stirring occasionally. Remove with a slotted spoon; drain on paper towels. Discard drippings, reserving 1½ tsp. in the pan. Add onion to drippings; cook and stir over medium-high heat until tender.
2. Meanwhile, place potatoes in a large saucepan; add water to cover. Bring to a boil over high heat. Reduce the heat to medium; cook potatoes, uncovered, for 10-15 minutes or until tender. Drain, reserving 1 cup potato water.
3. Add the corn, milk, salt, pepper and reserved potato water to saucepan; heat through. Stir in bacon and onion.
Per Serving: 1 cup equals 271 cal., 11g fat (5g sat. fat), 30mg chol., 555mg sodium, 34g carb. (9g sugars, 2g fiber), 10g pro.

MEAL PLANNER

SOUPS ♥ BREADS

WARM THE SOUL WITH A CLASSIC COMBO TONIGHT!

FAST & HEARTY

SOUP:
Bacon-Potato
Corn Chowder
page 244

BREAD:
Grandma's Biscuits
page 235

DESSERT:
Gooey Caramel-Topped
Gingersnaps
page 256

TAG YOUR MEAL
MEMORIES WITH
#100 FAMILYMEALS

GROCERY LIST

KITCHEN STAPLES
- ○ All-purpose flour
- ○ Baking powder
- ○ Shortening
- ○ Salt
- ○ Pepper

PRODUCE
- ○ 1 small onion
- ○ 1½ lbs. Yukon Gold potatoes (about 5 medium)

PANTRY
- ○ 1 can (14¾ oz.) cream-style corn
- ○ 1 can (12 oz.) evaporated milk
- ○ 1 bag (12 oz.) gingersnap cookies

MEAT
- ○ 1 package (12 oz.) bacon

DAIRY
- ○ ½ gallon 2% milk
- ○ 1 large egg

OTHER
- ○ 1 jar (16 oz.) honey-roasted peanuts
- ○ 1 package (14 oz.) caramels
- ○ 12 oz. white or dark chocolate candy coating
- ○ 1 jar (1.75 oz.) Chocolate jimmies

- ✂ - - -

SIMPLE DELIGHTS

SOUP:
Spinach &
Tortellini Soup
page 235

BREAD:
Herb Quick Bread
page 236

DESSERT:
White Almond
No-Bake Cookies
page 254

TAG YOUR MEAL
MEMORIES WITH
#100 FAMILYMEALS

GROCERY LIST

KITCHEN STAPLES
- ○ Olive oil
- ○ Canola oil
- ○ All-purpose flour
- ○ Sugar
- ○ Baking powder
- ○ Almond extract
- ○ Italian seasoning
- ○ Ground nutmeg
- ○ Dried thyme
- ○ Salt
- ○ Pepper

PRODUCE/SALAD BAR
- ○ 4 cups fresh baby spinach
- ○ 1 head of garlic

PANTRY
- ○ 1 can (14.5 oz.) no-salt-added diced tomatoes
- ○ 3 cans (14.5 oz. each) vegetable broth
- ○ 1 canister (18 oz.) old-fashioned oats

DAIRY
- ○ 1 large egg
- ○ 1 quart (32 oz.) fat-free milk

- ○ 1 quart (32 oz.) 2% milk
- ○ Butter
- ○ 1 bag (5 oz.) shredded Parmesan cheese

OTHER
- ○ 1 bottle (.9 oz.) caraway seed
- ○ 1 bag (12 oz.) white baking chips
- ○ 1 bag (5 oz.) dried cherries
- ○ 1 package (9 oz.) refrigerated cheese tortellini

MEAL PLANNER

SOUPS ♥ BREADS

WARM THE SOUL WITH A CLASSIC COMBO TONIGHT!

GET COZY

SOUP:
Chicken Barley Chowder
page 237

BREAD:
Cheese & Pesto Biscuits
page 243

DESSERT:
Browned Butter
Cereal Bars
page 270

TAG YOUR MEAL
MEMORIES WITH
#100 FAMILYMEALS

GROCERY LIST

KITCHEN STAPLES
- Olive oil
- All-purpose flour
- Baking powder
- Baking soda
- Vanilla extract
- Salt
- Pepper

PRODUCE
- 1 small onion
- 1 avocado
- 1 tomato
- 1 bunch chopped fresh cilantro
- 1 head of garlic

PANTRY
- 1 can (15 oz.) black beans
- 1 jar (6.3 oz.) prepared pesto
- 1 jar (15.5 oz.) salsa
- 1 carton (32 oz.) reduced-sodium chicken broth
- 1 bag (16 oz.) quick-cooking barley
- 1 box (14 oz.) Cap'n Crunch cereal
- 1 package (10.5 oz.) miniature marshmallows
- 3 packages (10 oz. each) large marshmallows

MEAT
- 1 lb. boneless skinless chicken breast

DAIRY
- Butter
- 1 quart (32 oz.) buttermilk
- 1 carton (16 oz.) half-and-half cream
- 1 cup (4 oz.) shredded Italian cheese blend

OTHER
- 1 packet (1 oz.) reduced-sodium taco seasoning
- 1 package (12 oz.) frozen mashed winter squash
- 1 package (14.4 oz.) frozen corn
- 4 cups white fudge-covered miniature pretzels
- 1 package (12 oz.) white baking chips

WEEKNIGHT EASE

SOUP:
Shortcut Sausage
Minestrone
page 243

BREAD:
Herbed Cheese Sticks
page 244

DESSERT:
Peanut Butter-Filled
Brownie Cupcakes
page 264

TAG YOUR MEAL
MEMORIES WITH
#100 FAMILYMEALS

GROCERY LIST

KITCHEN STAPLES
- Olive oil
- Sugar
- Confectioners' sugar
- Garlic powder
- Italian seasoning

PRODUCE
- 1 small green pepper
- 1 small onion
- 2 cups cut fresh green beans

PANTRY
- 1 can (16 oz.) kidney beans

- 1 can (14.5 oz.) diced tomatoes with basil, oregano and garlic
- 1 can (14.5 oz.) reduced-sodium chicken broth
- 1 jar (16 oz.) creamy peanut butter
- 1 box (16 oz.) ditalini pasta
- 1 jar (14 oz.) pizza sauce
- 1 package (6.5 oz.) pizza crust mix

MEAT
- ¾ lb. Italian turkey sausage links

DAIRY
- 1 large egg
- 1 container (8 oz.) cream cheese
- 1 bag (8 oz.) shredded part-skim mozzarella cheese
- 1 bag (5 oz.) shredded Parmesan cheese

OTHER
- 1 box (18.2 oz.) fudge brownie mix (8 in. square pan size)
- 1 package (12 oz.) miniature semisweet chocolate chips

Heart of Her Home

Catherine and her daughters, Jess and Jackie, are all smiles when spending time in the kitchen.

YOU MIGHT EXPECT the editor-in-chief of the world's largest food magazine, *Taste of Home,* to have a designer kitchen. But that's not Catherine Cassidy. She's been named one of America's 50 Most Powerful People in Food, but this wife and mom of four (two daughters, a stepdaughter and a stepson) keeps it real!

When Catherine and her husband, Steve, began a kitchen remodel a few years ago, she had one goal. "I wanted

that's where everyone ends up," says Catherine. "Our days started with eating breakfast there. My kids did homework there. We enjoyed our dinners there. It's always been our hangout."

They installed a large island that quickly became the family's favorite spot. A few built-in storage features underneath the island offered a place to stash family photo albums, among other things. "We would sit there for hours, looking at and laughing over

Times have changed. The kids are on their own, and Catherine and Steve sold their home to a couple who now enjoy that kitchen with their young children.

But gathering as a family around the table remains central to her life. "Food provides us something that little else can: the chance to share a part of our lives with each other," she says.

"Food brings everyone to the table and helps us bond with one another. Mealtime is an opportunity to live, laugh

"Real joy comes from making something. 'Bake' someone happy!"

-Helen Turner
Upland, Indiana

SWEET SURPRISES

BAKE UP a little magic in your home with a smile-inducing treat!

QUICK APPLE CRISP

This dessert can be assembled in a snap and cooks up in minutes, giving me more time to work on other things. It's super delicious served with a scoop of vanilla ice cream or whipped topping.
—Suzie Salle, Renton, WA

Takes: 30 min. • **Makes:** 8 servings

- 1 cup graham cracker crumbs (about 16 squares)
- ½ cup all-purpose flour
- ½ cup packed brown sugar
- 1 tsp. ground cinnamon
- ½ tsp. ground nutmeg
- ½ cup butter, melted
- 8 medium tart apples, peeled and sliced
  Whipped topping or ice cream

1. In a large bowl, combine the cracker crumbs, flour, brown sugar, cinnamon, nutmeg and butter. Place the apples in a greased microwave-safe 2½-qt. dish. Top with crumb mixture.
2. Microwave, uncovered, on high for 8-9 minutes or until apples are tender. Serve warm with whipped topping or ice cream.
Note: This recipe was tested in a 1,100-watt microwave.
Per serving: 1 cup equals 289 cal., 13g fat (7g sat. fat), 30mg chol., 150mg sodium, 44g carb. (30g sugars, 3g fiber), 2g pro.

PECAN BUTTERSCOTCH COOKIES

I come back to this recipe often when baking because these are the quickest, tastiest cookies I've ever made. Change the pudding flavor or type of nuts for an easy twist.
—Trisha Kruse, Eagle, ID

Takes: 25 min. • **Makes:** about 1½ dozen

- 1 cup complete buttermilk pancake mix
- 1 pkg. (3.4 oz.) instant butterscotch pudding mix
- ⅓ cup butter, melted
- 1 large egg
- ½ cup chopped pecans, toasted

1. In a large bowl, beat the pancake mix, dry pudding mix, butter and egg until blended. Stir in pecans.
2. Roll into 1½-in. balls. Place 2 in. apart on greased baking sheets. Flatten with the bottom of a glass. Bake at 350° for 8-10 minutes or until edges begin to brown. Remove to wire racks to cool.
Note: You may substitute regular biscuit/baking mix for the complete buttermilk pancake mix.
Per serving: 1 cookie equals 85 cal., 5g fat (2g sat. fat), 17mg chol., 178mg sodium, 9g carb. (4g sugars, 0 fiber), 1g pro. **Diabetic Exchanges:** ½ starch, 1 fat.

FUDGY S'MORES BROWNIES

I combined the perfect, simple summer snack with my favorite brownie recipe to get a treat that's sure to wow your family all year long. Best of all, the treats are ready for the oven in 15 minutes!
—Judy Cunningham, Max, ND

Prep: 15 min. • **Bake:** 25 min. + cooling
Makes: 1 dozen

- 1⅓ cups butter, softened
- 2⅔ cups sugar
- 4 large eggs
- 1 Tbsp. vanilla extract
- 2 cups all-purpose flour
- 1 cup baking cocoa
- ½ tsp. salt
- 1 cup Golden Grahams, coarsely crushed
- 1¾ cups miniature marshmallows
- 4 oz. milk chocolate, chopped

1. Preheat oven to 350°. In a large bowl, cream butter and sugar until light and fluffy. Beat in eggs and vanilla. In a bowl, mix flour, cocoa and salt; gradually beat into creamed mixture.
2. Spread into a greased 13x9-in. baking pan. Bake for 25-30 minutes or until a toothpick inserted in center comes out with moist crumbs (do not overbake).
3. Preheat the broiler. Sprinkle baked brownies with cereal and marshmallows; broil 5-6 in. from heat 30-45 seconds or until marshmallows are golden brown. Immediately sprinkle with the chopped chocolate. Cover with foil and let stand 5 minutes or until chocolate begins to melt. Remove foil and cool completely in pan on a wire rack. Cut into bars.
Per serving: 1 brownie equals 560 cal., 26g fat (15g sat. fat), 118mg chol., 321mg sodium, 80g carb. (56g sugars, 2g fiber), 7g pro.

Table Talk

What is the strangest dream you've ever had?

Maybe you had a little too much dessert one night, and your imagination ran wild once you hit the sheets. Take turns explaining your silliest, spookiest or happiest dreams.

TOFFEE PECAN BARS

Top off dinner with a hot cup of coffee and one of these oh-so-sweet treats. The golden topping and flaky crust give way to the heartwarming taste of old-fashioned pecan pie.
—Dianna Croskey, Gibsonia, PA

Prep: 15 min. • **Bake:** 40 min. + chilling
Makes: 3 dozen

- 2   cups all-purpose flour
- ½   cup confectioners' sugar
- 1   cup cold butter, cubed
- 1   large egg
- 1   can (14 oz.) sweetened condensed milk
- 1   tsp. vanilla extract
- 1   pkg. English toffee bits (10 oz.) or almond brickle chips (7½ oz.)
- 1   cup chopped pecans

1. Preheat oven to 350°. In a large bowl, mix flour and confectioners' sugar; cut in butter until mixture is crumbly.
2. Press into a greased 13x9-in. baking pan. Bake 15 minutes. Meanwhile, in a small bowl, mix egg, milk and vanilla. Fold in toffee bits and pecans. Spoon over crust. Bake 24-26 minutes or until golden brown. Refrigerate until firm.

Per serving: 1 bar equals 179 cal., 11g fat (5g sat. fat), 26mg chol., 112mg sodium, 18g carb. (13g sugars, 1g fiber), 2g pro.

COCONUT MACAROON PIE

Coconut macaroons are divine, but they can be a little messy to make. I turned the batter into a pie filling, and the luscious results speak for themselves.
—Becky Mollenkamp, St. Louis, MO

....

Prep: 15 min. • **Bake:** 35 min.
Makes: 10 servings

1	**sheet refrigerated pie pastry**
2	**large eggs**
1	**can (14 oz.) sweetened condensed milk**
¼	**cup butter, melted**
1	**tsp. almond extract**
¼	**tsp. salt**
¼	**cup all-purpose flour**
1	**pkg. (14 oz.) flaked coconut**

1. Preheat oven to 350°. Unroll pastry sheet into a 9-in. pie plate; flute edge. Refrigerate while preparing filling.
2. In a large bowl, beat the eggs, milk, melted butter, extract and salt until blended. Stir in flour. Reserve ½ cup coconut; stir remaining coconut into egg mixture. Transfer to pastry-lined pie plate. Sprinkle with reserved coconut.
3. Bake on a lower oven rack for 35-45 minutes or until golden brown and filling is set. Cool on a wire rack.
Per serving: 1 slice equals 490 cal., 29g fat (20g sat. fat), 67mg chol., 344mg sodium, 53g carb. (40g sugars, 2g fiber), 7g pro.

WHITE ALMOND NO-BAKE COOKIES

My daughter and I like to try new recipes. We were out of chocolate chips one day, so we came up with this cookie using white chips.

—Debbie Johnson, Winona Lake, IN

Prep: 25 min. • **Cook:** 5 min. + chilling
Makes: about 3½ dozen

- 2 cups sugar
- ½ cup butter, cubed
- ½ cup 2% milk
- 1 cup white baking chips
- ½ tsp. almond extract
- 3 cups old-fashioned oats
- 1 cup dried cherries or dried cranberries, optional

1. In a large saucepan, combine sugar, butter and milk. Cook and stir over medium heat until butter is melted and sugar is dissolved. Remove from heat. Stir in the baking chips and extract until smooth. Add oats and, if desired, the cherries; stir until coated.
2. Drop by rounded tablespoonfuls onto waxed paper-lined baking sheets. Refrigerate until set, about 30 minutes. Store cookies in an airtight container in the refrigerator.
Per serving: 1 cookie (calculated without dried cherries) equals 101 cal., 4g fat (2g sat. fat), 7mg chol., 23mg sodium, 16g carb. (12g sugars, 1g fiber), 1g pro.

---

(5)INGREDIENTS

CREAMY HAZELNUT PIE

I've always been a huge fan of peanut butter. Then I tried Nutella—I was hooked! I even changed one of my favorite pie recipes by subbing that yummy ingredient.

—Lisa Varner, El Paso, TX

Prep: 10 min. + chilling
Makes: 8 servings

- 1 pkg. (8 oz.) cream cheese, softened
- 1 cup confectioners' sugar
- 1¼ cups Nutella, divided
- 1 carton (8 oz.) frozen whipped topping, thawed
- 1 chocolate crumb crust (9 in.)

1. In a large bowl, beat cream cheese, confectioners' sugar and 1 cup Nutella until smooth. Fold in whipped topping. Spread evenly into crust.
2. Warm remaining Nutella in microwave for 15-20 seconds; drizzle over the pie. Refrigerate at least 4 hours or overnight.
Per serving: 1 slice equals 567 cal., 33g fat (13g sat. fat), 32mg chol., 224mg sodium, 65g carb. (51g sugars, 2g fiber), 6g pro.

BERRY DREAM CAKE

I use cherry gelatin to give a boxed cake mix an eye-appealing marbled effect. Try different gelatin flavors for different looks and tastes. You can top the cake with whatever fruit you like.
—Margaret McNeil, Germantown, TN

Prep: 15 min. + chilling
Bake: 30 min. + cooling
Makes: 15 servings

- 1 pkg. white cake mix (regular size)
- 1½ cups boiling water
- 1 pkg. (3 oz.) cherry gelatin
- 1 pkg. (8 oz.) cream cheese, softened
- 2 cups whipped topping
- 4 cups fresh strawberries, coarsely chopped

1. Prepare and bake the cake mix batter according to package directions, using a greased 13x9-in. baking pan.
2. In a small bowl, add boiling water to gelatin; stir for 2 minutes to completely dissolve. Cool the cake on a wire rack for 3-5 minutes. Using a wooden skewer, pierce top of cake to within 1 in. of edge; twist skewer gently to make slightly larger holes. Gradually pour gelatin over the cake, being careful to fill each hole. Cool cake for 15 minutes. Refrigerate, covered, 30 minutes.
3. In a large bowl, beat cream cheese until fluffy. Fold in whipped topping. Carefully spread over cake. Top with strawberries. Cover and refrigerate for at least 2 hours before serving.

Per serving: 1 piece equals 306 cal., 16g fat (6g sat. fat), 54mg chol., 315mg sodium, 37g carb. (22g sugars, 1g fiber), 5g pro.

CHOCOLATE CINNAMON TOAST

Cinnamon bread is toasted to perfection in a skillet, then topped with chocolate and fresh fruit. Add a small dollop of whipped cream to each slice to make it extra indulgent.
—Jeanne Ambrose, Milwaukee, WI

Takes: 10 min. • **Makes:** 1 serving

- 1 slice cinnamon bread
- 1 tsp. butter, softened
- 2 Tbsp. 60% cacao bittersweet chocolate baking chips
   Sliced banana and strawberries, optional

Spread both sides of bread with butter. In a small skillet, toast the bread over medium-high heat 2-3 minutes on each side, topping with chocolate chips after turning. Remove from heat; spread the melted chocolate evenly over toast. If desired, top with fruit.
Per serving: 1 slice (calculated without fruit) equals 235 cal., 13g fat (8g sat. fat), 10mg chol., 131mg sodium, 29g carb. (19g sugars, 3g fiber), 4g pro.

> *"Our kids pitch in when it comes to kitchen chores. The younger children clear the plates and wipe the table, and the older ones wash the dishes."*
>
> —ANN WEGENER, SPRINGVILLE, IN

GOOEY CARAMEL-TOPPED GINGERSNAPS

Making these cookies is therapeutic for me. They're so easy because they start with premade cookies! You can create new variations by changing the cookie base or varying the nuts.
—Deirdre Cox, Kansas City, MO

Prep: 30 min. + standing
Makes: 3½ dozen

- 42 gingersnap cookies
- 1 pkg. (14 oz.) caramels
- ¼ cup 2% milk or heavy whipping cream
- 1 cup chopped honey-roasted peanuts
- 12 oz. white or dark chocolate candy coating, melted
   Chocolate jimmies or finely chopped honey-roasted peanuts

1. Arrange cookies in a single layer on waxed paper-lined baking sheets. In a microwave, melt caramels with milk; stir until smooth. Stir in 1 cup chopped peanuts. Spoon about 1 tsp. caramel mixture over each cookie; refrigerate until set.
2. Dip each cookie halfway into candy coating; allow excess to drip off. Return to baking sheet; sprinkle with jimmies. Refrigerate until set.
Per serving: 1 cookie (calculated without jimmies) equals 128 cal., 5g fat (3g sat. fat), 1mg chol., 70mg sodium, 19g carb. (14g sugars, 0 fiber), 2g pro.

Easy Ideas

When freezing the bananas, you can also set them in a single layer on a baking sheet lined with waxed or parchment paper. Cover the slices and freeze. When it's time to mix up the soft serve, remember to scrape the sides of the processor a few times for best results.

RASPBERRY-BANANA SOFT SERVE

When I make this ice cream, I mix and match bananas for their ripeness. Very ripe ones add more banana flavor while less ripe ones have a fluffier texture.
—Melissa Hansen, Milwaukee, WI

Prep: 10 min. + freezing
Makes: 2½ cups

- 4 medium ripe bananas
- ½ cup fat-free plain yogurt
- 1 to 2 Tbsp. maple syrup
- ½ cup frozen unsweetened raspberries
  Fresh raspberries, optional

1. Thinly slice bananas; transfer to a large resealable plastic freezer bag. Arrange slices in a single layer; freeze overnight.
2. Pulse bananas in a food processor until finely chopped. Add yogurt, maple syrup and raspberries. Process just until smooth, scraping the sides as needed. Serve immediately, adding fresh berries if desired.

Note: For Chocolate-Peanut Butter Soft Serve, substitute 2 Tbsp. each creamy peanut butter and baking cocoa for the raspberries; proceed as directed.

Per serving: ½ cup (calculated without optional ingredients) equals 104 cal., 0 fat (0 sat. fat), 1mg chol., 15mg sodium, 26g carb. (15g sugars, 2g fiber), 2g pro.
Diabetic Exchanges: ½ starch, 1 fruit.

MEXICAN CRINKLE COOKIES

When it's baking time, my family lobbies for these Mexican crinkle cookies. No chocolate? Just use 3 tablespoons of cocoa powder plus 1 tablespoon butter, shortening or oil to replace each 1 ounce of unsweetened chocolate.

—Kim Kenyon, Greenwood, MO

Prep: 25 min. + chilling
Bake: 10 min./batch
Makes: about 2 dozen

- ¾ cup butter, cubed
- 2 oz. unsweetened chocolate, chopped
- 1 cup packed brown sugar
- ¼ cup light corn syrup
- 1 large egg
- 2 cups all-purpose flour
- 2 tsp. baking soda
- 1½ tsp. ground cinnamon, divided
- ¼ tsp. salt
- ½ cup confectioners' sugar

1. In a large microwave-safe bowl, melt butter and chocolate; stir until smooth. Beat in brown sugar and corn syrup until blended. Beat in egg. In another bowl, whisk flour, baking soda, 1 tsp. cinnamon and salt; gradually beat into brown sugar mixture. Refrigerate, covered, 1 hour or until firm.
2. Preheat oven to 350°. In a shallow bowl, mix confectioners' sugar and remaining cinnamon. Shape dough into 1½-in. balls; roll in confectioners' sugar mixture. Place 2 in. apart on greased baking sheets.
3. Bake 10-12 minutes or until set and the tops are cracked. Cool on pans 2 minutes. Remove from pans to wire racks to cool.
Per serving: 1 cookie equals 158 cal., 7g fat (4g sat. fat), 23mg chol., 184mg sodium, 22g carb. (13g sugars, 1g fiber), 2g pro.

(5) INGREDIENTS
COCONUT BROWNIES

Brownies are an easy way to make someone smile; no one seems to tire of the fudgy treats. Dress up a boxed mix to make them special.

—Barbara Carlucci, Orange Park, FL

Prep: 10 min. • **Bake:** 30 min. + cooling
Makes: 2 dozen

- 1 pkg. fudge brownie mix (13x9-in. pan size)
- 1 cup (8 oz.) sour cream
- 1 cup coconut-pecan frosting
- 2 large eggs
- ¼ cup water
- 1 cup (6 oz.) semisweet chocolate chips

1. Preheat oven to 350°. In a large bowl, combine the brownie mix, sour cream, frosting, eggs and water just until the ingredients are moistened.
2. Pour into a 13x9-in. baking dish coated with cooking spray. Bake 30-35 minutes or until center is set (do not overbake). Sprinkle with chocolate chips; let stand 5 minutes. Spread chips over brownies.
Per serving: 1 brownie equals 203 cal., 9g fat (4g sat. fat), 25mg chol., 117mg sodium, 29g carb. (21g sugars, 1g fiber), 3g pro.

FROSTY TOFFEE BITS PIE

It only takes me 10 minutes to mix up this sweet treat! Have the oh-so-good dessert after a family meal or for guests.

—LaDonna Reed, Ponca City, OK

Prep: 10 min. + freezing
Makes: 6-8 servings

- 3 oz. cream cheese, softened
- 2 Tbsp. sugar
- ½ cup half-and-half cream
- 1 carton (8 oz.) frozen whipped topping, thawed
- 1 pkg. (8 oz.) milk chocolate English toffee bits, divided
- 1 graham cracker crust (9 in.)

1. In a large bowl, beat the cream cheese and sugar until smooth. Beat in cream until blended. Fold in whipped topping and 1 cup toffee bits.
2. Spoon into the crust; sprinkle with remaining toffee bits. Cover and freeze overnight. Remove the pie from the freezer 10 minutes before serving.
Per serving: 1 slice equals 403 cal., 25g fat (14g sat. fat), 29mg chol., 262mg sodium, 41g carb. (34g sugars, 0g fiber), 2g pro.

NOTES

_____
_____
_____
_____
_____
_____
_____
_____
_____

CHOCOLATE-COVERED STRAWBERRY COBBLER

Our love of chocolate-covered strawberries shows up in a surprising cobbler. Why not stir a little chocolate syrup into the whipped cream topping?
—Andrea Bolden, Unionville, TN

Prep: 15 min. • **Bake:** 35 min. + standing
Makes: 12 servings

- 1 cup butter, cubed
- 1½ cups self-rising flour
- 2¼ cups sugar, divided
- ¾ cup 2% milk
- 1 tsp. vanilla extract
- ⅓ cup baking cocoa
- 4 cups fresh strawberries, quartered
- 2 cups boiling water
  Whipped cream and additional strawberries

1. Preheat oven to 350°. Place butter in a 13x9-in. baking pan; heat pan in oven 3-5 minutes or until the butter is melted. Meanwhile, in a large bowl, combine flour, 1¼ cups sugar, milk and vanilla until well blended. In a small bowl, mix cocoa and remaining sugar.

2. Remove baking pan from oven; add batter. Sprinkle with strawberries and cocoa mixture; pour boiling water evenly over top (do not stir). Bake 35-40 minutes or until a toothpick inserted into cake portion comes out clean. Let stand for 10 minutes. Serve warm with whipped cream and additional strawberries.

Per serving: 1 serving (calculated without whipped cream) equals 368 cal., 16g fat (10g sat. fat), 42mg chol., 316mg sodium, 55g carb. (41g sugars, 2g fiber), 3g pro.

⑤INGREDIENTS FAST FIX
CAKE WITH PINEAPPLE PUDDING

A dear friend shared her quick dessert recipe with me, and I make it often. It's so light and refreshing. Best of all, the yummy topping is ready in minutes. What could be easier?
—Judy Sellgren, Grand Rapids, MI

Takes: 10 min. • **Makes:** 6 servings

- 2 cups cold 2% milk
- 1 pkg. (3.4 oz.) instant French vanilla pudding mix
- 1 can (8 oz.) unsweetened crushed pineapple, drained
- 1 cup whipped topping
- 6 slices angel food cake

In a large bowl, whisk milk and pudding mix for 2 minutes. Let pudding stand for 2 minutes or until soft-set. Fold in pineapple and whipped topping. Chill until serving. Serve with cake.

Per serving: 1 serving equals 236 cal., 5g fat (4g sat. fat), 8mg chol., 470mg sodium, 43g carb. (21g sugars, 1g fiber), 4g pro.

MINI RUM CAKES

Mom kept sponge cakes in her freezer and pudding in the pantry. We tried many cakes with rum topping to find the best one. We think this one rises to the top!
—Dona Hoffman, Addison, IL

Takes: 10 min. • **Makes:** 6 servings

- 2 cups cold 2% milk
- 1 pkg. (3.4 oz.) instant vanilla pudding mix
- 1 tsp. rum extract
- 6 individual round sponge cakes
- 1½ cups whipped topping
  Fresh or frozen raspberries

1. In a small bowl, whisk milk and pudding mix for 2 minutes; stir in extract. Let stand for 2 minutes or until soft-set.
2. Place sponge cakes on dessert plates; top with pudding. Garnish with whipped topping and raspberries.
Per serving: 1 cake equals 238 cal., 7g fat (5g sat. fat), 34mg chol., 320mg sodium, 37g carb. (27g sugars, 0 fiber), 4g pro.

APPLE PIE OATMEAL DESSERT

A warm and comforting dessert brings back memories of time spent with my family around the kitchen table. Using a slow cooker makes this old-fashioned recipe new again.
—Carol Greer, Earlville, IL

Prep: 15 min. • **Cook:** 4 hours
Makes: 6 servings

- 1 cup quick-cooking oats
- ½ cup all-purpose flour
- ⅓ cup packed brown sugar
- 2 tsp. baking powder
- 1½ tsp. apple pie spice
- ¼ tsp. salt
- 3 large eggs
- 1⅔ cups 2% milk, divided
- 1½ tsp. vanilla extract
- 3 medium apples, peeled and finely chopped
  Vanilla ice cream, optional

1. In a large bowl, whisk the oats, flour, brown sugar, baking powder, pie spice and salt. In a small bowl, whisk eggs, 1 cup milk and vanilla until blended. Add to the oat mixture, stirring just until moistened. Fold in the apples.
2. Transfer to a greased 3-qt. slow cooker. Cook, covered, on low 4-5 hours or until apples are tender and top is set.
3. Stir in remaining milk. Serve warm or cold, with ice cream if desired.

Per serving: ¾ cup (calculated without ice cream) equals 238 cal., 5g fat (2g sat. fat), 111mg chol., 306mg sodium, 41g carb. (22g sugars, 3g fiber), 8g pro.

SPEEDY SWAPS!
Make it your own with a few changes.

DON'T HAVE VANILLA?
Use almond extract instead or leave it out altogether.

LOVE FRUIT?
Replace a few apples with pears and toss in fresh cranberries.

NUTELLA HAND PIES

Pint-size Nutella hand pies made with puff pastry are a great way to surprise your family!
—*Taste of Home* Test Kitchen

....

Prep: 10 min. • **Bake:** 20 min.
Makes: 9 servings

- 1 large egg
- 1 Tbsp. water
- 1 sheet frozen puff pastry, thawed
- 3 Tbsp. Nutella
- 1 to 2 tsp. grated orange peel

ICING
- ⅓ cup confectioners' sugar
- ½ tsp. orange juice
- ⅛ tsp. grated orange peel
   Additional Nutella, optional

1. Preheat oven to 400°. In a small bowl, whisk egg with water.

2. Unfold the puff pastry; cut into nine squares. Place 1 tsp. of Nutella in center of each; sprinkle with orange peel. Brush edges of pastry with egg mixture. Fold one corner over filling to form a triangle; press the edges to seal.

3. Transfer to an ungreased baking sheet. Bake 17-20 minutes or until golden brown. Cool slightly.

4. In a small bowl, mix confectioners' sugar, orange juice and orange peel; drizzle over pies. If desired, warm additional Nutella in a microwave and drizzle over tops.

Per serving: 1 hand pie equals 190 cal., 10g fat (2g sat. fat), 21mg chol., 100mg sodium, 24g carb. (8g sugars, 2g fiber), 3g pro.

BERRIED TREASURE ANGEL FOOD CAKE

My husband grills everything, even dessert! With his encouragement, I came up with an easy recipe that takes just a few minutes to prepare yet always hits the spot.
—Anita Archibald, Aurora, ON

Takes: 25 min. • **Makes:** 4 servings

8 slices angel food cake
   (1½ in. thick)
¼ cup butter, softened
½ cup heavy whipping cream
¼ tsp. almond extract
¼ cup almond cake and pastry filling
½ cup fresh blueberries
½ cup fresh raspberries
½ cup sliced fresh strawberries
¼ cup mixed nuts, coarsely chopped
   Confectioners' sugar

1. Using a 1½-in. round cookie cutter, cut out the centers of half of the cake slices (discard removed cake or save for another use). Spread butter over both sides of cake slices. Grill, covered, over medium heat or broil 4 in. from heat 1-2 minutes on each side or until toasted.
2. In a small bowl, beat the cream until it begins to thicken. Add extract; beat until soft peaks form.
3. To serve, stack one solid and one cutout slice of cake on each dessert plate, placing the outer edges on opposite sides for a more even thickness. Spoon almond filling into holes; top with the whipped cream, berries and nuts. Dust cake stacks with confectioners' sugar.
Per serving: 1 serving (calculated without confectioner's sugar) equals 486 cal., 29g fat (15g sat. fat), 72mg chol., 575mg sodium, 53g carb. (11g sugars, 3g fiber), 6g pro.

MONKEY BARS

Yum—two favorite foods together in one dessert. Smooth peanut butter and sweet banana combine to make these thick, muffin-like bars.
—Tina Haupert, Weymouth, MA

Prep: 15 min. • **Bake:** 25 min.
Makes: 16 servings

½ cup butter, softened
1 cup packed brown sugar
½ cup creamy peanut butter
1 large egg
1 medium ripe banana, mashed
1 tsp. vanilla extract
1 cup whole wheat flour
1 tsp. baking powder
⅛ tsp. salt
   Confectioners' sugar, optional

1. Preheat oven to 350°. In a large bowl, beat butter, brown sugar and peanut butter until blended. Gradually beat in egg, banana and vanilla. In another bowl, whisk the flour, baking powder and salt; gradually add to the butter mixture, mixing well.
2. Spread into an 8-in. square baking dish coated with cooking spray. Bake 25-30 minutes or until a toothpick inserted in center comes out clean. Cool on a wire rack. Cut into bars. If desired, dust with confectioners' sugar.
Per serving: 1 bar equals 188 cal., 10g fat (5g sat. fat), 27mg chol., 139mg sodium, 22g carb. (15g sugars, 1g fiber), 4g pro.

PEANUT BUTTER-FILLED BROWNIE CUPCAKES

Everyone loves brownies and cupcakes, so why not combine the two? Watch these sweet snacks disappear before your very eyes!
—Carol Gillespie, Chambersburg, PA

Prep: 15 min. • **Bake:** 15 min. + cooling
Makes: 1 dozen

- 1 pkg. fudge brownie mix (8-in. square pan size)
- ½ cup miniature semisweet chocolate chips
- ⅓ cup creamy peanut butter
- 3 Tbsp. cream cheese, softened
- 1 large egg
- ¼ cup sugar
   Confectioners' sugar

1. Preheat oven to 350°. Prepare brownie batter according to package directions; stir in chocolate chips. For filling, in a small bowl, beat peanut butter, cream cheese, egg and sugar until smooth.
2. Fill paper-lined muffin cups one-third full with batter. Drop peanut butter filling by teaspoonfuls into the center of each cupcake. Cover with remaining batter.
3. Bake 15-20 minutes or until a toothpick inserted in brownie portion comes out clean. Cool 10 minutes before removing cupcakes from pan to a wire rack to cool completely. Dust tops with confectioners' sugar. Store in the refrigerator.
Per serving: 1 cupcake equals 328 cal., 18g fat (5g sat. fat), 40mg chol., 201mg sodium, 39g carb. (27g sugars, 2g fiber), 5g pro.

⑤ INGREDIENTS
CHOCOLATY S'MORES BARS

One night when my husband had some friends over, he requested these s'mores bars. They polished off the pan and asked for some more. I shared the recipe, and now his friends' families enjoy them, too.
—Rebecca Shipp, Beebe, AR

Prep: 15 min. + cooling
Makes: 1½ dozen

- ¼ cup butter, cubed
- 1 pkg. (10 oz.) large marshmallows
- 1 pkg. (12 oz.) Golden Grahams
- ⅓ cup milk chocolate chips, melted

1. In a large saucepan, melt butter over low heat. Add marshmallows; cook and stir until blended. Remove from heat. Stir in cereal until coated.
2. Using a buttered spatula, press evenly into a greased 13x9-in. pan. Drizzle with melted chocolate chips. Cool completely. Cut into bars. Store in airtight container.
Per serving: 1 bar equals 159 cal., 4g fat (2g sat. fat), 7mg chol., 197mg sodium, 30g carb. (17g sugars, 1g fiber), 1g pro.

⑤ INGREDIENTS
LEMON-BERRY ICE CREAM PIE

I love the combination of fresh strawberries and lemon curd. It's so refreshing, especially in an easy make-ahead dessert like this.
—Roxanne Chan, Albany, CA

Prep: 15 min. + freezing
Makes: 8 servings

- 1 pint strawberry ice cream, softened
- 1 graham cracker crust (9 in.)
- 1 cup lemon curd
- 2 cups frozen whipped topping, thawed
- 1 pint fresh strawberries, halved

1. Spoon ice cream into pie crust; freeze for 2 hours or until firm.
2. Spread lemon curd over ice cream; top with whipped topping. Freeze, covered, for 4 hours or until firm.
3. Remove from freezer 10 minutes before serving. Serve with strawberries.
Per serving: 1 slice equals 370 cal., 13g fat (7g sat. fat), 40mg chol., 171mg sodium, 58g carb. (40g sugars, 1g fiber), 2g pro.

LOADED M&M OREO COOKIE BARS

We're all so busy and pressed for time that I find myself creating recipes that are generally fast to prepare. Here's proof you don't have to spend all day in the kitchen to obtain fabulous results .
—Averie Sunshine, San Diego, CA

Prep: 15 min. • **Bake:** 25 min. + cooling
Makes: 9 servings

- 1 large egg
- 1 cup packed light brown sugar
- ½ cup unsalted butter, melted
- 1 Tbsp. vanilla extract
- 1 cup all-purpose flour
- ¼ tsp. baking soda, optional
- ¼ tsp. salt, optional
- 18 Oreo cookies, coarsely chopped
- ½ cup milk chocolate M&M's

1. Preheat oven to 350°. Line an 8-in. square baking pan with foil, letting ends extend up sides of pan; grease foil.
2. In a large bowl, whisk egg, brown sugar, butter and vanilla until blended. If desired, mix flour with baking soda and salt; add to brown sugar mixture. Stir in cookies.
3. Spread into prepared pan; sprinkle with M&M's. Bake 25-30 minutes or until a toothpick inserted in center comes out with moist crumbs (do not overbake). Cool completely in pan on a wire rack. Lifting with foil, remove from pan. Cut into bars. Store in an airtight container.
Note: For a chewier cookie bar texture, be sure to add the baking soda and salt.
Per serving: 1 bar (calculated without the baking soda and salt) equals 403 cal., 18g fat (9g sat. fat), 49mg chol., 117mg sodium, 58g carb. (40g sugars, 1g fiber), 3g pro.

CARAMEL FLUFF & TOFFEE TRIFLE

With just five ingredients you can put together a stunning, quick, and completely irresistible dessert.
—Daniel Anderson, Kenosha, WI

Prep: 15 min. + chilling
Makes: 12 servings

- 2 cups heavy whipping cream
- ¾ cup packed brown sugar
- 1 tsp. vanilla extract
- 1 prepared angel food cake (8 to 10 oz.), cut into 1-in. cubes
- 1 cup milk chocolate English toffee bits

1. In a large bowl, beat cream, brown sugar and vanilla just until blended. Refrigerate, covered, for 20 minutes. Beat until stiff peaks form.
2. In a 4-qt. glass bowl, layer one-third of each of the following: cake cubes, whipped cream and toffee bits. Repeat layers twice. Refrigerate until serving.
Per serving: 1 serving equals 347 cal., 22g fat (13g sat. fat), 61mg chol., 227mg sodium, 38g carb. (27g sugars, 0 fiber), 2g pro.

EAT SMART **FAST FIX** ▶
BLUEBERRY CANTALOUPE CUPS

Freshen up dessert with these cute cups. The simple citrus dressing really jazzes up the fruit.
—R. Jean Rand, Edina, MN

Takes: 10 min. • **Makes:** 4 servings

- ¾ cup (6 oz.) orange yogurt
- 1½ tsp. lemon juice
- ¾ tsp. poppy seeds
- ½ tsp. grated orange peel
- 2 cups diced cantaloupe
- 1 cup fresh blueberries

In a small bowl, mix yogurt, lemon juice, poppy seeds and orange peel. To serve, divide the cantaloupe and blueberries among four dishes; top fruit with the yogurt mixture.
Per serving: ¾ cup with 3 Tbsp. dressing equals 76 cal., 1g fat (trace sat. fat), 1mg chol., 24mg sodium, 17g carb. (15g sugars, 1g fiber), 2g pro. **Diabetic Exchange:** 1 fruit.

BANANA PUDDING

We went to the airport to pick up my son, who had been in the Marines for 2 years. When we got to our house, the first thing he did was eat two bowls of his favorite banana pudding...all ready for him.
—Stephanie Harris, Montpelier, VA

....

Prep: 35 min. + chilling
Makes: 9 servings

¾ cup sugar
¼ cup all-purpose flour
¼ tsp. salt
3 cups 2% milk
3 large eggs
1½ tsp. vanilla extract
8 oz. vanilla wafers (about 60 cookies), divided
4 large ripe bananas, cut into ¼-in. slices

1. In a large saucepan, mix sugar, flour and salt. Whisk in the milk. Cook and stir over medium heat until thickened and bubbly. Reduce the heat to low; cook and stir 2 minutes longer. Remove from heat.
2. In a small bowl, whisk the eggs. Whisk a small amount of hot mixture into eggs; return all to the pan, whisking constantly. Bring to a gentle boil; cook and stir for 2 minutes. Remove from heat. Stir in vanilla. Cool 15 minutes, stirring occasionally.
3. In an ungreased 8-in. square baking dish, layer 25 vanilla wafers, half of the banana slices and half of the pudding. Repeat layers.
4. Press plastic wrap onto the surface of pudding. Refrigerate 4 hours or overnight. Just before serving, crush the remaining wafers and sprinkle over top.
Per serving: 1 serving equals 302 cal., 7g fat (2g sat. fat), 80mg chol., 206mg sodium, 55g carb. (37g sugars, 2g fiber), 7g pro.

UNDER
350
CALORIES

GRAPEFRUIT, LIME & MINT YOGURT PARFAIT

Tart grapefruit and lime are balanced with a bit of honey in a cool and easy parfait. Serve them for desserts, after-school snacks or even for a light and lively breakfast.

—Lois Enger, Colorado Springs, CO

Takes: 15 min. • **Makes:** 6 servings

- 4 **large grapefruit**
- 4 **cups (32 oz.) reduced-fat plain yogurt**
- 2 **tsp. grated lime peel**
- 2 **Tbsp. lime juice**
- 3 **Tbsp. honey**
  Torn fresh mint leaves, optional

1. Cut a thin slice from top and bottom of each grapefruit; stand upright on a cutting board. With a knife, cut off peel and outer membrane from grapefruit. Cut along the membranes of each segment to remove fruit.

2. In a large bowl, mix yogurt, lime peel and juice. Layer half of the grapefruit sections and the yogurt mixture into six parfait glasses. Repeat layers. Drizzle with honey; top with mint if desired.

Per serving: 1 parfait equals 207 cal., 3g fat (2g sat. fat), 10mg chol., 115mg sodium, 39g carb. (36g sugars, 3g fiber), 10g pro.

TEXAS TUMBLEWEEDS

Tumbleweeds blow across the roads in some parts of Texas, and I think these cute stacks resemble them. I've been make these sweet, crunchy little treats with my sister for years.
—Karen LeMay, Seabrook, TX

Prep: 20 min. + chilling
Makes: about 4 dozen

- 1 cup (6 oz.) butterscotch chips
- 1 cup creamy peanut butter
- 1 can (9 oz.) potato sticks (about 6 cups)

1. In a microwave, melt butterscotch chips and the peanut butter; stir until smooth. Stir in potato sticks.
2. Drop by rounded tablespoonfuls onto waxed paper-lined baking sheets. Refrigerate 10-15 minutes or until set.
Per serving: 1 cookie equals 76 cal., 5g fat (2g sat. fat), 0mg chol., 57mg sodium, 6g carb. (3g sugars, trace fiber), 2g pro.

BANANA CHIP CAKE

One of my favorite treats is Ben & Jerry's Chunky Monkey ice cream, so I decided to create a cake with the same flavors. The hardest part is waiting for it to cool!
—Barbara Pryor, Milford, MA

Prep: 25 min. • **Bake:** 40 min. + cooling
Makes: 16 servings

- 1 pkg. yellow cake mix (regular size)
- 1¼ cups water
- 3 large eggs
- ½ cup unsweetened applesauce
- 2 medium bananas, mashed
- 1 cup miniature semisweet chocolate chips
- ½ cup chopped walnuts

1. In a large bowl, combine the cake mix, water, eggs and applesauce; beat on low speed for 30 seconds. Beat on medium for 2 minutes. Stir in the bananas, chips and walnuts.
2. Transfer to a 10-in. fluted tube pan coated with cooking spray and sprinkled with flour. Bake at 350° for 40-50 minutes or until a toothpick inserted near the center comes out clean. Cool cake for 10 minutes before removing from pan to a wire rack to cool completely.
Per serving: 1 slice equals 233 cal., 9g fat (4g sat. fat), 40mg chol., 225mg sodium, 38g carb. (24g sugars, 1g fiber), 3g pro.

FROZEN BERRY & YOGURT SWIRLS

These are great treats to have on a warm summer day. Use clementines for a change of color and taste.
—Colleen Ludovice, Wauwatosa, WI

Prep: 15 min. + freezing • **Makes:** 10 pops

- 2¾ cups fat-free honey Greek yogurt
- 10 plastic or paper cups (3 oz. each) and wooden pop sticks
- 1 cup mixed fresh berries
- ¼ cup water
- 2 Tbsp. sugar

1. Divide yogurt among cups. Place the berries, water and sugar in a food processor; pulse until combined. Spoon over yogurt. Using a pop stick, stir the mixture to swirl.
2. Top cups with foil and insert sticks through foil. Freeze until firm.
Note: For Frozen Clementine & Yogurt Swirls, use 1 cup clementine segments (about 5 medium, seeded if necessary) and ¼ cup orange juice in place of berries, water and sugar; proceed as directed.
Per serving: 1 pop equals 60 cal., 0 fat (0 sat. fat), 0 chol., 28mg sodium, 9g carb. (8g sugars, 1g fiber), 6g pro.

> *"The kitchen is the heart of the home. I love coming together as a family and talking over a homemade supper."*
> —HELEN TURNER, UPLAND, IN

BROWNED BUTTER CEREAL BARS

Crispy rice treats were one of the first recipes I ever made as a kid. My entire family thinks that using Cap'n Crunch and browned butter is a great touch.
—Kelly Krauss, Lebanon, NJ

Prep: 15 min. + freezing
Cook: 20 min. + cooling • **Makes:** 5 dozen

- 4 cups white fudge-covered miniature pretzels
- 1 pkg. (10½ oz.) miniature marshmallows
- 1 pkg. (10 to 12 oz.) white baking chips
- 2 cups butter, cubed
- 3 pkg. (10 oz. each) large marshmallows
- 2 tsp. vanilla extract
- 1 tsp. salt
- 8 cups Cap'n Crunch

1. Line a 15x10x1-in. pan with parchment paper, letting ends extend over sides; set aside. Freeze the pretzels, miniature marshmallows and baking chips 1 hour.
2. Remove pretzels, marshmallows and baking chips from freezer; combine in a large bowl. In a Dutch oven, melt butter over medium heat. Heat 10-13 minutes or until golden brown, stirring constantly. Add the large marshmallows; cook and stir until blended. Remove from heat; stir in vanilla and salt.
3. Stir in cereal until coated. Stir in pretzel mixture; transfer to the prepared pan, pressing evenly with a buttered spatula. Cool completely.
4. Lifting with parchment paper, remove cereal mixture from pan. Cut into bars. Store in airtight containers.
Per serving: 1 bar equals 186 cal., 9g fat (6g sat. fat), 17mg chol., 172mg sodium, 27g carb. (18g sugars, 0 fiber), 1g pro.

FAST FIX

GRANDMA BRUBAKER'S ORANGE COOKIES

At least two generations of my family have enjoyed the recipe for these light, delicate, orange-flavored cookies.
—Sheri DeBolt, Huntington, IN

Takes: 30 min. • **Makes:** about 6 dozen

- 1 cup shortening
- 2 cups sugar
- 2 large eggs, separated
- 1 cup buttermilk
- 5 cups all-purpose flour
- 2 tsp. baking powder
- 2 tsp. baking soda
- Pinch salt
- Juice and grated peel of 2 medium navel oranges

ICING
- 2 cups confectioners' sugar
- ¼ cup orange juice
- 1 Tbsp. butter
- 1 Tbsp. grated orange peel

1. In a bowl, cream shortening and sugar. Beat in egg yolks and buttermilk. Sift together flour, baking powder, soda and salt; add alternately with orange juice and peel to creamed mixture. Add egg whites and beat until smooth.
2. Drop by rounded teaspoonfuls onto greased cookie sheets. Bake at 325° for 10 minutes.
3. For icing, combine all the ingredients and beat until smooth. Frost the cookies when cool.
Per serving: 2 cookies equals 194 cal., 6g fat (2g sat. fat), 11mg chol., 153mg sodium, 32g carb. (19g sugars, 1g fiber), 2g pro.

FROSTY KEY LIME PIE

The secret behind my smooth-textured, fluffy version of the luscious classic pie is whipped cream in the filling—and on top.
—Lisa Feld, Grafton, WI

Prep: 20 min. + freezing
Makes: 6 servings

- 1 can (14 oz.) sweetened condensed milk
- 6 Tbsp. key lime juice
- 2 cups heavy whipping cream, whipped, divided
- 1 graham cracker crust (9 in.)

1. In a large bowl, combine milk and lime juice. Refrigerate ¼ cup whipped cream for garnish. Fold a fourth of the remaining whipped cream into lime mixture; fold in the remaining whipped cream. Spoon into crust. Cover and freeze overnight.
2. Remove from the freezer 10-15 minutes before serving. Garnish with the reserved whipped cream.

Per serving: 1 slice equals 474 cal., 32g fat (18g sat. fat), 99mg chol., 207mg sodium, 43g carb. (39g sugars, 0 fiber), 6g pro.

CANDY BAR CHEESECAKE BROWNIES

I came up with these brownies as a way to use up my son's leftover Halloween candy. For a seasonal touch, you can tint the cream cheese orange.
—Elisabeth Larsen, Pleasant Grove, UT

Prep: 15 min. • **Cook:** 30 min. + chilling
Makes: 2 dozen

- 1 cup butter, cubed
- 2 cups sugar
- ⅓ cup baking cocoa
- 2 tsp. vanilla extract
- 4 large eggs
- 2 cups all-purpose flour
- 1 tsp. salt
- 1 cup chopped assorted miniature candy bars (about 18)

TOPPING
- 1 pkg. (8 oz.) cream cheese, softened
- ⅓ cup sugar
- ½ tsp. vanilla extract
- 1 large egg
- ½ cup chopped assorted miniature candy bars (about 10)

1. Preheat oven to 350°. Grease a 13x9-in. baking pan. In a microwave, melt butter in a large microwave-safe bowl. Stir in sugar, cocoa and vanilla. Add eggs, one at a time, whisking to blend after each addition. Add flour and salt; stir just until combined. Stir in 1 cup candy bars.
2. Spread into prepared pan. In a large bowl, beat cream cheese and sugar until smooth. Beat in vanilla. Add egg; beat on low speed just until blended. Drop by tablespoonfuls over batter. Cut through batter with a knife to swirl. Sprinkle with ½ cup candy bars.
3. Bake 30-35 minutes or until filling in center is almost set. Cool 1 hour in pan on a wire rack. Refrigerate for at least 2 hours. Cut into bars.

Per serving: 1 brownie equals 282 cal., 14g fat (8g sat. fat), 71mg chol., 233mg sodium, 36g carb. (25g sugars, 1g fiber), 4g pro.

GRANDMA DAVIDSON'S BAKED APPLE PUDDING

During the Depression years my savvy grandmother whipped up recipes that many of us still use today, like this homey, cinnamon-scented apple pudding.
—Holly Sharp, Warren, ON

Prep: 15 min. • **Bake:** 40 min. + standing
Makes: 6 servings

- 1 cup packed brown sugar
- 1 cup all-purpose flour
- 2 tsp. baking powder
- ½ tsp. salt
- ½ tsp. ground cinnamon
- ½ cup 2% milk
- 3 medium tart apples, peeled and chopped
- 2 Tbsp. butter, cubed
- 2 cups boiling water
  Vanilla ice cream, optional

1. Preheat oven to 400°. In a large bowl, mix the first five ingredients. Add milk; stir just until blended. Fold in the apples. Transfer to a greased 2½-qt. deep baking dish. Dot with butter.
2. Pour boiling water over the top. Bake, uncovered, 40-45 minutes or until golden brown. Let stand for 15 minutes before serving. If desired, serve with ice cream.
Per serving: 1 cup equals 291 cal., 5g fat (3g sat. fat), 12mg chol., 381mg sodium, 61g carb. (43g sugars, 2g fiber), 3g pro.

Sweet Substitution

Don't have mint candy? Don't worry! Chop up whatever chocolate bars you have at home and toss them into the pudding mixture. Depending on the flavor, you may want to forgo the mint extract.

EASY GRASSHOPPER PIE

This no-bake pie with chocolate mint candies is a classic in our family. I make it all year long.
—Melissa Sokasits, Warrenville, IL

Prep: 15 min. + chilling
Makes: 8 servings

- 1½ cups cold 2% milk
- 1 pkg. (3.9 oz.) instant chocolate pudding mix
- 2¾ cups whipped topping, divided
- 1 pkg. (4.67 oz.) Andes mint candies, chopped, divided
- 1 chocolate crumb crust (9 in.)
- ¼ tsp. mint extract
- 2 drops green food coloring, optional

1. In a small bowl, whisk milk and pudding mix 2 minutes. Stir in ¾ of cup whipped topping. Fold in ¾ cup of the mint candies. Spoon into crust.
2. Place the remaining whipped topping in another bowl. Fold in extract and, if desired, the food coloring. Spread over pudding mixture; top with remaining candies. Refrigerate, covered, 4 hours or until set.
Per serving: 1 slice equals 332 cal., 16g fat (11g sat. fat), 4mg chol., 196mg sodium, 44g carb. (26g sugars, 1g fiber), 4g pro.

DATE-WALNUT PINWHEELS

Every time someone drops in for coffee, I bake up a batch of these fruit and nut cookies—I always keep the ingredients in my pantry. The recipe's a cinch to double, too, so it's good for parties and potlucks.
—Lori McLain, Denton, TX

Takes: 25 min. • **Makes:** 1 dozen

- 3 Tbsp. sugar
- ½ tsp. ground cinnamon
- 1 refrigerated pie pastry
- 1 Tbsp. apricot preserves
- ⅔ cup finely chopped pitted dates
- ½ cup finely chopped walnuts

1. Preheat oven to 350°. Mix sugar and cinnamon. On a lightly floured surface, unroll pastry sheet; roll pastry into a 12-in. square. Spread preserves over the top; sprinkle with the dates, walnuts and cinnamon sugar.

2. Roll up jelly-roll style; pinch seam to seal. Cut crosswise into 12 slices, about 1 in. thick. Place the slices 1 in. apart on an ungreased baking sheet. Bake for 12-14 minutes or until golden brown. Remove from pan to a wire rack to cool.

Per serving: 1 pastry equals 155 cal., 8g fat (2g sat. fat), 3mg chol., 68mg sodium, 21g carb. (11g sugars, 1g fiber), 2g pro.

UNDER 200 CALORIES

BLOND BUTTERSCOTCH BROWNIES

Toffee and chocolate dot the golden brown batter of these delightful brownies. I do a lot of cooking for the police officers I work with, and they always line up for these treats.

—Jennifer Ann Sopko, Battle Creek, MI

Prep: 15 min. • **Bake:** 20 min. + cooling
Makes: 2 dozen

- 2 **cups all-purpose flour**
- 2 **cups packed brown sugar**
- 2 **tsp. baking powder**
- ¼ **tsp. salt**
- ½ **cup butter, melted and cooled**
- 2 **large eggs**
- 1 **tsp. vanilla extract**
- 1 **cup semisweet chocolate chunks**
- 4 **Heath candy bars (1.4 oz. each), coarsely chopped**

1. In a large bowl, combine the flour, brown sugar, baking powder and salt. In another bowl, beat the butter, eggs and vanilla until smooth. Stir into dry ingredients just until combined (the batter will be thick).
2. Spread into a 13x9-in. baking pan coated with cooking spray. Sprinkle with chocolate chunks and chopped candy bars; press gently into batter.
3. Bake at 350° for 20-25 minutes or until a toothpick inserted near the center comes out clean. Cool on a wire rack. Cut into bars.
Per serving: 1 bar equals 218 cal., 9g fat (5g sat. fat), 29mg chol., 126mg sodium, 35g carb. (26g sugars, 1g fiber), 2g pro.

(5) INGREDIENTS
WATERMELON CHOCOLATE CHIP SORBET

With just a tiny bit of planning, I can surprise my gang with this refreshing melon sorbet. It's fresh and fruity and free of the gluten, dairy and eggs you find in other frozen desserts.

—Rachel Lewis, Danville, VA

Prep: 15 min. + chilling
Process: 30 min. + freezing • **Makes:** 1 qt.

- 1 **cup sugar**
- ½ **cup water**
- 3 **cups chopped seedless watermelon**
- 1 **cup orange juice**
- 2 **Tbsp. lime juice**
- ½ **cup miniature semisweet chocolate chips, optional**

1. In a small saucepan, bring sugar and water to a boil. Reduce heat; simmer mixture, uncovered, for 5 minutes, stirring occasionally to dissolve sugar. Cool slightly.
2. Place watermelon in a food processor; process until pureed. Add orange juice, lime juice and cooled syrup; process until blended. Transfer to a large bowl; refrigerate, covered, 3 hours or until cold.
3. Pour into cylinder of ice cream freezer. Freeze according to the manufacturer's directions; if desired, add chocolate chips during the last 10 minutes of processing. Transfer the sorbet to freezer containers, allowing headspace for expansion. Freeze 2-4 hours or until firm.
Per serving: ½ cup equals 129 cal., 0 fat (0 sat. fat), 0 chol., 1mg sodium, 33g carb. (32g sugars, 0 fiber), 1g pro.

MEAL PLANNER

SWEET ♥ SURPRISES

IT'S EASY TO BAKE UP SOME SWEET MEMORIES TODAY!

EASY COMFORT

ENTREE:
Three-Cheese Meatball
Mostaccioli
page 20

SIDE:
Green Salad with
Tangy Basil Vinaigrette
page 181

DESSERT:
Raspberry-Banana
Soft Serve
page 257

TAG YOUR MEAL
MEMORIES WITH
#100 FAMILYMEALS

GROCERY LIST

KITCHEN STAPLES
- Olive oil
- Brown sugar
- Italian seasoning
- Garlic powder
- Salt
- Pepper

PRODUCE
- 1 pint fresh raspberries
- 4 medium ripe bananas
- 1 medium onion
- 2 packages (12 oz. each) mixed salad greens

- 1 pint cherry tomatoes
- 1 bunch fresh parsley
- 1 bunch fresh basil

PANTRY
- 1 package (16 oz.) mostaccioli
- 2 jars (24 oz. each) pasta sauce with meat

MEAT
- 1 lb. ground beef

DAIRY
- 2 large eggs
- 1 carton (6 oz.) fat-free plain yogurt
- 1 carton (15 oz.) part-skim ricotta cheese

- 1 carton (5 oz.) grated Romano cheese
- 1 carton (5 oz.) shaved Parmesan cheese

FREEZER SECTION
- 1 package (12 oz.) frozen unsweetened raspberries
- 1 package (12 oz.) frozen fully cooked Italian meatballs

OTHER
- 1 bottle (12 oz.) honey
- 1 bottle (8.5 oz.) maple syrup
- 1 bottle (12.7 oz.) white wine vinegar

FUN FAMILY MEAL

ENTREE:
Pigs in a Poncho
page 96

SIDE:
Eddie's Favorite
Fiesta Corn
page 206

DESSERT:
Blueberry
Cantaloupe Cups
page 265

TAG YOUR MEAL
MEMORIES WITH
#100 FAMILYMEALS

GROCERY LIST

KITCHEN STAPLES
- Oil for frying
- Sugar
- Salt
- Pepper

PRODUCE
- 1 medium cantaloupe
- 1 orange
- 1 pint fresh blueberries
- 1 medium sweet red pepper
- 1 medium sweet yellow pepper

PANTRY
- 1 can (16 oz.) refried beans
- 2 cans (4 oz. each) chopped green chilies
- 1 can (2¼ oz.) sliced ripe olives

MEAT
- 1 package (16 oz.) hot dogs
- 1 package (8 oz.) bacon

DAIRY
- 2 cups (8 oz.) shredded Monterey Jack cheese
- 1 package (8 oz.) reduced-fat cream cheese

- 1 carton (16 oz.) half-and-half cream
- 1 container (6 oz.) orange yogurt

REFRIGERATED/ FREEZER SECTION
- 1 package (25 oz.) flour tortillas (10 in.)
- 2 packages (16 oz. each) frozen super sweet corn

OTHER
- 1 bottle (8 oz.) lemon juice
- 1 bottle (1.25 oz.) poppy seeds
- 1 jar (16 oz.) salsa

MEAL PLANNER

SWEET ♥ SURPRISES

IT'S EASY TO BAKE UP SOME SWEET MEMORIES TODAY!

SOUP & SANDWICH

ENTREE:
Bacon, Mushroom &
Onion Grilled Cheese
Sandwiches
page 106

SIDE:
The Ultimate
Chicken Noodle Soup
page 230

DESSERT:
Fudgy S'mores Brownies
page 250

TAG YOUR MEAL
MEMORIES WITH
#100 FAMILYMEALS

GROCERY LIST

KITCHEN STAPLES
- ○ Canola oil
- ○ All-purpose flour
- ○ Sugar
- ○ Bay leaves
- ○ Vanilla extract
- ○ Salt
- ○ Pepper

PRODUCE
- ○ 8 oz. sliced baby portobello mushrooms
- ○ 1 small onion
- ○ 1 large onion
- ○ 1 bunch celery
- ○ 4 medium carrots
- ○ 1 bunch fresh thyme

- ○ 1 bunch fresh parsley
- ○ 1 head of garlic

PANTRY
- ○ 1 carton (32 oz.) chicken broth
- ○ 1 can (49.5 oz.) chicken broth
- ○ 1 box (12 oz.) Golden Grahams cereal

MEAT
- ○ 2½ lbs. bone-in chicken thighs
- ○ 1 package (8 oz.) bacon

DAIRY
- ○ 4 large eggs
- ○ Butter

- ○ 1 package (7.6 oz.) thin-sliced cheddar cheese

OTHER
- ○ 1 loaf (24 oz.) Texas toast
- ○ 1 package (16 oz.) kluski or egg noodles
- ○ 1 bottle (8 oz.) lemon juice
- ○ 1 can (8 oz.) baking cocoa
- ○ 1 package (10 oz.) miniature marshmallows
- ○ 4 oz. milk chocolate

SEAFOOD STAPLE

ENTREE:
One-Dish
Seafood Meal
page 132

SIDE:
Easy Cheesy Biscuits
page 228

DESSERT:
Frozen Berry &
Yogurt Swirls
page 268

TAG YOUR MEAL
MEMORIES WITH
#100 FAMILYMEALS

GROCERY LIST

KITCHEN STAPLES
- ○ Olive oil
- ○ All-purpose flour
- ○ Baking powder
- ○ Sugar
- ○ Crushed red pepper flakes
- ○ Seafood seasoning
- ○ Cream of tartar
- ○ Salt
- ○ Pepper

PRODUCE
- ○ 1 lemon
- ○ 2 medium ears sweet corn

- ○ Mixed fresh (1 cup) berries
- ○ 1 head of garlic

MEAT/SEAFOOD
- ○ 2 salmon fillets (6 oz. each)
- ○ ¾ lb. uncooked shrimp (31-40 per lb.)
- ○ ½ lb. summer sausage

DAIRY
- ○ Butter
- ○ 1 quart (32 oz.) 2% milk

- ○ 1 package (8 oz.) shredded sharp cheddar cheese
- ○ 1 container (24 oz.) fat-free honey Greek yogurt

OTHER
- ○ 1 package (20 oz.) refrigerated red potato wedges
- ○ 10 plastic or paper cups (3 oz. each) and wooden pop sticks

Small Bites, Big Fun

Emma and Jenni make memories in the kitchen (above) and invite a few friends in on the fun, too (left).

SPRINKLE SOME MAGIC around your kitchen when you bring your little one in for a bit of decorating fun! That's just what Jenni Hagen does with her 5-year-old stepdaughter, Emma.

"Emma is a girly girl," says Jenni. "She adores pink and sprinkles and cupcakes, so decorating baked goods together is a great way to share some girl time."

For this duo, spending time together is key, but they're also creating happy memories. "I know she will remember these events for years to come," Jenni

adds. "I adore the look on her face as she proudly presents her custom-made dessert to her dad."

The pair love to decorate cupcakes and cookies all year long. "It's not just a holiday thing with us," Jenni says. "Kids are always up for frosting and decorating , so let them put the finishing touches on cakes and brownies. The treats don't have to be fancy. I just whip up cupcakes from a boxed mix."

Jenni has even hosted a decorating party for a birthday. "It was actually

pretty easy, and the kids loved it,'" she explains. "I baked the cupcakes early, so when the girls arrived everything was ready. I set out bowls of sprinkles, jimmies and crushed candies for them.

"When the two of us decorate, however, I use a muffin tin to hold the toppings," she says. "Decorating over a jelly roll pan also eases cleanup as everything simply falls onto the pan."

Why not bake up some fun with your little helper today? As Jenni notes, "There's always room for dessert!"

"Each day is a gift! That's why I prepare meals every day regardless of our schedules."

−Suzie Salle
Renton, Washington

ODDS
and ENDS

CREATE the perfect meal with these fun and tasty change-of-pace ideas.

SHRIMP WITH ORZO

This pretty dish always brings smiles at my table. It's a tasty change-of-pace from pasta salads. I serve it with my own vinaigrette to make it even better.
—Ginger Johnson, Pottstown, PA

Takes: 30 min. • **Makes:** 8 servings

- 1 pkg. (16 oz.) orzo pasta
- ¾ lb. peeled and deveined cooked shrimp (31-40 per lb.), cut into thirds
- 1 can (14 oz.) water-packed quartered artichoke hearts, rinsed and drained
- 1 cup finely chopped green pepper
- 1 cup finely chopped sweet red pepper
- ¾ cup finely chopped red onion
- ½ cup pitted Greek olives
- ½ cup minced fresh parsley
- ⅓ cup chopped fresh dill
- ¾ cup Greek vinaigrette

1. Cook orzo according to the package directions. Drain; rinse with cold water and drain well.

2. In a large bowl, combine orzo, shrimp, vegetables, olives and herbs. Add the vinaigrette; toss to coat. Refrigerate, covered, until serving.

Per serving: 1½ cups equals 397 cal., 12g fat (2g sat. fat), 65mg chol., 574mg sodium, 52g carb. (4g sugars, 3g fiber), 18g pro.

(5) INGREDIENTS | FAST FIX

MEXICAN CHOCOLATE DIP

Chocolate, cinnamon and a touch of heat are a classic Mexican trio. Any fruit goes well with fudgy dip. Don't forget to try it with churros!
—*Taste of Home* Test Kitchen

Takes: 10 min. • **Makes:** ½ cup dip

- ¾ cup semisweet chocolate chips
- ⅓ cup heavy whipping cream
- ⅛ tsp. ground cinnamon
- ⅛ tsp. cayenne pepper
   Assorted fresh fruit

In a small heavy saucepan, combine chocolate chips and cream. Using a whisk, heat and stir over medium-low heat for 4-5 minutes or until smooth. Remove from heat; stir in cinnamon and cayenne. Cool slightly. Serve with fruit.

Per serving: 2 tablespoons (calculated without fruit) equals 221 cal., 17g fat (10g sat. fat), 27mg chol., 11mg sodium, 21g carb. (18g sugars, 2g fiber), 2g pro.

FAMILY *FAVORITE*

PANNA COTTA WITH PAPAYA COULIS

Panna cotta means "cooked cream" in Italian. My friend and I developed a version of this rich, creamy dessert that is also tangy and refreshing.
—Shauna Havey, Roy, UT

Prep: 15 min. + chilling
Cook: 5 min. + chilling
Makes: 4 servings

- 2½ tsp. unflavored gelatin
- ¼ cup 2% milk
- 2 cups heavy whipping cream
- ¼ cup sugar
- 1 tsp. vanilla extract

PAPAYA COULIS
- 2 cups coarsely chopped papaya
- 2 to 3 Tbsp. lime juice
- 1 Tbsp. sugar
  Fresh raspberries and fresh mint leaves

1. In a small bowl, sprinkle gelatin over milk; let stand 5 minutes. Meanwhile, in a small saucepan, combine cream and sugar; cook and stir over medium heat until sugar is dissolved. Add the gelatin mixture and vanilla, stirring mixture until the gelatin is completely dissolved.
2. Divide mixture among four dessert dishes. Refrigerate, covered, 2 hours or until set.
3. For coulis, place the papaya, lime juice and sugar in a food processor; process until smooth, scraping down sides of the bowl as needed. Transfer to a small bowl. Refrigerate, covered, until cold.
4. To serve, spoon papaya coulis over panna cotta. Top with the raspberries and mint.
Per serving: 524 cal., 45g fat (28g sat. fat), 166mg chol., 62mg sodium, 28g carb. (26g sugars, 1g fiber), 5g pro.

Table Talk

What would your own radio show be like?

Discuss the type of radio show everyone at the table would host. What sort of music would you play? Would your show be on during the morning drive? Who would be the guests?

ASIAN CHICKEN WRAPS

My kids love all kinds of wraps and Asian foods. An easy go-to in our house, these bundles work for everyone.
—Mary Lou Timpson, Colorado City, AZ

Takes: 25 min. • **Makes:** 4 servings

- 8 frozen breaded chicken tenders (about 10 oz.)
- 2 cups coleslaw mix
- ½ cup sweet chili sauce
- 2 green onions, chopped
- 2 Tbsp. chopped fresh cilantro
- 1 tsp. soy sauce
- 4 flour tortillas (8 in.), warmed
- ½ cup dry roasted peanuts, chopped

1. Bake chicken tenders according to package directions. Meanwhile, in a large bowl, toss coleslaw mix with chili sauce, green onions, cilantro and soy sauce.

2. Arrange chicken down center of each tortilla; top with coleslaw mixture and peanuts. Fold sides of tortillas over filling and roll up. Cut each diagonally in half.
Per serving: 1 wrap equals 519 cal., 21g fat (3g sat. fat), 13mg chol., 1250mg sodium, 66g carb. (19g sugars, 7g fiber), 19g pro.

CHOCOLATE BANANA BRAN MUFFINS

So easy-to-make, these healthy treats still satisfy my chocolate-loving family. Stir in raisin bran instead of bran flakes for a little extra flavor.

—Tracy Chappell, Hamiota, MB

Takes: 25 min. • **Makes:** 1 dozen

- 1 cup all-purpose flour
- ½ cup sugar
- 2 Tbsp. baking cocoa
- 1 tsp. baking powder
- 1 tsp. baking soda
- ½ tsp. salt
- 1 cup bran flakes
- 2 large eggs
- 1 cup mashed ripe bananas (about 2 medium)
- ⅓ cup canola oil
- ¼ cup buttermilk

1. Preheat oven to 400°. In a large bowl, whisk the first six ingredients. Stir in bran flakes. In another bowl, whisk the eggs, bananas, oil and buttermilk until blended. Add to the flour mixture; stir just until ingredients are moistened.
2. Fill foil-lined muffin cups three-fourths full. Bake for 12-14 minutes or until a toothpick inserted in center comes out clean. Cool 5 minutes before removing from pan to a wire rack. Serve warm.
Per serving: 1 muffin equals 169 cal., 7g fat (1g sat. fat), 35mg chol., 278mg sodium, 24g carb. (12g sugars, 2g fiber), 3g pro. **Diabetic Exchanges:** 1½ starch, 1½ fat.

DILL PICKLE HAMBURGER PIZZA

My husband's favorite foods are pizza and cheeseburgers, so I combined the two in a crazy good pizza with mayo and dill pickle juice topping.

—Angie Zimmerman, Eureka, IL

Takes: 30 min. • **Makes:** 6 servings

- ½ lb. ground beef
- 1 prebaked 12-in. pizza crust
- ½ cup ketchup
- ¼ cup prepared mustard
- 1½ cups (6 oz.) shredded cheddar cheese
- 2 cups shredded lettuce
- ½ cup chopped dill pickle
- ¼ cup chopped onion
- ½ cup mayonnaise
- 2 to 3 Tbsp. dill pickle juice

1. Preheat the oven to 425°. In a large skillet, cook and crumble beef over medium heat until no longer pink, about 3-4 minutes; drain.
2. Meanwhile, place the crust on an ungreased baking sheet or pizza pan. Mix ketchup and mustard; spread over crust. Add ground beef; bake 5 minutes. Sprinkle with cheese; bake until cheese is bubbly and crust is lightly browned, 8-10 minutes more.
3. Top with lettuce, pickle and onion. Whisk mayonnaise and enough pickle juice to reach the desired consistency; drizzle over the pizza.
Per serving: 1 slice equals 521 cal., 32g fat (10g sat. fat), 59mg chol., 1192mg sodium, 36g carb. (7g sugars, 2g fiber), 21g pro.

Have It Your Way

It's easy to customize this pizza. Don't like pickles? Leave them off. Add a little cooked and crumbled bacon or toss on a handful of diced onion. Sprinkle with chopped tomatoes for color, too!

TZATZIKI POTATO SALAD

My son has an egg allergy, so potato salad with a yogurt dressing is perfect for him—and for most everyone who finds it on the dinner or buffet table.
—Cindy Romberg, Mississauga, ON

Prep: 25 min. + chilling
Makes: 12 servings

- 3 lbs. small red potatoes, halved
- 1 carton (12 oz.) refrigerated tzatziki sauce
- 2 celery ribs, thinly sliced
- ½ cup plain Greek yogurt
- 2 green onions, chopped
- 2 Tbsp. snipped fresh dill
- 2 Tbsp. minced fresh parsley
- ½ tsp. salt
- ¼ tsp. celery salt
- ¼ tsp. pepper
- 1 Tbsp. minced fresh mint, optional

1. Place potatoes in a Dutch oven; add water to cover. Bring to a boil. Reduce heat; cook, uncovered, 10-15 minutes or until tender. Drain and place in a large bowl. Refrigerate, covered, until chilled.
2. In a small bowl, mix the tzatziki sauce, celery, yogurt, green onions, dill, parsley, salt, celery salt, pepper and the mint if desired. Spoon over potatoes; gently toss to coat.
Per serving: ¾ cup equals 128 cal., 3g fat (2g sat. fat), 7mg chol., 190mg sodium, 21g carb. (3g sugars, 2g fiber), 4g pro.

---

⑤INGREDIENTS

GARLIC LOAF

This golden loaf has garlicky goodness in every bite. People go wild over its savory flavor. Try serving it with an herb-infused or lightly salted olive oil for dunking.
—*Taste of Home* Cooking School

Prep: 15 min. + rising • **Bake:** 20 min.
Makes: 1 loaf (24 pieces)

- 2 loaves (1 lb. each) frozen bread dough or 24 frozen unbaked white dinner rolls, thawed
- ½ cup finely chopped sweet onion
- ½ cup butter, melted
- 2 garlic cloves, minced
- 1 tsp. dried parsley flakes
- ¼ tsp. salt
   Herb-seasoned olive oil, optional

1. Divide dough into 24 pieces. In a small bowl, combine the onion, butter, garlic, parsley and salt. Dip each piece of dough into butter mixture; place in a 10-in. fluted tube pan coated with cooking spray. Cover and let rise in a warm place until doubled, about 1 hour.
2. Bake at 375° for 20-25 minutes or until golden brown. Serve warm with the olive oil if desired.
Per serving: 1 piece equals 141 cal., 5g fat (2g sat. fat), 10mg chol., 263mg sodium, 19g carb. (2g sugars, 2g fiber), 4g pro.

> **Dress It Up**
> To add a bit of color, flavor and crunch to her potato salad, Cindy Romberg says she stirs in a few sliced radishes, chopped apple bits and diced garlic dill pickles.

QUICK AMBROSIA FRUIT SALAD

I mix in a little coconut and just enough marshmallows so my ambrosia tastes like the creamy version I grew up with. Now everyone in my home loves it too.

—Trisha Kruse, Eagle, ID

Takes: 10 min. • **Makes:** 6 servings

- 1 can (8¼ oz.) fruit cocktail, drained
- 1 can (8 oz.) unsweetened pineapple chunks, drained
- 1 cup green grapes
- 1 cup seedless red grapes
- 1 cup miniature marshmallows
- 1 medium banana, sliced
- ¾ cup vanilla yogurt
- ½ cup flaked coconut

In a large bowl, combine all ingredients. Chill until serving.

Per serving: ¾ cup equals 191 cal., 4g fat (3g sat. fat), 2mg chol., 48mg sodium, 40g carb. (34g sugars, 2g fiber), 3g pro.

ALMOND-VANILLA YOGURT PARFAITS

I'm a night-shift nurse. When I get home, I make a crunchy parfait with yogurt as a protein boost before heading off to a good day's sleep.

—Meredith Brazinski, Neptune, NJ

Takes: 15 min. • **Makes:** 4 servings

- 4 cups reduced-fat plain Greek yogurt
- 1 pkg. (3.4 oz.) instant vanilla or cheesecake pudding mix
- ½ cup almond butter
- 1 cup granola with fruit and nuts Toasted chopped almonds, optional

READY IN 15 MINUTES

In a large bowl, mix yogurt and pudding mix until well blended; gently fold in the almond butter to swirl. Layer ½ cup of the yogurt mixture and 2 tablespoons granola in each of four parfait glasses. Repeat layers. If desired, sprinkle with almonds. Serve immediately.

Per serving: 1 serving (calculated without almonds) equals 560 cal., 26g fat (5g sat. fat), 13mg chol., 508mg sodium, 56g carb. (34g sugars, 5g fiber), 32g pro.

MEDITERRANEAN TORTELLINI SALAD

One of my childhood friends moved to Italy 20 years ago. During a recent visit to see her, I enjoyed a scrumptious salad made with tortellini and fresh vegetables, and here's my re-creation.
—Kelly Mapes, Fort Collins, CO

Takes: 30 min. • **Makes:** 6 servings

- 1 **pkg. (19 oz.) frozen cheese tortellini**
- 1 **pkg. (14 oz.) smoked turkey sausage, sliced**
- ¾ **cup prepared pesto**
- 2 **cups fresh baby spinach, chopped**
- 2 **cups sliced baby portobello mushrooms**
- 1 **can (15 oz.) white kidney or cannellini beans, rinsed and drained**
- 1 **cup roasted sweet red peppers, chopped**
- 1 **cup (4 oz.) crumbled feta cheese**
- ¼ **cup pitted Greek olives, sliced**

1. Cook the cheese tortellini according to package directions.
2. Meanwhile, in a large nonstick skillet coated with cooking spray, cook and stir sausage over medium heat 6-7 minutes or until lightly browned. Transfer to a bowl.
3. Drain tortellini; add to sausage. Stir in pesto. Add remaining ingredients; toss to combine. Serve salad warm or refrigerate until chilled.
Per serving: 1½ cups equals 334 cal., 17g fat (6g sat. fat), 45mg chol., 981mg sodium, 25g carb. (2g sugars, 4g fiber), 19g pro.

BUTTERMILK PEACH ICE CREAM

Making a batch of homemade ice cream is a great way to bring the family into the kitchen, give kids a quick science lesson and get creative with ingredients...all at the same time!
—Kim Higginbotham, Knoxville, TN

Prep: 15 min. + chilling
Process: 30 min./batch + freezing
Makes: 2 qt.

- 2 **lbs. ripe peaches (about 7 medium), peeled and quartered**
- ½ **cup sugar**
- ½ **cup packed brown sugar**
- 1 **Tbsp. lemon juice**
- 1 **tsp. vanilla extract**
  Pinch salt
- 2 **cups buttermilk**
- 1 **cup heavy whipping cream**

1. Place the peaches in a food processor; process until smooth. Add sugar, brown sugar, lemon juice, vanilla and salt; process until blended.
2. In a large bowl, mix the buttermilk and cream. Stir in peach mixture. Refrigerate, covered, 1 hour or until cold.
3. Fill cylinder of ice cream maker no more than two-thirds full. Freeze according to manufacturer's directions, refrigerating any remaining mixture to process later. Transfer ice cream to freezer containers, allowing headspace for expansion. Freeze for 2-4 hours or until firm. Let ice cream stand at room temperature 10 minutes before serving.
Per serving: ½ cup equals 137 cal., 6g fat (4g sat. fat), 22mg chol., 75mg sodium, 20g carb. (19g sugars, 1g fiber), 2g pro. **Diabetic Exchanges:** 1 starch, 1 fat.

(5) INGREDIENTS | FAST FIX

BBQ HOT DOG & POTATO PACKS

The kids will have fun helping assemble these nifty foil packs, then savoring the tasty results in short order. They're perfect for any camping trip—or for camping in the backyard.
—Kelly Westphal, Wind Lake, WI

Takes: 20 min. • **Makes:** 4 servings

1   **pkg. (20 oz.) refrigerated red potato wedges**
4   **hot dogs**
1   **small onion, cut into wedges**
¼   **cup shredded cheddar cheese**
½   **cup barbecue sauce**

1. Divide the potato wedges among four pieces of heavy-duty foil (about 18 in. square). Top each with a hot dog, onion wedges and shredded cheese. Drizzle with barbecue sauce. Fold foil around mixture, sealing tightly.
2. Grill, covered, over medium heat for 10-15 minutes or until heated through. Open the foil carefully to allow the steam to escape.
Per serving: 293 cal., 16g fat (7g sat. fat), 33mg chol., 1227mg sodium, 25g carb. (9g sugars, 4g fiber), 11g pro.

FRESH CRANBERRY RELISH

This no-cook cranberry sauce is a little different from the traditional version you're probably used to. The fresh taste is slightly more tart but will mellow the longer it sits in the refrigerator.
—Deborah Williams, Peoria, AZ

Prep: 15 min. + chilling • **Makes:** 4 cups

1   **pkg. (12 oz.) fresh or frozen cranberries, chopped**
1   **can (8 oz.) unsweetened crushed pineapple, drained**
1   **medium apple, chopped**
1   **medium orange, chopped**
1   **cup sugar**
¾   **cup chopped pecans, toasted**
1   **Tbsp. lemon juice**
½   **tsp. ground cinnamon**
½   **tsp. minced fresh gingerroot**

Place all the ingredients in a large bowl; toss to combine. Refrigerate the relish, covered, overnight to blend.
Note: To toast nuts, bake in a shallow pan in a 350° oven for 5-10 minutes or cook in a skillet over low heat until lightly browned, stirring nuts occasionally.
Per serving: ¼ cup equals 113 cal., 4g fat (trace sat. fat), 0 chol., 1mg sodium, 20g carb. (17g sugars, 2g fiber), 1g pro.

NOTES

_____
_____
_____
_____
_____
_____
_____
_____

BERRY TASTY
FROZEN LEMONADE

This quick treat is just as pretty as it is delicious. With raspberries, blueberries and lemon juice, it's a great way to cool off summer meals or add a bit of fun to dreary winter days.

—Shawn Carleton, San Diego, CA

....

Prep: 10 min. • **Makes:** 4 servings

- 1 **cup lemon juice**
- 1 **cup sugar**
- 4 **cups ice cubes**
- 1 **cup fresh or frozen blueberries**
   Maraschino cherries

Place lemon juice, sugar and ice in a blender; cover and process until slushy. Divide blueberries among four chilled glasses; muddle slightly. Add lemon slush; top with cherries.

Per serving: ¾ cup (calculated without cherries): 229 cal., trace fat (trace sat. fat), 0 chol., 1mg sodium, 60g carb. (55g sugars, 1g fiber), trace pro.

GERMAN APPLES

In culinary school, I had to make a salad with Granny Smith apples. I remembered my mother's German potato salad and swapped out the potatoes.

—Sharyn Hill, Las Cruces, NM

Prep: 10 min. • **Cook:** 25 min.
Makes: 6 servings

- 6 bacon strips, cut crosswise into ½-in. slices
- ½ cup chopped onion
- 2 Tbsp. all-purpose flour
- 1 tsp. salt
- ½ tsp. pepper
- 1 cup water
- ½ cup cider vinegar
- ¼ cup sugar
- 5½ cups Granny Smith apples (about 4 large), cut into ½-in. slices

1. In a large skillet, cook the bacon over medium heat until crisp; drain on paper towels. Discard all but 2 Tbsp. drippings. Add onion; cook until tender, 2-3 minutes. Stir in flour, salt and pepper until blended. Add water and vinegar; cook and stir until slightly thickened, about 1 minute. Stir in sugar until dissolved.
2. Return bacon to pan; gently add apple slices. Cook, stirring constantly, until the apples are wilted and slightly caramelized, about 10-12 minutes. Remove from heat; serve warm.
Per serving: ¾ cup equals 232 cal., 11g fat (4g sat. fat), 18mg chol., 582mg sodium, 29g carb. (22g sugars, 3g fiber), 4g pro.

EAT SMART FAST FIX

CHICKEN CUCUMBER BOATS

I've tended a garden for decades, and these colorful cucumber boats hold my fresh tomatoes, peas and dill perfectly. It's absolute garden greatness.

—Ronna Farley, Rockville, MD

Takes: 15 min. • **Makes:** 2 servings

- 2 medium cucumbers
- ½ cup fat-free plain Greek yogurt
- 2 Tbsp. mayonnaise
- ½ tsp. garlic salt
- 3 tsp. snipped fresh dill, divided
- 1 cup chopped cooked chicken breast
- 1 cup chopped seeded tomato (about 1 large), divided
- ½ cup fresh or frozen peas, thawed

1. Cut each cucumber lengthwise in half; scoop out pulp, leaving a ¼-in. shell. In a bowl, mix yogurt, mayonnaise, garlic salt and 1 tsp. dill; gently stir in chicken, ¾ cup tomato and peas.
2. Spoon into cucumber shells. Top with the remaining tomato and dill.
Per serving: 2 filled cucumber halves equals 322 cal., 13g fat (2g sat. fat), 59mg chol., 398mg sodium, 18g carb. (10g sugars, 6g fiber), 34g. pro. **Diabetic Exchanges:** ½ starch, 4 lean meat, 2 vegetable, 2 fat.

(5)INGREDIENTS
ROSEMARY LEMONADE

A friend suggested that I add a sprig of rosemary to lemonade. The herb makes a familiar beverage fresh and bright.
—Dixie Graham, Rancho Cucamonga, CA

Prep: 10 min. • **Cook:** 15 min. + chilling
Makes: 8 servings

- 2 cups water
- 2 fresh rosemary sprigs
- ½ cup sugar
- ½ cup honey
- 1¼ cups fresh lemon juice
- 6 cups cold water
  Ice cubes
  Additional lemon slices and fresh rosemary sprigs, optional

1. In a small saucepan, bring 2 cups water to a boil; add the rosemary sprigs. Reduce heat; simmer, covered, for 10 minutes.
2. Strain water; discarding the rosemary. Stir in the sugar and honey until dissolved. Transfer liquid to a pitcher; refrigerate for 15 minutes.
3. Add lemon juice; stir in the cold water. Serve the lemonade over ice. If desired, top with additional lemon slices and rosemary sprigs.
Per serving: 1 cup equals 121 cal., 0 fat (0 sat. fat), 0 chol., 1mg sodium, 33g carb. (31g sugars, 0 fiber), 0 pro.

PEAR-PECAN SAUSAGE QUICHE

For a distinctive quiche, combine the savory flavor of sausage with the sweetness of pear slices. It's an easy dinner or brunch or, when served in narrow slices, a hearty side dish.
—Patricia Harmon, Baden, PA

Prep: 15 min. • **Bake:** 35 min.
Makes: 8 servings

- 1 sheet refrigerated pie pastry
- ½ lb. bulk hot Italian sausage
- ⅓ cup chopped sweet onion
- 1 medium pear, sliced
- ⅓ cup chopped pecans
- 4 large eggs
- 1½ cups half-and-half cream
- ½ tsp. salt
- ½ tsp. dried thyme
- ⅛ tsp. ground nutmeg
- 1 cup (4 oz.) shredded cheddar cheese
- 8 pecan halves

1. Line a 9-in. pie plate with pastry. Trim pastry to ½ in. beyond edge of pie plate; flute edges.
2. In a large skillet, cook the sausage and onion over medium heat for 4-5 minutes or until the meat is no longer pink; drain. Arrange pear slices in the crust; top with sausage. Sprinkle with pecans. In a large bowl, whisk eggs, cream, salt, thyme and nutmeg. Stir in cheese. Pour over sausage.
3. Bake at 350° for 35-40 minutes or until a knife inserted near the center comes out clean and crust is golden brown. Cover edges with foil during the last 15 minutes to prevent overbrowning if necessary. Garnish with pecan halves. Let stand for 5 minutes before slicing.
Per serving: 1 slice equals 375 cal., 27g fat (12g sat. fat), 160mg chol., 520mg sodium, 20g carb. (6g sugars, 1g fiber), 12g pro.

(5)INGREDIENTS FAST FIX ▶
WALNUT BUTTER SPREAD

Try this healthy alternative spread and I bet you'll start making more of your own homemade spreads. It's so simple, takes just minutes, and you always know exactly what's in it. Yum!
—Bryan Kennedy, Kaneohe, HI

Takes: 10 min. • **Makes:** ⅔ cup

- 2 cups walnut halves, toasted
- 2 tsp. grated orange peel
- ½ tsp. coarsely ground pepper
- ⅛ tsp. salt
  Whole wheat bread slices, toasted
  Apricot preserves, optional
  Brie cheese, optional

Place the walnuts, orange peel, pepper and salt in a food processor; cover and process until creamy. Spread on toast, with preserves and Brie if desired.
Per serving: 2 Tbsp. (calculated without bread, preserves and cheese) equals: 263 cal., 26g fat (2g sat. fat), 0 chol., 60mg sodium, 6g carb. (1g sugars, 3g fiber), 6g pro.

PEANUT BUTTER-BANANA YOGURT PARFAITS

For a fast breakfast or lunch, I layer vanilla yogurt with bananas, peanuts and multigrain cereal. It's crunchy, easy and perfect for kids.
—Teresa Miller, Hamilton, IN

Takes: 5 min. • **Makes:** 4 servings

- 3 cups vanilla yogurt
- 1 cup dried banana chips, crushed
- 1 cup Peanut Butter Multi Grain Cheerios
- 2 large ripe bananas, sliced
- ¼ cup unsalted dry roasted peanuts, chopped

Layer ¾ cup of yogurt, ¼ cup of banana chips, ¼ cup of cereal into four parfait glasses. Top with the banana slices and the peanuts.

Per serving: 1 parfait equals 457 cal., 17g fat (11g sat. fat), 9mg chol., 152mg sodium, 67g carb. (47g sugars, 5g fiber), 14g pro.

MAKEOVER FLUFFY LIME SALAD

Loaded with crunchy walnuts, tangy pineapple and lip-smacking lime flavor, this delicious salad could even double as a fun dessert!
—*Taste of Home* Test Kitchen

Prep: 15 min. + chilling
Makes: 8 servings

- 1 can (8 oz.) unsweetened crushed pineapple, undrained
- 1 pkg. (.3 oz.) sugar-free lime gelatin
- 3 Tbsp. water
- 6 oz. reduced-fat cream cheese
- 1 cup miniature marshmallows
- ½ cup chopped walnuts
- 1 carton (8 oz.) frozen reduced-fat whipped topping, thawed

1. Drain pineapple, reserving juice; set the pineapple aside. In a small saucepan, combine the gelatin, water and reserved juice. Cook and stir over low heat until the gelatin is dissolved. Refrigerate until syrupy, about 30 minutes.
2. In a small bowl, beat the cream cheese until fluffy. Stir in the gelatin mixture, marshmallows, walnuts and pineapple. Fold in whipped topping.
3. Transfer to a serving bowl. Cover and refrigerate for 2 hours or until set.
Per serving: ¾ cup equals 206 cal., 12g fat (7g sat. fat), 15mg chol., 125mg sodium, 21g carb. (11g sugars, 1g fiber), 4g pro.

PESTO BUTTERMILK DRESSING

A good dressing is hard to beat; a great one is brilliant. My family loves a tangy blend of buttermilk and Greek yogurt.
—Liz Bellville, Havelock, NC

Prep: 10 min. + chilling • **Makes:** 1¾ cups

- ⅔ cup buttermilk
- ½ cup fat-free plain Greek yogurt
- ½ cup prepared pesto
- ¼ cup shredded Parmesan cheese
- 1 Tbsp. white wine vinegar
- 1 Tbsp. grated lemon peel
- 1 garlic clove, minced
- ½ tsp. coarsely ground pepper
- ⅛ tsp. salt

Place all the ingredients in a jar with a tight-fitting lid; shake well. Refrigerate for 1 hour. Just before serving, shake dressing again.
Per serving: 2 Tbsp. equals 50 cal., 4g fat (1g sat. fat), 2mg chol., 165mg sodium, 2g carb. (1g sugars, trace fiber), 2g pro.
Diabetic Exchange: 1 fat.

FAST FIX

CHIP-CRUSTED GRILLED CORN

For my version of Mexican street corn, I roll the ears in crushed chips. For extra pizzazz, try different chip flavors like ranch dressing and jalapeno.
—Crystal Schlueter, Northglenn, CO

Takes: 30 min. • **Makes:** 6 servings

- ¾ cup mayonnaise
- ¼ cup sour cream
- 2 Tbsp. minced fresh cilantro
- ½ tsp. salt
- ¼ tsp. cayenne pepper
- ¼ tsp. pepper
- 1 cup crushed tortilla chips
- 6 medium ears sweet corn, husks removed
  Lime wedges

1. In a small bowl, combine the first six ingredients. Refrigerate, covered, until serving. Place tortilla chips in a shallow bowl. Grill corn, covered, over medium heat for 15-20 minutes or until tender, turning occasionally.
2. When cool enough to handle, spread corn with mayonnaise mixture; roll in chips. Grill corn, covered, 1-2 minutes longer or until lightly browned. Serve with lime wedges.
Per serving: 1 ear of corn equals 355 cal., 27g fat (5g sat. fat), 17mg chol., 405mg sodium, 26g carb. (7g sugars, 2g fiber), 4g pro.

ITALIAN PATTIES

While trying to think of a new way to fix hamburgers with the same old ground beef, I came up with an easy Italian spin. They're great with or without a bun.
—Rebekah Beyer, Sabetha, KS

Takes: 20 min. • **Makes:** 4 servings

- 1 cup (4 oz.) shredded part-skim mozzarella cheese, divided
- 1 tsp. Worcestershire sauce
- ¼ tsp. Italian seasoning
- ⅛ tsp. salt
- ⅛ tsp. pepper
- 1 lb. ground beef
  Marinara or spaghetti sauce, warmed

1. In a large bowl, combine ½ cup cheese and next 4 ingredients. Add beef; mix lightly but thoroughly. Shape into four ½-in.-thick patties.

2. Grill burgers, covered, over medium heat or broil 4 in. from heat 4-5 minutes on each side or until a thermometer reads 160°. Sprinkle with remaining cheese; grill, covered, for 1-2 minutes longer or until cheese is melted. Serve the patties with marinara sauce.

Per serving: 1 burger (calculated without marinara sauce) equals: 279 cal., 18g fat (8g sat. fat), 86mg chol., 282mg sodium, 1g carb. (1g sugars, trace fiber), 27g pro.

UNDER
300
CALORIES

LEMON FLUFF

Sweet, lemony and light, fluff is even better when you slice fresh strawberries over the top.

—Nancy Brown, Dahinda, IL

Prep: 15 min. + chilling
Makes: 20 servings

- 1 can (12 oz.) evaporated milk
- 1½ cups graham cracker crumbs
- ⅓ cup butter, melted
- 1 pkg. (.3 oz.) sugar-free lemon gelatin
- 1 cup boiling water
- 3 Tbsp. lemon juice
- 1 pkg. (8 oz.) reduced-fat cream cheese
- ¾ cup sugar
- 1 tsp. vanilla extract

1. Pour the milk into a large metal bowl; place mixer beaters in the bowl. Cover and refrigerate for at least 2 hours.
2. In a small bowl, combine the graham cracker crumbs and butter; set aside 1 Tbsp. for topping. Press the remaining crumb mixture into a 13x9-in. baking dish. Chill until set.
3. Meanwhile, in a small bowl, dissolve the gelatin in boiling water. Stir in the lemon juice; cool.
4. In another bowl, beat the cream cheese, sugar and vanilla until smooth. Add gelatin mixture and mix well. Beat evaporated milk until soft peaks form; fold into cream cheese mixture. Pour over crust. Sprinkle with reserved crumbs. Refrigerate for at least 2 hours before serving. Refrigerate any leftovers.

Per serving: 1 piece equals 135 cal., 7g fat (4g sat. fat), 21mg chol., 136mg sodium, 15g carb. (12g sugars, trace fiber), 3g pro.
Diabetic Exchanges: 1 starch, 1 fat.

GRAPES WITH LEMON-HONEY YOGURT

We like to sweeten up our Greek yogurt with honey, cinnamon and vanilla. It's a tasty counterpoint to plump grapes and crunchy nuts.

—Julie Sterchi, Campbellsville, KY

Takes: 10 min. • **Makes:** 8 servings

- 1 cup fat-free plain Greek yogurt
- 2 Tbsp. honey
- 1 tsp. vanilla extract
- ½ tsp. grated lemon peel
- ⅛ tsp. ground cinnamon
- 3 cups seedless red grapes
- 3 cups green grapes
- 3 Tbsp. sliced almonds, toasted

In a small bowl, combine the first five ingredients. Divide grapes among eight serving bowls. Top with yogurt mixture; sprinkle with almonds.

Note: To toast nuts, bake in a shallow pan in a 350° oven for 5-10 minutes or cook in a skillet over low heat until lightly browned, stirring nuts occasionally.

Per serving: ¾ cup grapes with 2 Tbsp. yogurt mixture and about 1 tsp. almonds equals 138 cal., 2g fat (trace sat. fat), 0 chol., 20mg sodium, 28g carb. (26g sugars, 2g fiber), 6g. pro. **Diabetic Exchanges:** 1½ fruit, ½ starch.

STROMBOLI SLICES

I've served this dish to teens, college students and a women's group. Easy and delicious, it's sure to please at your table as well.
—Rachel Jackson, Pennsville, NJ

Takes: 25 min. • **Makes:** 1½ dozen slices

- 1 tube (11 oz.) refrigerated crusty French loaf
- 2 Tbsp. olive oil
- ½ tsp. dried basil
- 1 pkg. (3½ oz.) sliced pepperoni
- 2 cups (8 oz.) shredded part-skim mozzarella cheese
- 1 cup meatless spaghetti sauce, warmed

1. Preheat oven to 350°. Unroll loaf of dough at the seam into a square; cut in half. Combine the oil and basil; brush lengthwise down half of each rectangle to within ½ in. of edges. Layer brushed side with the pepperoni and cheese. Fold plain dough over filling and pinch edges to seal. Place on greased baking sheets.
2. Bake for 10-15 minutes or until golden brown. Cut into slices. Serve warm with spaghetti sauce.
Per serving: 119 cal., 7g fat (3g sat. fat), 12mg chol., 331mg sodium, 9g carb. (2g sugars, 1g fiber), 6g pro.

"My mother insisted on sit-down meals every night. We want our kids to have that experience, too."
—YVONNE NAVE, LYONS, KS

GRILLED CORN RELISH

To get kids to eat their veggies, serve up this colorful relish. It's an instant upgrade for hot dogs!
—Ellen Riley, Murfreesboro, TN

Takes: 25 min. • **Makes:** 2 cups

- 1 large sweet red pepper
- 2 medium ears sweet corn, husks removed
- 5 Tbsp. honey Dijon vinaigrette, divided
- 2 green onions, thinly sliced
- ½ tsp. coarsely ground pepper
- ¼ tsp. salt

1. Cut the red pepper lengthwise in half; remove seeds. Grill red pepper and corn, covered, over medium heat 10-15 minutes or until tender, turning and basting pieces occasionally with 3 Tbsp. vinaigrette.
2. Remove corn from cobs and chop red pepper; transfer to a small bowl. Add the green onions, pepper, salt and remaining vinaigrette; toss to combine.
Per serving: ¼ cup equals 42 cal., 1g fat (trace sat. fat), 0 chol., 157mg sodium, 8g carb. (4g sugars, 1g fiber), 1g pro. **Diabetic Exchange:** ½ starch.

ICED TEA PARFAITS

Here's a gelatin parfait for a quick, light, refreshing bite. Adults like the unexpected flavor of tea, and kids have fun finding the cherry at the bottom.
—Teena Petrus, Johnstown, PA

Prep: 15 min. + chilling
Makes: 4 servings

- 2 **cups water**
- 3 **tea bags**
- 1 **pkg. (3 oz.) lemon gelatin**
- 4 **maraschino cherries**
- 1½ **cups whipped topping, divided**
- 4 **lemon slices**

1. In a small saucepan, bring the water to a boil. Remove from the heat; add the tea bags. Cover and steep for 5 minutes. Discard tea bags. Stir gelatin into tea until completely dissolved. Cool slightly.
2. Pour ¼ cup gelatin mixture into each of four parfait glasses. Place a cherry in each glass; refrigerate until set but not firm, about 1 hour. Transfer remaining gelatin mixture to small bowl; refrigerate for 1 hour or until soft-set.
3. Whisk gelatin mixture for 2-3 minutes or until smooth. Stir in ½ cup of whipped topping; spoon into the parfait glasses. Refrigerate for at least 2 hours. Just before serving, top with the remaining whipped topping and garnish with the lemon slices.
Per serving: 1 parfait equals 162 cal., 5g fat (5g sat. fat), 0 chol., 48mg sodium, 27g carb. (24g sugars, 0 fiber), 2g pro. **Diabetic Exchanges:** 1½ starch, 1 fat.

PEPPERONI ROLL-UPS

Each bite of this fast treat has gooey, melted cheese and real pizza flavor. It's a big hit at my house, especially when I serve it with pizza sauce for dipping.
—Debra Purcell, Safford, AZ

Takes: 20 min. • **Makes:** 8 appetizers

- 1 **tube (8 oz.) refrigerated crescent rolls**
- 16 **slices pepperoni, cut into quarters**
- 2 **pieces string cheese (1 oz. each), cut into quarters**
- ¾ **tsp. Italian seasoning, divided**
- ¼ **tsp. garlic salt**

1. Unroll crescent dough; separate into eight triangles. Place eight pepperoni pieces on each. Place a piece of cheese on the short side of each triangle; sprinkle with ½ tsp. Italian seasoning. Roll up each, starting with the short side; pinch seams to seal. Sprinkle with the garlic salt and remaining Italian seasoning.
2. Place 2 in. apart on a greased baking sheet. Bake at 375° for 10-12 minutes or until golden brown. Serve warm.
Per serving: 2 roll-ups equals 282 cal., 17g fat (5g sat. fat), 12mg chol., 766mg sodium, 22g carb. (4g sugars, trace fiber), 7g pro.

KiDS in the KiTCHeN

Pepperoni Roll-Ups are a great treat for teens to make themselves, but younger kids can get into the act, too! Let them set the pepperoni and cheese in place, sprinkle on the seasonings and roll it all up!

ORANGE-BERRY YOGURT MUFFINS

These are my family's favorite muffins, so I love to keep them on hand. The treats freeze and reheat beautifully. Just warm them in the oven and you're ready to go.
—Amber Cummings, Indianapolis, IN

Prep: 15 min. • **Bake:** 25 min.
Makes: 15 regular muffins

- 1 cup all-purpose flour
- 1 cup whole wheat flour
- ¾ cup sugar
- 3 tsp. baking powder
- ¼ tsp. salt
- 1 cup fat-free plain Greek yogurt
- ½ cup orange juice
- ⅓ cup unsweetened applesauce
- 2 large egg whites
- 1 large egg
- 4 tsp. grated orange peel
- 1 cup fresh blueberries or frozen unsweetened blueberries, unthawed

1. Preheat oven to 350°. In a large bowl, whisk flours, sugar, baking powder and salt. In another bowl, whisk the yogurt, orange juice, applesauce, egg whites, egg and orange peel until blended. Add to flour mixture; stir just until moistened. Fold in blueberries.

2. Coat muffin cups with cooking spray; fill three-fourths full with batter. Bake for 24-26 minutes or until a toothpick inserted in center comes out clean. Cool 5 minutes before removing from pans to wire racks. Serve warm.

Per serving: 1 muffin equals 126 cal., 1g fat (trace sat. fat), 14mg chol., 140mg sodium, 26g carb. (13g sugars, 2g fiber), 5g pro.
Diabetic Exchange: 1½ starch.

"My family's health and happiness are my top priorities, so I strive to prepare good food for them, no matter how little time I have."

—NANCY BROWN, DAHINDA, IL

Homemade Touch

Mix up this tasty butter and store it in the fridge to add fast flair to everything from frozen waffles to deli chicken sandwiches.

⑤ INGREDIENTS FAST FIX

EASY STRAWBERRY BUTTER

After strawberry picking for the first time, I developed this fruity butter spread. Try other fruit spreads using raspberries, blackberries or even seedless jams like apricot, my favorite.
—Julie Herrera-Lemler, Rochester, MN

Takes: 5 min. • **Makes:** 2¼ cup

- 6 **large fresh strawberries, stems removed and room temperature**
- 1 **cup butter, softened**
- ¾ **to 1 cup confectioners' sugar**

Pulse strawberries in a food processor until chopped. Add the butter and ½ cup confectioners' sugar; process until blended. Add enough of the remaining confectioners' sugar to reach the desired spreading consistency and sweetness. Refrigerate the remaining strawberry butter.

Per serving: 1 tablespoon equals 56 cal., 5g fat (3g sat. fat), 14mg chol., 41mg sodium, 3g carb. (3g sugars, 0 fiber), 0 pro.

Get social with us!
The next time you bake up
a treat for your gang,
share it on Facebook or
Twitter. Be sure to use
#100FamilyMeals.

FAST FIX

MEAT 'N' VEGGIE POCKETS

*For a quick, hearty, handheld meal, omit
any ingredients you don't like and replace
them with others.*
—Danielle Binkley, Huber Heights, OH

Takes: 10 min. • **Makes:** 4 servings

- 1   small cucumber, chopped
- ½   cup chopped onion
- 1   can (2¼ oz.) sliced ripe
      olives, drained
- ½   cup Italian salad dressing
- 4   pita breads (6 in.), halved
- ½   lb. thinly sliced deli ham
- ½   lb. thinly sliced deli turkey
- 4   slices process American cheese

In a small bowl, combine the cucumber,
onion, olives and salad dressing. Fill pita
halves with the ham, turkey and cheese;
top with cucumber mixture.

Per serving: 2 pita halves equals 479 cal., 20g
fat (5g sat. fat), 64mg chol., 2342mg sodium,
44g carb. (5g sugars, 2g fiber), 31g pro.

FAST FIX

HOT DOG PIE

*A co-worker who loves hot dogs shared
this recipe with me. Baked in a purchased
pastry shell, the pie is easy to assemble
and is on the table in just 30 minutes.*
—Amy Bullis, Henryville, PA

Takes: 30 min. • **Makes:** 6 servings

- ½   lb. ground beef
- 4   hot dogs, cut in half
      lengthwise and sliced
- 1   can (16 oz.) baked beans
- ½   cup ketchup
- 2   Tbsp. brown sugar
- 2   Tbsp. prepared mustard
- 2   oz. process cheese
      (Velveeta), cubed
- 1   unbaked deep-dish
      pastry shell (9 in.)
- 4   slices American cheese

1. In a large saucepan, cook the beef over
medium heat until no longer pink; drain.
Add the hot dogs, beans, ketchup, brown
sugar, mustard and cheese cubes. Cook
and stir until cheese is melted.
2. Meanwhile, prick pastry shell with a
fork. Bake at 400° for 10 minutes. Fill
with hot beef mixture. Cut each cheese
slice into four strips; make lattice topping
over pie. Bake for 5-10 minutes longer or
until cheese is melted.
Per serving: 1 slice equals 487 cal., 27g fat
(11g sat. fat), 62mg chol., 1321mg sodium,
43g carb. (13g sugars, 5g fiber), 21g pro.

TOMATO BASIL SNACKERS

Fresh basil, summer-ripe tomatoes and melted mozzarella cheese cover toasted English muffins in a fabulous pick-me-up. It's a fun way to get teens into the kitchen and teach them a new dish they can make for themselves.
—Taste of Home *Test Kitchen*

Takes: 15 min. • **Makes:** 4 servings

- 2　English muffins, split and toasted
- 2　Tbsp. fat-free mayonnaise
- 3　plum tomatoes, cut into ¼-in. slices
- 6　fresh basil leaves, thinly sliced
- ⅛　tsp. pepper
- ½　cup shredded part-skim mozzarella cheese

Place the English muffin halves on an ungreased baking sheet; spread with mayonnaise. Top with the tomatoes, basil, pepper and cheese. Broil 4 in. from the heat for 3-4 minutes or until cheese is melted.

Per serving: 1 muffin half equals 118 cal., 3g fat (2g sat. fat), 9mg chol., 261mg sodium, 17g carb. (3g sugars, 1g fiber), 6g pro. **Diabetic Exchanges:** 1 starch, ½ fat.

CREAMY BEEF & POTATOES

One of my husband's favorite childhood memories was his Grandma Barney's Tater Tot casserole. One day I started preparing it using O'Brien potatoes instead. Now I always make it this way.
—Heather Matthews, Keller, TX

Takes: 20 min. • **Makes:** 4 servings

- 4　cups frozen O'Brien potatoes
- 1　Tbsp. water
- 1　lb. ground beef
- ½　tsp. salt
- ¼　tsp. pepper
- 2　cans (10¾ oz. each) condensed cream of mushroom soup, undiluted
- ⅔　cup 2% milk
- 2　cups (8 oz.) shredded Colby-Monterey Jack cheese

1. Place the potatoes and water in a microwave-safe bowl. Microwave, covered, on high for 8-10 minutes or until tender, stirring twice.

2. Meanwhile, in a Dutch oven, cook beef over medium heat for 6-8 minutes or until no longer pink, breaking into crumbles; drain. Stir in salt and pepper. In a small bowl, whisk soup and milk until blended; add to beef. Stir in potatoes. Sprinkle with the cheese. Reduce the heat to low; cook, covered, until cheese is melted.

Note: This recipe was tested in a 1,100-watt microwave.

Per serving: 1¾ cups equals 664 cal., 38g fat (19g sat. fat), 130mg chol., 1851mg sodium, 40g carb. (5g sugars, 6g fiber), 37g pro.

MY FAMILY MEALS

AT-A-GLANCE JOURNAL
MAKING MEMORIES ONE MEAL AT A TIME.

RECIPE NAME	PAGE	DATE
1.		
2.		
3.		
4.		
5.		
6.		
7.		
8.		
9.		
10.		
11.		
12.		
13.		
14.		
15.		
16.		
17.		
18.		
19.		
20.		
21.		
22.		
23.		
24.		
25.		

RECIPE NAME	PAGE	DATE
26.		
27.		
28.		
29.		
30.		
31.		
32.		
33.		
34.		
35.		
36.		
37.		
38.		
39.		
40.		
41.		
42.		
43.		
44.		
45.		
46.		
47.		
48.		
49.		
50.		

RECIPE NAME	PAGE	DATE
51.		
52.		
53.		
54.		
55.		
56.		
57.		
58.		
59.		
60.		
61.		
62.		
63.		
64.		
65.		
66.		
67.		
68.		
69.		
70.		
71.		
72.		
73.		
74.		
75.		

RECIPE NAME	PAGE	DATE
76.		
77.		
78.		
79.		
80.		
81.		
82.		
83.		
84.		
85.		
86.		
87.		
88.		
89.		
90.		
91.		
92.		
93.		
94.		
95.		
96.		
97.		
98.		
99.		
100.		

GENERAL RECIPE INDEX
Find every recipe by food category and major ingredient.

APPETIZERS & SNACKS
DIP
Mexican Chocolate Dip 281
HOT APPETIZERS
Garlic Loaf 286
Herbed Cheese Sticks. 244
SNACKS
Grapes with Lemon-Honey
  Yogurt 298
Pepperoni Roll-Ups 300
Tomato Basil Snackers 305
SPREADS
Easy Strawberry Butter 303
Walnut Butter Spread 294

APPLES
Apple Maple Pecan Salad. 173
Apple-Pecan Salad with
  Honey Vinaigrette 177
Apple Pie Oatmeal Dessert. 261
Apple-Topped Ham Steak 109
Barbecue Pork Tacos with
  Apple Slaw. 105
Easy Homemade Chunky
  Applesauce 205
German Apples. 293
Grandma Davidson's Baked
  Apple Pudding 272
Quick Apple Crisp 250
Thyme-Baked Apple Slices 206

ASPARAGUS
Lemon-Roasted Asparagus. 203

AVOCADOS
Chipotle Lime Avocado Salad. 170
Citrus Avocado Spinach Salad 183
Grilled Mango & Avocado
  Salad 172

BACON
Bacon & Swiss Chicken Sandwiches . . 56
Bacon Cheeseburger Tater Tot
  Bake 30
Bacon, Mushroom & Onion Grilled
  Cheese Sandwiches 106
Bacon-Potato Corn Chowder. 244
Bacon-Tomato Salad. 183
Bean & Bacon Griddle Burritos 115

BANANAS
Banana Chip Cake 268
Banana Pudding 266
Chocolate Banana Bran Muffins 284
Monkey Bars 263
Peanut Butter-Banana
  Yogurt Parfaits 295
Raspberry-Banana Soft Serve 257

BEANS, GREEN
Easy Green Beans with
  Mushrooms 212
Tomato-Onion Green Beans 210

BEEF
(also see Ground Beef)
MAIN DISHES
Beef Brisket 22
Cocoa-Crusted Beef
  Tenderloin. 17
Fajita in a Bowl 46
Hash Brown-Topped Steak 38
Slow-Cooked Round Steak 21
Slow Cooker Beef Tips 14
Sweet & Tangy Beef Roast 37
Weekday Beef Stew. 40
SANDWICHES
Balsamic Beef Hoagies. 29
Tomato Steak Sandwiches 25

BEVERAGE
Rosemary Lemonade 294

BISCUITS
Cheese & Pesto Biscuits. 243
Easy Cheesy Biscuits. 228
Grandma's Biscuits 235
Ham & Green Onion Biscuits 232
Monkey Bread Biscuits. 225

BLACKBERRIES
Honey-Yogurt Berry Salad 188

BLUEBERRIES
Berried Treasure Angel Food
  Cake 263
Berry Tasty Frozen Lemonade. 292
Blueberry Cantaloupe Cups 265
Honey-Yogurt Berry Salad 188
Orange-Berry Yogurt Muffins 302

BREADS
(also see Biscuits; Corn Bread & Cornmeal;
Muffins & Quick Breads)
Chimichurri Monkey Bread 232
Chocolate Cinnamon Toast 256
Garlic Loaf 286
Great Garlic Bread. 230
Herbed Cheese Sticks. 244
Herby Parmesan Bread 233
Pesto Breadsticks 237

BROCCOLI
Broccoli-Mushroom Bubble
  Bake 227
Broccoli Slaw with Lemon
  Dressing. 176
Lemon Pepper Roasted
  Broccoli 218

BRUSSELS SPROUTS
Brussels Sprouts with Garlic &
    Goat Cheese. 209

BURGERS
(also see Sandwiches & Wraps)
Italian Patties. 297

BUTTERNUT SQUASH
Butternut Squash & Potato Mash. . . 215

CABBAGE & SAUERKRAUT
Apple Maple Pecan Salad. 173
Blue Cheese & Grape Coleslaw 185
Broccoli Slaw with Lemon
    Dressing. 176
Easy Peasy Slaw 187
Jazzed-Up Slaw. 178

CAKES & CUPCAKES
Banana Chip Cake 268
Berried Treasure Angel Food
    Cake 263
Berry Dream Cake. 255
Cake with Pineapple Pudding. 260
Mini Rum Cakes 261
Peanut Butter-Filled Brownie
    Cupcakes. 264

CARAMEL
Caramel Fluff & Toffee Trifle 265
Gooey Caramel-Topped
    Gingersnaps 256

CARROTS
Edamame Corn Carrot Salad 176
Honey-Butter Peas and Carrots 199
Orange Spice Carrots. 203
Pina Colada Carrot Salad. 187

CASSEROLES
(also see Lasagna, Pasta & Noodles)
Bacon Cheeseburger Tater Tot
    Bake 30

Broccoli-Mushroom Bubble
    Bake 227
Burrito Bake 28
Chicken Penne Casserole 71
Creamy Beef & Potatoes 305
Easy Stuffed Shells 44
Favorite Baked Spaghetti. 24
Florentine Spaghetti Bake. 112
Ham & Veggie Casserole 102
Hearty Beef Casserole 41
Mom's Chicken Tetrazzini 74
Pizza Macaroni & Cheese. 121
Pizza Macaroni Bake 17
Pork Shepherd's Pie 111
Slow Cooker Tuna Noodle
    Casserole. 156
Three-Cheese Meatball Mostaccioli. . 20
Turkey Mushroom Tetrazzini 58

CAULIFLOWER
Browned Butter Roasted
    Cauliflower 209

CHEESE
BREADS
Cheddar Corn Dog Muffins. 229
Cheese & Pesto Biscuits 243
Easy Cheesy Biscuits. 228
Herbed Cheese Sticks. 244
Herby Parmesan Bread 233
DESSERT
Candy Bar Cheesecake
    Brownies 271
MAIN DISHES
Beef & Cheese Skillet
    Cobbler 43
Buffalo Shrimp Mac & Cheese. 147
Cheesy Summer Squash
    Flatbreads. 161
Mozzarella Corn Bread Pizza 151
Parmesan Fish Sticks 159
Quick Chicken Parmesan. 57
Sausage & Swiss Chard
    Lasagna 124

Slow Cooker Cheesy White
    Lasagna 82
Three-Cheese Meatball
    Mostaccioli 20
SALADS
Blue Cheese & Grape
    Coleslaw. 185
Feta Garbanzo Bean Salad 189
SANDWICHES
Bacon & Swiss Chicken
    Sandwiches. 56
Bacon, Mushroom & Onion Grilled
    Cheese Sandwiches 106
SIDE DISHES & CONDIMENTS
Baked Parmesan Breaded
    Squash 201
Brussels Sprouts with Garlic &
    Goat Cheese. 209
Parmesan Creamed
    Spinach 202
SOUP
Cheeseburger Soup 224

CHERRIES
Michigan Cherry Salad. 178

CHICKEN
MAIN DISHES
Barbecue Chicken
    Quesadillas 68
Buffalo Chicken Pasta. 88
Chicken & Wild Rice
    Strudels 64
Chicken Caesar Pizza 66
Chicken Penne Casserole 71
Chicken-Stuffed Cubanelle
    Peppers 87
Crispy Fried Chicken 64
Crumb-Coated Ranch
    Chicken 76
Garden Pasta with Chicken. 79
Mom's Chicken Tetrazzini 74
Pecan-Crusted Chicken
    Nuggets. 61

CHICKEN

MAIN DISHES (CONTINUED)

Quick Chicken Parmesan 57
Roasted Chicken Thighs with
  Peppers & Potatoes 63
Roasted Chicken with Potato
  Wedges 84
Slow Cooker Cheesy White
  Lasagna 82
Slow Cooker Chicken Tacos 55
Spanish Rice with Chicken &
  Peas 81
Speedy Chicken Marsala 60
Sweet Tea Barbecued
  Chicken 73
Thai Chicken Tacos 77

SALADS

Chicken Cucumber Boats 293
Spaghetti Salad 80

SANDWICHES

Asian Chicken Wraps 283
Bacon & Swiss Chicken
  Sandwiches 56

SOUPS & CHILI

Chicken Barley Chowder 237
Creamy Chicken Soup 242
Easy Chicken Corn
  Chowder 241
Speedy Chicken Chowder 226
Spring-Thyme Chicken Stew 73
The Ultimate Chicken Noodle
  Soup 230
Tuscan Chicken Soup 239

CHILI

Chili Beef Noodle Skillet 32
Chili Sloppy Joes 19

CHOCOLATE

BREAD

Chocolate Banana Bran
  Muffins 284
Chocolate Cinnamon
  Toast 256

CAKE & CUPCAKES

Banana Chip Cake 268
Peanut Butter-Filled Brownie
  Cupcakes 264

COOKIES, BARS & BROWNIES

Blond Butterscotch
  Brownies 274
Candy Bar Cheesecake
  Brownies 271
Chocolaty S'mores Bars 264
Coconut Brownies 259
Fudgy S'mores Brownies 250
Loaded M&M Oreo Cookie
  Bars 265
Mexican Crinkle Cookies 259

DESSERTS

Chocolate-Covered Strawberry
  Cobbler 260
Creamy Hazelnut Pie 254
Easy Grasshopper Pie 272
Mexican Chocolate Dip 281
Nutella Hand Pies 262
Watermelon Chocolate Chip
  Sorbet 274

CINNAMON

Chocolate Cinnamon Toast 256

COCONUT

Coconut Acorn Squash 208
Coconut Brownies 259
Coconut Macaroon Pie 253

CONDIMENTS

Easy Strawberry Butter 303
Fresh Cranberry Relish 291
Grilled Corn Relish 299
Walnut Butter Spread 294

COOKIES, BARS & BROWNIES

Browned Butter Cereal Bars 270
Candy Bar Cheesecake Brownies . . . 271
Chocolaty S'mores Bars 264
Coconut Brownies 259

Date-Walnut Pinwheels 273
Fudgy S'mores Brownies 250
Gooey Caramel-Topped
  Gingersnaps 256
Grandma Brubaker's Orange
  Cookies 270
Loaded M&M Oreo Cookie
  Bars 265
Mexican Crinkle Cookies 259
Monkey Bars 263
Pecan Butterscotch Cookies 250
Texas Tumbleweeds 268
Toffee Pecan Bars 252
White Almond No-Bake
  Cookies 254

CORN

Bacon-Potato Corn Chowder 244
Cheese Tortellini with Tomatoes
  and Corn 197
Chip-Crusted Grilled Corn 296
Crazy-Quick Corn & Black Bean
  Salad 190
Easy Chicken Corn Chowder 241
Edamame Corn Carrot Salad 176
Eddie's Favorite Fiesta Corn 206
Grilled Corn Relish 299
Ham & Corn Chowder 228
Marina's Golden Corn
  Fritters 238
Shrimp & Corn Stir Fry 154

CORN BREAD & CORNMEAL

Cheddar Corn Dog Muffins 229
Mozzarella Corn Bread Pizza 151
Savory Corn Bread 239

CRANBERRIES

Fresh Cranberry Relish 291
Mixed Green Salad with
  Cranberry Vinaigrette 186

CRISPS & COBBLERS

Apple Pie Oatmeal Dessert 261

Chocolate-Covered Strawberry
   Cobbler 260
Quick Apple Crisp 250

DESSERTS

(also see Cakes & Cupcakes; Cookies,
Bars & Brownies; Crisps & Cobblers; Ice
Cream & Frozen Desserts; Pies)
Almond-Vanilla Yogurt Parfaits 287
Apple Pie Oatmeal Dessert 261
Banana Pudding 266
Blueberry Cantaloupe Cups 265
Caramel Fluff & Toffee Trifle 265
Frozen Berry & Yogurt Swirls 268
Grandma Davidson's Baked Apple
   Pudding 272
Grapefruit, Lime & Mint Yogurt
   Parfait 267
Iced Tea Parfaits 300
Lemon Fluff 298
Nutella Hand Pies 262
Panna Cotta with Papaya
   Coulis 282
Quick Ambrosia Fruit Salad 287

DIP

Mexican Chocolate Dip 281

DRESSING

(see Stuffing & Dressing)

FISH

(also see Seafood)
Family-Favorite Fish Tacos 137
Fish & Chips with Dipping Sauce 140
Ginger Salmon with
   Brown Rice 162
Lemon-Parsley Baked Cod 134
Oven-Roasted Salmon 142
Parmesan Fish Sticks 159
Salmon Wraps 150
Slow Cooker Tuna Noodle
   Casserole 156
Southwestern Catfish 138

FRUIT

(also see specific kinds)
Berried Treasure Angel Food
   Cake 263
Blue Cheese & Grape Coleslaw 185
Blueberry Cantaloupe Cups 265
Frozen Berry & Yogurt Swirls 268
Grapefruit, Lime & Mint Yogurt
   Parfait 267
Grapes with Lemon-Honey
   Yogurt 298
Grilled Mango & Avocado Salad 172
Honey-Yogurt Berry Salad 188
Panna Cotta with Papaya Coulis 282
Pork Tenderloin with Mango
   Relish 94
Quick Ambrosia Fruit Salad 287
Summer Buzz Fruit Salad 176
Tropical Ginger Rice 212
Watermelon Chocolate Chip
   Sorbet 274

GARLIC

Brussels Sprouts with Garlic &
   Goat Cheese 209
Garlic Loaf 286
Great Garlic Bread 230

GINGER

Ginger Salmon with Brown Rice 162
Tropical Ginger Rice 212

GNOCCHI

Garden Vegetable Gnocchi 142

GRILLED & BROILED RECIPES

BBQ Hot Dog & Potato Packs 291
Chip-Crusted Grilled Corn 296
Citrus-Glazed Pork Chops 123
Cocoa-Crusted Beef Tenderloin 17
Family-Favorite Fish Tacos 137
Grilled Corn Relish 299
Grilled Mango & Avocado
   Salad 172

Grilled Romaine with Chive-
   Buttermilk Dressing 187
No-Fry Black Bean
   Chimichangas 153
One-Dish Seafood Meal 132
Salmon Wraps 150
Southwestern Catfish 138

GROUND BEEF

MAIN DISHES
Bacon Cheeseburger Tater Tot
   Bake 30
Beef & Cheese Skillet
   Cobbler 43
Beef Potato Meat Loaf 26
Burrito Bake 28
Cheeseburger Soup 224
Chili Beef Noodle Skillet 32
Creamy Beef & Potatoes 305
Dill Pickle Hamburger
   Pizza 284
Favorite Baked Spaghetti 24
Hearty Beef Casserole 41
Hot Dog Pie 304
Meatball Pizza 32
One-Pot Saucy Beef Rotini 37
One Skillet Lasagna 35
Pizza Macaroni Bake 17
Sloppy Joe Biscuit Cups 45
Speedy Shepherd's Pie 48
Three-Cheese Meatball
   Mostaccioli 20
SANDWICHES
Chili Sloppy Joes 19
Italian Patties 297
SIDE DISH
Mom's Spanish Rice 205

HAM

Apple-Topped Ham Steak 109
Ham & Corn Chowder 228
Ham & Green Onion Biscuits 232
Ham & Veggie Casserole 102
Ham Barbecue 97

HAM (CONTINUED)

Family Quilt Pizza 129
Meat 'n' Veggie Pockets 304
Waffle Monte Cristos 117

HERBS

Basil Tomato Soup with Orzo 233
Chimichurri Monkey Bread 232
Dill Garden Salad 190
Green Salad with Tangy Basil
    Vinaigrette 181
Grilled Romaine with Chive-
    Buttermilk Dressing 187
Herb Quick Bread 236
Herbed Cheese Sticks. 244
Herbed Noodles with
    Edamame 216
Herby Parmesan Bread 233
Lemon-Parsley Baked Cod 134
Roasted Vegetables with
    Sage 218
Rosemary Lemonade 294
Spring-Thyme Chicken Stew. 73
Thyme-Baked Apple Slices 206
Thyme-Roasted Vegetables 202
Tomato Basil Snackers 305

HONEY

Grapes with Lemon-Honey
    Yogurt 298
Honey Beer Bread 238
Honey-Yogurt Berry Salad 188

ICE CREAM & FROZEN DESSERTS

Berry Tasty Frozen Lemonade. 292
Buttermilk Peach Ice Cream 289
Frosty Key Lime Pie. 271
Frosty Toffee Bits Pie 259
Frozen Berry & Yogurt Swirls. 268
Lemon-Berry Ice Cream Pie 264
Raspberry-Banana Soft Serve 257
Watermelon Chocolate Chip
    Sorbet 274

LASAGNA

Muffin Tin Lasagnas 139
One Skillet Lasagna. 35
Sausage & Swiss Chard Lasagna 124
Slow Cooker Cheesy White
    Lasagna 82

LEGUMES & LENTILS

Crazy-Quick Corn & Black Bean
    Salad. 190
Feta Garbanzo Bean Salad 189
Lentil & Chickpea Stew. 147
No-Fry Black Bean Chimichangas . . . 153
Quick Barbecued Beans. 196
Quinoa & Black Bean-Stuffed
    Peppers 158
Simple Vegetarian Slow-Cooked
    Beans 213
Sweet Potato & Chickpea Salad. 182
White Beans & Bow Ties 133

LEMONS

Berry Tasty Frozen Lemonade. 292
Broccoli Slaw with Lemon
    Dressing. 176
Grapes with Lemon-Honey
    Yogurt 298
Lemon-Berry Ice Cream Pie 264
Lemon Date Couscous 210
Lemon Fluff. 298
Lemon Mushroom Orzo 216
Lemon-Parsley Baked Cod 134
Lemon Pepper Roasted Broccoli. . . . 218
Lemon-Roasted Asparagus. 203
Lemony Zucchini Ribbons 198
Rosemary Lemonade 294

LIMES

Chipotle Lime Avocado Salad. 170
Frosty Key Lime Pie. 271
Grapefruit, Lime & Mint Yogurt
    Parfait. 267
Makeover Fluffy Lime Salad 295
Thai Lime Shrimp & Noodles. 145

MEAT LOAVES & MEATBALLS

Beef Potato Meat Loaf 26
Easy Stuffed Shells 44
Meatball Pizza 32
Three-Cheese Meatball
    Mostaccioli 20

MEAT PIES

Hot Dog Pie 304
Sloppy Joe Biscuit Cups. 45
Speedy Shepherd's Pie. 48

MINT

Grapefruit, Lime & Mint Yogurt
    Parfait. 267
Minty Watermelon-Cucumber
    Salad. 175

MUFFINS & QUICK BREADS

Cheddar Corn Dog Muffins. 229
Chocolate Banana Bran Muffins 284
Herb Quick Bread 236
Herby Parmesan Bread 233
Honey Beer Bread 238
Olive & Onion Quick Bread. 240
Orange-Berry Yogurt Muffins 302
Tender Whole Wheat Muffins 239

MUSHROOMS

Bacon, Mushroom & Onion Grilled
    Cheese Sandwiches 106
Broccoli-Mushroom Bubble
    Bake 227
Easy Green Beans with
    Mushrooms 212
Lemon Mushroom Orzo 216
Mushroom & Peas Rice Pilaf. 202
Turkey Mushroom Tetrazzini 58

NUTS & PEANUT BUTTER

Apple-Pecan Salad with Honey
    Vinaigrette 177
Date-Walnut Pinwheels 273
Monkey Bars 263

Peanut Butter-Banana Yogurt
   Parfaits............................ 295
Peanut Butter-Filled Brownie
   Cupcakes.......................... 264
Pear-Pecan Sausage Quiche........ 294
Pecan Butterscotch Cookies 250
Pecan-Crusted Chicken
   Nuggets............................ 61
Texas Tumbleweeds 268
Toffee Pecan Bars 252
Walnut Butter Spread 294

OATS & GRANOLA
Almond-Vanilla Yogurt Parfaits..... 287
Apple Pie Oatmeal Dessert......... 261

OLIVES
Olive & Onion Quick Bread........ 240

ONIONS
Ham & Green Onion Biscuits 232
Olive & Onion Quick Bread........ 240
Sauteed Squash with Tomatoes
   & Onions 213
Tomato-Onion Green Beans 210

ORANGE
Grandma Brubaker's Orange
   Cookies 270
Orange-Berry Yogurt Muffins 302

PASTA & NOODLES
(also see Casseroles; Lasagna)
MAIN DISHES
Buffalo Chicken Pasta............... 88
Buffalo Shrimp Mac &
   Cheese........................... 147
Chicken Penne Casserole 71
Chipotle Manicotti Bake........... 164
Easy Stuffed Shells 44
Egg Roll Noodle Bowl............. 126
Favorite Baked Spaghetti.......... 24
Florentine Spaghetti Bake......... 112
Garden Pasta with Chicken........ 79

Garden Vegetable Gnocchi........ 142
Mom's Chicken Tetrazzini 74
One-Pot Saucy Beef
   Rotini 37
Pizza Macaroni & Cheese 121
Pizza Macaroni Bake.............. 17
Slow Cooker Tuna Noodle
   Casserole......................... 156
Sun-Dried Tomato Pasta.......... 155
Thai Lime Shrimp & Noodles...... 145
Three Cheese Meatball
   Mostaccioli....................... 20
Turkey Mushroom Tettrazini 58
White Beans & Bow Ties 133
SALADS
Mediterranean Tortellini
   Salad............................. 289
Shrimp with Orzo 280
Spaghetti Salad................... 80
Vermicelli Pasta Salad............. 175
SIDE DISHES
Cheese Tortellini with Tomatoes
   and Corn 197
Herbed Noodles with
   Edamame 216
Lemon Date Couscous............. 210
Lemon Mushroom Orzo 216
Pesto Pasta & Potatoes 205
SOUPS
Basil Tomato Soup with
   Orzo 233
Hearty Macaroni Vegetable
   Soup 229
Shortcut Sausage
   Minestrone....................... 243
Spicy Sausage Soup with
   Tortellini 226
Spinach & Tortellini Soup 235
The Ultimate Chicken Noodle
   Soup 230
Tortellini Primavera Soup 238

PEACHES
Buttermilk Peach Ice Cream........ 289

PEARS
Pear-Pecan Sausage Quiche........ 294

PEAS
Easy Peasy Slaw 187
Honey-Butter Peas and
   Carrots........................... 199
Mushroom & Peas Rice Pilaf........ 202
Snap Pea Salad 185
Spanish Rice with Chicken
   & Peas............................ 81

PEPPERS & CHILIES
Chicken-Stuffed Cubanelle
   Peppers 87
Quinoa & Black Bean-Stuffed
   Peppers 158
Roasted Chicken Thighs with
   Peppers & Potatoes.............. 63

PESTO
Cheese & Pesto Biscuits............ 243
Pesto Breadsticks 237
Pesto Buttermilk Dressing.......... 295
Pesto Pasta & Potatoes 205

PIES
Coconut Macaroon Pie 253
Creamy Hazelnut Pie.............. 254
Easy Grasshopper Pie.............. 272
Frosty Key Lime Pie............... 271
Frosty Toffee Bits Pie.............. 259
Lemon-Berry Ice Cream Pie........ 264
Nutella Hand Pies................. 262

PINEAPPLE
Cake with Pineapple Pudding....... 260
Pineapple Shrimp Stir-Fry.......... 148

PIZZA
Cheesy Summer Squash
   Flatbreads........................ 161
Chicken Caesar Pizza 66
Dill Pickle Hamburger Pizza 284

PIZZA (CONTINUED)

Family Quilt Pizza. 129
Meatball Pizza. 32
Mozzarella Corn Bread Pizza 151
Triple Tomato Flatbread 242

PORK

*(also see Bacon; Ham; Sausage
& Pepperoni)*

Barbecue Pork Tacos with
   Apple Slaw. 105
BBQ Country-Style Ribs. 116
Busy-Day Pork Chops. 109
Citrus-Glazed Pork Chops. 123
Egg Roll Noodle Bowl. 126
PB&J Pork Sandwiches 118
Pork Shepherd's Pie 111
Pork Tenderloin with Mango
   Relish 94
Sesame Pulled Pork
   Sandwiches. 102
Slow-Cooked Pork Stew 100
Sweet Barbecued Pork Chops 110

POTATOES

(also see Sweet Potatoes)

MAIN DISHES

Bacon Cheeseburger Tater Tot
   Bake 30
BBQ Hot Dog & Potato Packs 291
Beef Potato Meat Loaf. 26
Creamy Beef & Potatoes 305
Fish & Chips with Dipping
   Sauce 140
Hash Brown-Topped Steak 38
Pork Shepherd's Pie 111
Roasted Chicken Thighs with
   Peppers & Potatoes. 63
Roasted Chicken with Potato
   Wedges 84
Speedy Shepherd's Pie. 48

SALAD & SIDE DISHES

Butternut Squash & Potato
   Mash. 215

Oh-So-Good Creamy Mashed
   Potatoes 212
Pesto Pasta & Potatoes 205
Quick & Easy au Gratin
   Potatoes 207
Tzatziki Potato Salad. 286

SOUP

Bacon-Potato Corn Chowder. 244

QUICK BREADS

(see Biscuits; Muffins & Quick Breads)

RAISINS & DATES

Date-Walnut Pinwheels 273
Lemon Date Couscous. 210

RASPBERRIES

Berried Treasure Angel Food
   Cake 263
Honey-Yogurt Berry Salad 188
Raspberry-Banana Soft Serve 257

RICE & GRAINS

California Quinoa. 201
Chicken & Wild Rice Strudels. 64
Chicken Barley Chowder 237
Colorful Quinoa Salad 177
Ginger Salmon with Brown Rice 162
Mom's Spanish Rice. 205
Mushroom & Peas Rice Pilaf. 202
Quinoa & Black Bean-Stuffed
   Peppers 158
Spanish Rice with Chicken & Peas. . . . 81
Tropical Ginger Rice 212

SALADS

FRUIT SALADS

Apple Maple Pecan Salad. 173
Apple-Pecan Salad with Honey
   Vinaigrette 177
Color It Ruby Salad 186
Garden Tomato Salad. 184
Grilled Mango & Avocado
   Salad. 172

Honey-Yogurt Berry Salad 188
Makeover Fluffy Lime Salad 295
Michigan Cherry Salad. 178
Minty Watermelon-Cucumber
   Salad. 175
Pina Colada Carrot Salad. 187
Quick Ambrosia Fruit Salad 287
Summer Buzz Fruit Salad 176
Tomatoes with Buttermilk
   Vinaigrette 207

GREEN SALADS

Apple-Pecan Salad with Honey
   Vinaigrette 177
Bacon-Tomato Salad. 183
Citrus Avocado Spinach Salad 183
Green Salad with Tangy Basil
   Vinaigrette 181
Grilled Romaine with Chive-
   Buttermilk Dressing. 187
Kale Salad. 186
Michigan Cherry Salad. 178
Mixed Green Salad with Cranberry
   Vinaigrette 186
Spinach Salad with Poppy Seed
   Dressing. 184
Sweet Potato & Chickpea
   Salad. 182

MAIN-DISH SALADS

Chicken Cucumber Boats 293
Fajita in a Bowl 46
Mediterranean Tortellini
   Salad. 289
Shrimp with Orzo 280

PASTA SALADS

Mediterranean Tortellini
   Salad. 289
Shrimp with Orzo 280
Spaghetti Salad. 80
Vermicelli Pasta Salad. 175

VEGETABLE SALADS

Blue Cheese & Grape
   Coleslaw. 185
Broccoli Slaw with Lemon
   Dressing. 176

Chipotle Lime Avocado
   Salad 170
Color It Ruby Salad 186
Colorful Quinoa Salad 177
Crazy-Quick Corn & Black
   Bean Salad 190
Dill Garden Salad 190
Edamame Corn Carrot Salad 176
Feta Garbanzo Bean Salad 189
Garden Bounty Salad 171
Garden Cucumber Salad 181
Garden Tomato Salad 184
Grilled Mango & Avocado
   Salad 172
Jazzed-Up Slaw 178
Lemony Zucchini Ribbons 198
Minty Watermelon-Cucumber
   Salad 175
Pina Colada Carrot Salad 187
Sicilian Salad 177
Snap Pea Salad 185
Sweet Potato & Chickpea
   Salad 182
Tzatziki Potato Salad 286

SANDWICHES & WRAPS
(also see Burgers)
COLD SANDWICH
Meat 'n' Veggie Pockets 304
HOT SANDWICHES
Asian Chicken Wraps 283
Bacon & Swiss Chicken
   Sandwiches 56
Bacon, Mushroom & Onion
   Grilled Cheese Sandwiches 106
Balsamic Beef Hoagies 29
Chili Sloppy Joes 19
Ham Barbecue 97
PB&J Pork Sandwiches 118
Pigs in a Poncho 96
Salmon Wraps 150
Sesame Pulled Pork
   Sandwiches 102
Tomato Basil Snackers 305

Tomato Steak Sandwiches 25
Waffle Monte Cristos 117

SAUSAGE & PEPPERONI
BBQ Hot Dog & Potato Packs 291
Cheddar Corn Dog Muffins 229
Florentine Spaghetti Bake 112
Hot Dog Pie 304
Mediterranean Tortellini Salad 289
Pear-Pecan Sausage Quiche 294
Pepperoni Pizza Soup 235
Pepperoni Roll-Ups 300
Pigs in a Poncho 96
Pizza Macaroni Bake 17
Pizza Pancakes 99
Sausage & Swiss Chard Lasagna 124
Shortcut Sausage Minestrone 243
Sicilian Salad 177
Spaghetti Squash & Sausage
   Easy Meal 120
Spicy Sausage Soup with
   Tortellini 226
Stromboli Slices 299

SEAFOOD
(also see Fish)
MAIN DISHES
Buffalo Shrimp Mac &
   Cheese 147
One-Dish Seafood Meal 132
Pineapple Shrimp Stir-Fry 148
Shrimp & Corn Stir Fry 154
Thai Lime Shrimp &
   Noodles 145
SALAD
Shrimp with Orzo 280

SIDE DISHES
MISCELLANEOUS
Easy Homemade Chunky
   Applesauce 205
Fresh Cranberry Relish 291
German Apples 293
Grilled Corn Relish 299

Simple Vegetarian Slow-Cooked
   Beans 213
Thyme-Baked Apple Slices 206
PASTA
Cheese Tortellini with Tomatoes
   and Corn 197
Herbed Noodles with
   Edamame 216
Lemon Date Couscous 210
Lemon Mushroom Orzo 216
Pesto Pasta & Potatoes 205
POTATOES & SWEET POTATOES
Butternut Squash & Potato
   Mash 215
Oh-So-Good Creamy Mashed
   Potatoes 212
Pesto Pasta & Potatoes 205
Quick & Easy au Gratin
   Potatoes 207
Roasted Sweet Potato
   Wedges 214
RICE & GRAINS
California Quinoa 201
Mom's Spanish Rice 205
Mushroom & Peas Rice Pilaf 202
Tropical Ginger Rice 212
VEGETABLES
Baked Parmesan Breaded
   Squash 201
Browned Butter Roasted
   Cauliflower 209
Butternut Squash & Potato
   Mash 215
Cheese Tortellini with
   Tomatoes and Corn 197
Coconut Acorn Squash 208
Easy Green Beans with
   Mushrooms 212
Eddie's Favorite Fiesta Corn 206
Garden-Fresh Rainbow
   Chard 213
Herbed Noodles with Edamame . . . 216
Honey-Butter Peas and
   Carrots 199

SIDE DISHES
VEGETABLES (CONTINUED)
Lemon Pepper Roasted
  Broccoli 218
Lemon-Roasted
  Asparagus 203
Lemony Zucchini Ribbons 198
Marina's Golden Corn
  Fritters 238
Orange Spice Carrots 203
Oven-Dried Tomatoes 203
Parmesan Creamed
  Spinach 202
Quick Barbecued Beans 196
Roasted Vegetables with
  Sage 218
Sauteed Squash with Tomatoes
  & Onions 213
Thyme-Roasted
  Vegetables 202
Tomato-Onion Green
  Beans 210

SKILLET & STOVETOP ENTREES
BEEF
Beef & Cheese Skillet
  Cobbler 43
Chili Beef Noodle Skillet 32
Chili Sloppy Joes 19
One Skillet Lasagna 35
FISH & SEAFOOD
Pineapple Shrimp Stir-Fry 148
Shrimp & Corn Stir Fry 154
Thai Lime Shrimp
  & Noodles 145
PORK & SAUSAGE
Apple-Topped Ham Steak 109
Bean & Bacon Griddle
  Burritos 115
Egg Roll Noodle Bowl 126
Spaghetti Squash & Sausage
  Easy Meal 120
Sweet Barbecued Pork
  Chops 110

MEATLESS
Sun-Dried Tomato Pasta 155
White Beans & Bow Ties 133

SLOW COOKER RECIPES
DESSERTS
Apple Pie Oatmeal Dessert 261
MAIN DISHES
Balsamic Beef Hoagies 29
Barbecue Pork Tacos with
  Apple Slaw 105
BBQ Country-Style Ribs 116
Beef Brisket 22
Buffalo Chicken Pasta 88
Buffalo Shrimp Mac & Cheese 147
Ham Barbecue 97
PB&J Pork Sandwiches 118
Sesame Pulled Pork
  Sandwiches 102
Slow-Cooked Pork Stew 100
Slow-Cooked Round Steak 21
Slow Cooker Beef Tips 14
Slow Cooker Cheesy White
  Lasagna 82
Slow Cooker Chicken
  Tacos 55
Slow Cooker Tuna Noodle
  Casserole 156
Sweet & Tangy Beef Roast 37
SIDE DISHES
Easy Green Beans with
  Mushrooms 212
Honey-Butter Peas and
  Carrots 199
Orange Spice Carrots 203
Simple Vegetarian Slow-Cooked
  Beans 213
Slow Cooker Dressing 198
SOUPS & CHILI
Cheeseburger Soup 224
Ham & Corn Chowder 228
Lentil & Chickpea Stew 147
Pepperoni Pizza Soup 235
Spring-Thyme Chicken Stew 73

SOUPS
(also see Chili; Stews)
Bacon-Potato Corn Chowder 244
Basil Tomato Soup with Orzo 233
Cheeseburger Soup 224
Chicken Barley Chowder 237
Creamy Chicken Soup 242
Easy Chicken Corn Chowder 241
Ham & Corn Chowder 228
Hearty Macaroni Vegetable
  Soup 229
Pepperoni Pizza Soup 235
Shortcut Sausage Minestrone 243
Speedy Chicken Chowder 226
Spicy Sausage Soup with
  Tortellini 226
Spinach & Tortellini Soup 235
The Ultimate Chicken Noodle
  Soup 230
Tortellini Primavera Soup 238
Tuscan Chicken Soup 239

SPINACH
Citrus Avocado Spinach Salad 183
Florentine Spaghetti Bake 112
Parmesan Creamed Spinach 202
Spinach Salad with Poppy Seed
  Dressing 184
Spinach & Tortellini Soup 235

SPREADS
Easy Strawberry Butter 303
Walnut Butter Spread 294

SQUASH
(also see Butternut Squash; Zucchini
& Summer Squash)
Coconut Acorn Squash 208
Spaghetti Squash & Sausage
  Easy Meal 120

STEWS
Lentil & Chickpea Stew 147
Slow-Cooked Pork Stew 100

Spring-Thyme Chicken Stew......... 73
Turkey Biscuit Stew................ 84
Weekday Beef Stew.............. 40

STRAWBERRIES
Berried Treasure Angel Food
  Cake 263
Berry Dream Cake................ 255
Chocolate-Covered Strawberry
  Cobbler 260
Easy Strawberry Butter........... 303
Honey-Yogurt Berry Salad 188
Lemon-Berry Ice Cream Pie....... 264

STUFFING & DRESSINGS
Slow Cooker Dressing............. 198

SWEET POTATOES
Roasted Sweet Potato Wedges..... 214
Sweet Potato & Chickpea
  Salad........................ 182

TACOS, ENCHILADAS BURRITOS & QUESADILLAS
Barbecue Chicken Quesadillas....... 68
Barbecue Pork Tacos with
  Apple Slaw.................... 105
Bean & Bacon Griddle Burritos..... 115
Family-Favorite Fish Tacos 137
No-Fry Black Bean
  Chimichangas.................. 153
Slow Cooker Chicken Tacos 55
Thai Chicken Tacos 77

TOFFEE
Caramel Fluff & Toffee Trifle 265
Frosty Toffee Bits Pie............. 259
Toffee Pecan Bars 252

TOMATOES
Bacon-Tomato Salad.............. 183
Basil Tomato Soup with Orzo 233
Cheese Tortellini with Tomatoes
  and Corn 197

Color It Ruby Salad 186
Garden Tomato Salad.............. 184
Oven-Dried Tomatoes 203
Sauteed Squash with Tomatoes &
  Onions 213
Sun-Dried Tomato Pasta.......... 155
Tomato Basil Snackers 305
Tomato-Onion Green Beans 210
Tomato Steak Sandwiches 25
Tomatoes with Buttermilk
  Vinaigrette 207
Triple Tomato Flatbread 242

TORTILLAS
Barbecue Chicken
  Quesadillas 68
No-Fry Black Bean
  Chimichangas.................. 153
Pigs in a Poncho................... 96
Salmon Wraps 150

TURKEY & TURKEY SAUSAGE
Asian Turkey Lettuce Cups 69
Meat 'n' Veggie Pockets........... 304
Turkey Biscuit Stew................ 84
Turkey Mushroom Tetrazzini 58
Waffle Monte Cristos 117

VEGETABLES
(also see specific kinds)
Brussels Sprouts with Garlic &
  Goat Cheese................... 209
Chicken Cucumber Boats 293
Garden-Fresh Rainbow Chard 213
Garden Vegetable Gnocchi........ 142
Ham & Veggie Casserole.......... 102
Hearty Macaroni Vegetable
  Soup 229
Herbed Noodles with
  Edamame 216
Roasted Vegetables with
  Sage 218
Thyme-Roasted Vegetables 202
Tortellini Primavera Soup 238

VEGETARIAN ENTREES
Cheesy Summer Squash
  Flatbreads 161
Chipotle Manicotti Bake........... 164
Garden Vegetable Gnocchi........ 142
Grilled Mango & Avocado Salad 172
Lentil & Chickpea Stew............ 147
Mozzarella Corn Bread Pizza 151
No-Fry Black Bean
  Chimichangas.................. 153
Quinoa & Black Bean-Stuffed
  Peppers 158
Sun-Dried Tomato Pasta.......... 155
Vermicelli Pasta Salad............. 175
White Beans & Bow Ties 133

WHITE CHOCOLATE
White Almond No-Bake Cookies.... 254

ZUCCHINI & SUMMER SQUASH
Baked Parmesan Breaded
  Squash 201
Cheesy Summer Squash
  Flatbreads 161
Lemony Zucchini Ribbons.......... 198
Sauteed Squash with Tomatoes &
  Onions 213

ALPHABETICAL RECIPE INDEX

A

Almond-Vanilla Yogurt Parfaits..... 287
Apple Maple Pecan Salad........... 173
Apple-Pecan Salad with
  Honey Vinaigrette 177
Apple Pie Oatmeal Dessert......... 261
Apple-Topped Ham Steak 109
Asian Chicken Wraps 283
Asian Turkey Lettuce Cups 69

B

Bacon & Swiss Chicken
  Sandwiches...................... 56
Bacon Cheeseburger Tater Tot
  Bake 30
Bacon, Mushroom & Onion Grilled
  Cheese Sandwiches 106
Bacon-Potato Corn Chowder....... 244
Bacon-Tomato Salad.............. 183
Baked Parmesan Breaded
  Squash 201
Balsamic Beef Hoagies............. 29
Banana Chip Cake 268
Banana Pudding 266
Barbecue Chicken Quesadillas....... 68
Barbecue Pork Tacos with
  Apple Slaw..................... 105
Basil Tomato Soup with Orzo 233
BBQ Country-Style Ribs............ 116
BBQ Hot Dog & Potato Packs 291
Bean & Bacon Griddle Burritos 115
Beef & Cheese Skillet Cobbler 43
Beef Brisket....................... 22
Beef Potato Meat Loaf.............. 26
Berried Treasure Angel Food
  Cake 263
Berry Dream Cake................. 255
Berry Tasty Frozen Lemonade...... 292
Blond Butterscotch Brownies 274

Blue Cheese & Grape Coleslaw 185
Blueberry Cantaloupe Cups 265
Broccoli-Mushroom Bubble Bake... 227
Broccoli Slaw with Lemon
  Dressing....................... 176
Browned Butter Cereal Bars........ 270
Browned Butter Roasted
  Cauliflower 209
Brussels Sprouts with Garlic &
  Goat Cheese.................... 209
Buffalo Chicken Pasta.............. 88
Buffalo Shrimp Mac & Cheese...... 147
Burrito Bake 28
Busy-Day Pork Chops............. 109
Buttermilk Peach Ice Cream........ 289
Butternut Squash & Potato
  Mash.......................... 215

C

Cake with Pineapple Pudding....... 260
California Quinoa.................. 201
Candy Bar Cheesecake Brownies ... 271
Caramel Fluff & Toffee Trifle 265
Cheddar Corn Dog Muffins......... 229
Cheese & Pesto Biscuits........... 243
Cheese Tortellini with Tomatoes
  and Corn 197
Cheeseburger Soup 224
Cheesy Summer Squash
  Flatbreads..................... 161
Chicken & Wild Rice Strudels........ 64
Chicken Barley Chowder 237
Chicken Caesar Pizza 66
Chicken Cucumber Boats 293
Chicken Penne Casserole 71
Chicken-Stuffed Cubanelle
  Peppers 87
Chili Beef Noodle Skillet............ 32
Chili Sloppy Joes 19

Chimichurri Monkey Bread......... 232
Chip-Crusted Grilled Corn 296
Chipotle Lime Avocado Salad....... 170
Chipotle Manicotti Bake............ 164
Chocolate Banana Bran Muffins 284
Chocolate Cinnamon Toast 256
Chocolate-Covered Strawberry
  Cobbler 260
Chocolaty S'mores Bars............ 264
Citrus Avocado Spinach Salad 183
Citrus-Glazed Pork Chops......... 123
Cocoa-Crusted Beef Tenderloin 17
Coconut Acorn Squash 208
Coconut Brownies................. 259
Coconut Macaroon Pie 253
Color It Ruby Salad 186
Colorful Quinoa Salad 177
Crazy-Quick Corn & Black Bean
  Salad.......................... 190
Creamy Beef & Potatoes 305
Creamy Chicken Soup............. 242
Creamy Hazelnut Pie.............. 254
Crispy Fried Chicken 64
Crumb-Coated Ranch Chicken....... 76

D

Date-Walnut Pinwheels 273
Dill Garden Salad 190
Dill Pickle Hamburger Pizza 284

E

Easy Cheesy Biscuits.............. 228
Easy Chicken Corn Chowder 241
Easy Grasshopper Pie............. 272
Easy Green Beans with
  Mushrooms 212
Easy Homemade Chunky
  Applesauce.................... 205
Easy Peasy Slaw 187

Easy Strawberry Butter 303
Easy Stuffed Shells 44
Edamame Corn Carrot Salad 176
Eddie's Favorite Fiesta Corn 206
Egg Roll Noodle Bowl 126

F
Fajita in a Bowl 46
Family-Favorite Fish Tacos 137
Family Quilt Pizza 129
Favorite Baked Spaghetti 24
Feta Garbanzo Bean Salad 189
Fish & Chips with Dipping Sauce 140
Florentine Spaghetti Bake 112
Fresh Cranberry Relish 291
Frosty Key Lime Pie 271
Frosty Toffee Bits Pie 259
Frozen Berry & Yogurt Swirls 268
Fudgy S'mores Brownies 250

G
Garden Bounty Salad 171
Garden Cucumber Salad 181
Garden-Fresh Rainbow Chard 213
Garden Pasta with Chicken 79
Garden Tomato Salad 184
Garden Vegetable Gnocchi 142
Garlic Loaf 286
German Apples 293
Ginger Salmon with Brown Rice 162
Gooey Caramel-Topped
    Gingersnaps 256
Grandma Brubaker's Orange
    Cookies 270
Grandma Davidson's Baked
    Apple Pudding 272
Grandma's Biscuits 235
Grapefruit, Lime & Mint Yogurt
    Parfait 267
Grapes with Lemon-Honey
    Yogurt 298
Great Garlic Bread 230
Green Salad with Tangy Basil
    Vinaigrette 181

Grilled Corn Relish 299
Grilled Mango & Avocado Salad 172
Grilled Romaine with Chive-
    Buttermilk Dressing 187

H
Ham & Corn Chowder 228
Ham & Green Onion Biscuits 232
Ham & Veggie Casserole 102
Ham Barbecue 97
Hash Brown-Topped Steak 38
Hearty Beef Casserole 41
Hearty Macaroni Vegetable
    Soup 229
Herb Quick Bread 236
Herbed Cheese Sticks 244
Herbed Noodles with Edamame 216
Herby Parmesan Bread 233
Honey Beer Bread 238
Honey-Butter Peas and Carrots 199
Honey-Yogurt Berry Salad 188
Hot Dog Pie 304

I
Iced Tea Parfaits 300
Italian Patties 297

J
Jazzed-Up Slaw 178

K
Kale Salad 186

L
Lemon-Berry Ice Cream Pie 264
Lemon Date Couscous 210
Lemon Fluff 298
Lemon Mushroom Orzo 216
Lemon-Parsley Baked Cod 134
Lemon Pepper Roasted Broccoli 218
Lemon-Roasted Asparagus 203
Lemony Zucchini Ribbons 198
Lentil & Chickpea Stew 147
Loaded M&M Oreo Cookie Bars 265

M
Makeover Fluffy Lime Salad 295
Marina's Golden Corn Fritters 238
Meat 'n' Veggie Pockets 304
Meatball Pizza 32
Mediterranean Tortellini Salad 289
Mexican Chocolate Dip 281
Mexican Crinkle Cookies 259
Michigan Cherry Salad 178
Mini Rum Cakes 261
Minty Watermelon-Cucumber
    Salad 175
Mixed Green Salad with Cranberry
    Vinaigrette 186
Mom's Chicken Tetrazzini 74
Mom's Spanish Rice 205
Monkey Bars 263
Monkey Bread Biscuits 225
Mozzarella Corn Bread Pizza 151
Muffin Tin Lasagnas 139
Mushroom & Peas Rice Pilaf 202

N
No-Fry Black Bean
    Chimichangas 153
Nutella Hand Pies 262

O
Oh-So-Good Creamy Mashed
    Potatoes 212
Olive & Onion Quick Bread 240
One-Dish Seafood Meal 132
One-Pot Saucy Beef Rotini 37
One Skillet Lasagna 35
Orange-Berry Yogurt Muffins 302
Orange Spice Carrots 203
Oven-Dried Tomatoes 203
Oven-Roasted Salmon 142

P
Panna Cotta with Papaya Coulis 282
Parmesan Creamed Spinach 202
Parmesan Fish Sticks 159
PB&J Pork Sandwiches 118

Peanut Butter-Banana Yogurt Parfaits 295
Peanut Butter-Filled Brownie Cupcakes 264
Pear-Pecan Sausage Quiche 294
Pecan Butterscotch Cookies 250
Pecan-Crusted Chicken Nuggets 61
Pepperoni Pizza Soup 235
Pepperoni Roll-Ups 300
Pesto Breadsticks 237
Pesto Buttermilk Dressing 295
Pesto Pasta & Potatoes 205
Pigs in a Poncho 96
Pina Colada Carrot Salad 187
Pineapple Shrimp Stir-Fry 148
Pizza Macaroni & Cheese 121
Pizza Macaroni Bake 17
Pizza Pancakes 99
Pork Shepherd's Pie 111
Pork Tenderloin with Mango Relish 94

Q
Quick Ambrosia Fruit Salad 287
Quick & Easy au Gratin Potatoes . . . 207
Quick Apple Crisp 250
Quick Barbecued Beans 196
Quick Chicken Parmesan 57
Quinoa & Black Bean-Stuffed Peppers 158

R
Raspberry-Banana Soft Serve 257
Roasted Chicken Thighs with Peppers & Potatoes 63
Roasted Chicken with Potato Wedges 84
Roasted Sweet Potato Wedges 214
Roasted Vegetables with Sage 218
Rosemary Lemonade 294

S
Salmon Wraps 150
Sausage & Swiss Chard Lasagna 124

Sauteed Squash with Tomatoes & Onions 213
Savory Corn Bread 239
Sesame Pulled Pork Sandwiches 102
Shortcut Sausage Minestrone 243
Shrimp & Corn Stir Fry 154
Shrimp with Orzo 280
Sicilian Salad 177
Simple Vegetarian Slow-Cooked Beans 213
Sloppy Joe Biscuit Cups 45
Slow-Cooked Pork Stew 100
Slow-Cooked Round Steak 21
Slow Cooker Beef Tips 14
Slow Cooker Cheesy White Lasagna 82
Slow Cooker Chicken Tacos 55
Slow Cooker Dressing 198
Slow Cooker Tuna Noodle Casserole 156
Snap Pea Salad 185
Southwestern Catfish 138
Spaghetti Salad 80
Spaghetti Squash & Sausage Easy Meal 120
Spanish Rice with Chicken & Peas 81
Speedy Chicken Chowder 226
Speedy Chicken Marsala 60
Speedy Shepherd's Pie 48
Spicy Sausage Soup with Tortellini 226
Spinach & Tortellini Soup 235
Spinach Salad with Poppy Seed Dressing 184
Spring-Thyme Chicken Stew 73
Stromboli Slices 299
Summer Buzz Fruit Salad 176
Sun-Dried Tomato Pasta 155
Sweet & Tangy Beef Roast 37
Sweet Barbecued Pork Chops 110
Sweet Potato & Chickpea Salad 182
Sweet Tea Barbecued Chicken 73

T
Tender Whole Wheat Muffins 239
Texas Tumbleweeds 268
Thai Chicken Tacos 77
Thai Lime Shrimp & Noodles 145
The Ultimate Chicken Noodle Soup 230
Three-Cheese Meatball Mostaccioli 20
Thyme-Baked Apple Slices 206
Thyme-Roasted Vegetables 202
Toffee Pecan Bars 252
Tomato Basil Snackers 305
Tomato-Onion Green Beans 210
Tomato Steak Sandwiches 25
Tomatoes with Buttermilk Vinaigrette 207
Tortellini Primavera Soup 238
Triple Tomato Flatbread 242
Tropical Ginger Rice 212
Turkey Biscuit Stew 84
Turkey Mushroom Tetrazzini 58
Tuscan Chicken Soup 239
Tzatziki Potato Salad 286

V
Vermicelli Pasta Salad 175

W
Waffle Monte Cristos 117
Walnut Butter Spread 294
Watermelon Chocolate Chip Sorbet 274
Weekday Beef Stew 40
White Almond No-Bake Cookies 254
White Beans & Bow Ties 133